2015 Revision
CSET Foundational Mathematics
Study Guides I and II
Number and Quantity; Algebra
Geometry; Probability and Statistics

Copyright 2015 by Christopher Goff

University of the Pacific

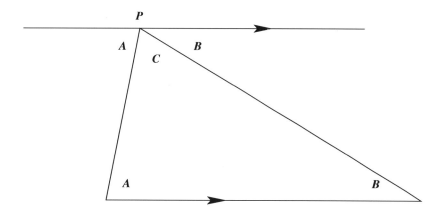

Domains Covered:

SUBTEST I

Number and Quantity; Algebra

1.1 The Real and Complex Number Systems

a. Demonstrate knowledge of the properties of the real number system and of its subsets

1. What are the real numbers?

   On a superficial level, each real number corresponds to a point on the number line, and vice versa. The real numbers include not only the whole numbers and ratios of whole numbers, but also all the numbers in between, including the "irrational" numbers.

   On a deeper level, the question of the nature of the real numbers is really more philosophical, getting at the very notion of number itself. In some textbooks, the real numbers are assumed to exist as a starting point of the discussion. This means there is no need to deduce their existence mathematically; it is just assumed by fiat. Other books construct the real numbers from the rational numbers. (We will define the rational numbers below.) The German mathematician Richard Dedekind (1831-1916) defined a real number in terms of two sets of rational numbers, all those less than or equal to the real number, and all those greater than it. (This is known as a Dedekind "cut.") We will choose the informal approach with which we began, namely, that the real numbers are in one-to-one correspondence with the points on the number line.

2. What are some properties of the real numbers?

   Many properties of the real numbers come from the fact that the set of all real numbers is a field. For a list of field properties, see below in section **2.1 Algebraic Structures**, part **a.** For now, we will just state that the real numbers are closed under addition and multiplication, each of which is commutative and associative. Also, addition and multiplication have their respective identity elements, and each element has an additive inverse. Every element except zero has a multiplicative inverse. Multiplication distributes over addition.

   There are also properties involving ordering, such as "greater than". See section **2.1.b** for more information about ordering properties.

   Finally, what sets the real numbers apart from the rational numbers (defined below) is the idea of "completeness". Sometimes it is phrased that any convergent sequence of rational numbers has to converge to a real number. But a more common way to say it is that any set of real numbers that is bounded above has a least upper bound that is itself a real number.

   For instance, consider the interval $[0, 1)$. This is the set of all real numbers that are greater than or equal to 0 and less than 1. The numbers 1, 1.5, 2, $\pi/2$, and e are upper bounds for this interval (and there are many more upper bounds). But of all the upper bounds, there is a least one, that is, one that is smaller than all the others. In this case, that is the number 1. Notice that 1 is not part of the interval in question, but it is the smallest upper bound for that interval.

   To see why this property is not shared by the rational numbers, see the Sample Problems.

3. What are some of the subsets of real numbers?

   Let's begin with what many would call the first infinite set: the natural numbers. Also called the counting numbers, the natural numbers contain 1, 2, 3, 4, etc. One can describe the natural numbers by saying that they contain the number 1, and that for every natural number n, the number $n+1$ is also a natural number. The number 0 is not considered natural (in most mathematics textbooks), nor is -2, for instance.

Some books list the whole numbers as a separate set from the natural numbers. For these books, the whole numbers begin at 0 and continue upward to 1, 2, 3, etc. (Some books call *this* set the natural numbers. Check your textbook to be sure.) Numbers like -2 and -5 are not considered whole numbers.

Next come the integers, which are basically the smallest set to contain the natural numbers as well as each natural number's additive inverse, as well as zero. So the integers contain $0, 1, -1, 2, -2, 3, -3$, etc. Numbers like 2.5 and π are not integers.

The next important set is the rational numbers, which can be described as all the ratios of two integers, provided that you do not divide by zero. In other words, every rational number can be written as $\frac{p}{q}$, where p and q are integers, and $q \neq 0$. Moreover, every number that can be written in this form is rational. Some examples of rational numbers are: $\frac{22}{7}, \frac{1}{4}, -\frac{2}{23}, -5, 0,$ and $\frac{22349}{34}$. Some numbers that are not rational are $\sqrt{2}, \pi$, and e.

4. What properties differ among the subsets of the real numbers?

The following table compiles key properties. All the sets described so far are closed under addition and multiplication, are ordered by $<$, and each contains 1, the multiplicative identity.

Number set	Additive identity in set	Additive inverses in set	Multiplicative inverses in set	Complete
Natural numbers	No	No	No	No
Whole numbers	Yes	No	No	No
Integers	Yes	Yes	No	No
Rational numbers	Yes	Yes	Yes	No
Real numbers	Yes	Yes	Yes	Yes

5. Sample Problems

   (a) Why aren't the rational numbers "complete"?

   (b) True or false. Explain your answers.

      i. The set of even integers is closed under addition.

      ii. The set of even integers is closed under multiplication.

      iii. The set of odd integers is closed under addition.

      iv. The set of odd integers is closed under multiplication.

6. Answers to Sample Problems

   (a) Why aren't the rational numbers "complete"?

      The main reason that the rational numbers are not complete is that there are sets that are bounded above, but do not have a smallest rational number as a least upper bound.

For instance, consider the set of all rational numbers less than $\sqrt{2}$. Clearly, $\sqrt{2}$ is an upper bound for this set (as is 2, 3, 4, etc.). But $\sqrt{2} \approx 1.414\ldots$ is not a rational number. (Euclid gave a proof of this fact in his *Elements* c. 300 BCE.) Let's suppose that we choose 1.415 as an upper bound. Since $1.415 = \frac{1415}{1000} = \frac{283}{200}$, then 1.415 is rational. And since $1.415^2 = 2.002225 > 2$, we know by taking square roots that $1.415 > \sqrt{2}$. So yes, 1.415 really is an upper bound for the set of rational numbers that are smaller than $\sqrt{2}$. But is it the least upper bound? The answer is no. There is another rational number, 1.4143 that is smaller than 1.415 but still larger than $\sqrt{2}$, because $1.4143^2 = 2.00024449 > 2$. Is 1.4143 the least upper bound? The answer is again no because we can go to the next decimal place and choose an upper bound there: 1.41422 is smaller than 1.4143, but is still larger than $\sqrt{2}$. Dedekind explained that there is always another rational number between $\sqrt{2}$ and any rational number greater than $\sqrt{2}$, and he found a formula for how to find it. I will let you look up Dedekind's work if you wish (or figure it out for yourself), but I hope that the consideration of subsequent decimal places will at least convince you that there is no way to find a smallest rational number that is greater than $\sqrt{2}$. (We used $\sqrt{2}$ here as an example, as did Dedekind, but of course any other irrational number would prove the same point.)

(b) True or false. Explain your answers.

    i. The set of even integers is closed under addition. True.

       Even integers can be written as $2k$, where k is an integer. So if you had two of them, say $2k$ and 2ℓ, then their sum would be $2k + 2\ell = 2(k + \ell)$. This is again an even integer, because it is twice the integer $k + \ell$. (We know $k + \ell$ is an integer because k and ℓ are each integers, and we know that the set of integers is closed under addition - see the chart above.) Hence the set of even integers is closed under addition.

    ii. The set of even integers is closed under multiplication. True.

       As before, choose $2k$ and 2ℓ as our even integers, where k and l are integers. Then their product, $(2k)(2\ell) = 4k\ell = 2(2k\ell)$, is again an even integer because it is twice the integer $2k\ell$. How do we know $2k\ell$ is an integer? We know because $2, k$, and ℓ are integers and the set of integers is closed under multiplication. Hence the set of even integers is also closed under multiplication.

    iii. The set of odd integers is closed under addition. False.

       The set of odd integers is not closed under addition. We could prove that the sum of two odd integers is even, but the way the question is asked, we only need to provide a single counterexample to disprove the statement. In other words, we only need to find two odd numbers whose sum is not odd. So consider the numbers 3 and 5. $3 + 5 = 8 = 2(4)$. Since 8 is even (being twice the integer 4), it is not odd. Therefore the set of odd integers is not closed under addition.

    iv. The set of odd integers is closed under multiplication. True.

       Unlike even numbers, odd numbers have the form $2k + 1$, where k is an integer. So let us pick two odd integers, $2k + 1$ and $2\ell + 1$, where k and ℓ are integers. Then the product is

$$(2k + 1)(2\ell + 1) = 4k\ell + 2k + 2\ell + 1 = 2(2k\ell + k + \ell) + 1,$$

which is again in the form $2m + 1$, where m is the integer $2k\ell + k + \ell$. How do we know m is an integer? We know because $2, k$ and ℓ are integers and we know that the set of integers is closed under addition and multiplication. Therefore the set of odd integers is closed under multiplication.

b. Perform operations and recognize equivalent expressions using various representations of real numbers (e.g., fractions, decimals, exponents)

1. What is the difference between fractions, decimals, and exponents?

This is perhaps not the most precise language we could use. Instead, we will talk about the difference between rational numbers, decimal representations of numbers, and numbers that are powers.

We defined rational numbers earlier as the ratio of two integers, provided that the denominator is not zero. In contrast, a decimal representation of a number involves writing it as a sum of powers of 10, including negative powers. As an example, the number 1.5 is a decimal representation of the rational number $\frac{3}{2}$. In its decimal form, we have the following meaning:

$$1.5 = (1)(10^0) + (5)(10^{-1}) = 1 + \frac{5}{10} = \frac{15}{10} = \frac{3}{2}.$$

Some numbers are easier to write as rational numbers, like $\frac{1}{3}$. The corresponding decimal representation repeats: $0.333333\ldots$. So while the rational number is easy to write, the decimal representation never terminates. Other numbers may be easier to write as decimals, especially if the numbers are longer, or involve integer parts, like 1032.49975.

We mentioned powers of 10 earlier. So what is a power, exactly? The term "power" is often defined as a base (usually an integer or rational number) raised to an integer exponent. For example, $2^2 = 4$. We say that 4 is a power of 2. Similarly, 100 is a power of 10, as is $\frac{1}{100}$ (since $10^{-2} = \frac{1}{100}$). Growing up using decimal representations usually makes people pretty comfortable with powers of 10. Computers have made powers of 2 very important as well through their use of binary representations of numbers.

2. How do you add, subtract, multiply, divide, exponentiate, or take roots of real numbers in these representations?

We will not comprehensively review how to perform operations with rational numbers, decimals, or powers here. Those can be found in any basic arithmetic or algebra text. We will only point out some key properties in each case.

- Rational Numbers.
$$\frac{a}{b} + \frac{c}{d} = \frac{ad + bc}{bd} \quad \text{and} \quad \frac{a}{b} \cdot \frac{c}{d} = \frac{ac}{bd}.$$

- Decimal representations. Addition and multiplication follow the usual integer rules and algorithms. The only difference is that the decimal point needs to be kept track of. For addition, align the decimal points and the add the values as you would for integers, leaving the decimal point in place. For multiplication, the rule of thumb is that the number of digits after the decimal place in the product should equal the sum of the numbers of digits after the decimal place in each factor. You will be asked to explain this rule in the Sample Problems.

- Powers

$$n^a \cdot n^b = n^{a+b} \quad \text{and} \quad (n^a)^b = n^{ab}.$$

Many of the other formulas can be derived from these. See the Sample Problems.

3. How do you convert between equivalent expressions involving real numbers?

We saw a little of this above. To convert from a terminating decimal representation to a rational number, simply write each power of 10 as a fraction, via $10^{-n} = \dfrac{1}{10^n}$. Then add each term using the rules for adding fractions.

To write a repeating decimal as a rational number, there is an algorithm that depends on how many digits repeat. As an example, we will find the rational equivalent of $1.\overline{36}$. Let $x = 1.\overline{36}$. Then $100x = 136.\overline{36}$. Subtracting the former equation from the latter, we get $99x = 135$. So $x = \dfrac{135}{99} = \dfrac{15}{11}$.

To convert a rational number to a decimal, you can use long division. The algorithm is the same as for integers, but keeping track of the decimal point along the way. So the decimal equivalent of $\dfrac{5}{6}$ can be found by dividing $5.000\ldots$ by 6.

$$
\begin{array}{r}
0.833\ldots \\
6 \; \overline{\big)5.000\ldots} \\
\underline{48} \\
20 \\
\underline{18} \\
20 \\
\underline{18} \\
2
\end{array}
$$

$\ldots$ and so on. So $\dfrac{5}{6} = 0.8\overline{3}$. In general, you might have to go a long way until the pattern repeats, but a nice property of rational numbers is that their decimal representations always either terminate or eventually repeat (forever).

4. How do you recognize equivalent expressions involving real numbers?

To me, this question is more about experience and having a good memory. I am personally reminded of my sixth-grade math teacher, Mrs. Peters, who made us memorize the squares of the integers from 1 to 25, and the cubes of the integers from 1 to 12. She also made us memorize the decimal equivalents for rational numbers in lowest terms having denominators at most 11. I have lost count as to how many times this knowledge has come in handy. Granted, I became a math professor, but I use the rational-decimal equivalences more in my day-to-day life than in my professional career. Because of my teacher, I can recognize these equivalences when I encounter them in the "real world." Mrs. Peters has inspired me to ask the same of you in the Sample Problems. (She also made us learn the percentage equivalents, but those are so close to the decimal representation that I will skip it here.) (PS - thank you, Mrs. Peters!)

5. Sample Problems

(a) Using the formula $\frac{a}{b} \cdot \frac{c}{d} = \frac{ac}{bd}$, how can you deduce that that $\frac{1}{\frac{a}{b}} = \frac{b}{a}$ (assuming $a, b \neq 0$)?

(b) Let $n > 0$. Using the formula $n^a \cdot n^b = n^{a+b}$, how can you deduce that $n^0 = 1$? ...that $n^{-a} = \frac{1}{n^a}$? ...that $n^{1/2} = \sqrt{n}$?

(c) Why was $1.\overline{36}$ multiplied by 100 in order to find its rational representation?

(d) Find rational representations for: $0.\overline{4}, 2.\overline{232}$, and $-1.12\overline{3}$.

(e) Explain why the the number of digits after the decimal place in the product of two decimal representations should equal the sum of the numbers of digits after the decimal place in the decimal representation of each factor.

(f) (Recognition of powers) List the squares of the numbers from 1 to 25 and the cubes of the numbers from 1 to 12.

(g) (Recognition of decimal equivalents of rational numbers) List the decimal equivalents of all the rational numbers in lowest terms having denominators at most 11. Notice any patterns?

6. Answers to Sample Problems

(a) Using the formula $\frac{a}{b} \cdot \frac{c}{d} = \frac{ac}{bd}$, how can you deduce that $\frac{1}{\frac{a}{b}} = \frac{b}{a}$ (assuming $a, b \neq 0$)?

First, assume $a, b \neq 0$. To answer the questions asked, let's start by answering another question: what is $\frac{a}{b} \cdot \frac{b}{a}$? Well, according to the formula, the product is $\frac{ab}{ab} = 1$. So $\frac{a}{b} \cdot \frac{b}{a} = 1$. If we divide both sides by $\frac{a}{b}$, then we get the desired result.

(b) Let $n > 0$. Using the formula $n^a \cdot n^b = n^{a+b}$, how can you deduce that $n^0 = 1$? ...that $n^{-a} = \frac{1}{n^a}$? ...that $n^{1/2} = \sqrt{n}$?

These answers go in order and build on each other. Let's start by considering the formula if $b = 0$, $n \neq 0$. Then $n^a \cdot n^0 = n^{a+0} = n^a$. Dividing both sides by n^a gives the result $n^0 = 1$. For the next result, let $b = -a$ in the formula. Then $n^a \cdot n^{-a} = n^{a+(-a)} = n^0 = 1$. Dividing both sides by n^a gives $n^{-a} = \frac{1}{n^a}$. For the last equation, consider $a = b = \frac{1}{2}$. Then $n^{1/2} \cdot n^{1/2} = n^1 = n$. Since $(n^{1/2})^2 = n$, taking the square root of both sides gives $n^{1/2} = \sqrt{n}$. Notice that this method could be tweaked to show that $n^{1/3} = \sqrt[3]{n}$, etc.

(c) Why was $1.\overline{36}$ multiplied by 100 in order to find its rational representation?

The reason is that we need all of the repeated decimals to align in the subtraction, thereby canceling them out. Since it is a two-digit repeating pattern, multiplying by $10^2 = 100$ will align the repeated digits.

(d) Find rational representations for: $0.\overline{4}, 2.\overline{232}$, and $-1.12\overline{3}$.

$$0.\overline{4} = \frac{4}{9}, \quad 2.\overline{232} = \frac{2230}{999} = 2\frac{232}{999}, \quad \text{and} \quad -1.12\overline{3} = -\frac{337}{300} = -1\frac{37}{300}$$

To see the last one, multiply the original by 10. Then subtract the original from this, giving $9x = -10.11$. Since this still has decimals in it, we can multiply both sides by 100, giving $900x = -1011$, or $300x = -337$.

(e) Explain why the the number of digits after the decimal place in the product of two decimal representations should equal the sum of the numbers of digits after the decimal place in the decimal representation of each factor.

Before we give a general reason, let's calculate $0.128 \cdot 0.45$. According to the rule, we should multiply 128 times 45 and then force there to be $3 + 2$, or 5 digits to the right of the decimal in the answer. So, $128 \cdot 45 = 5760$. In order to get this right, we need to count the final zero as one of the digits. So the final answer should be $0.05760 = 0.0576$. You can verify this with a calculator of course.

The question though is why does this algorithm work? Let's look at it another way, after converting each decimal representation to a sum of integers times powers of 10 and then multiplying out all the terms using the distributive property.

$$\begin{aligned} 0.128 \cdot 0.45 &= \left(1 \cdot 10^{-1} + 2 \cdot 10^{-2} + 8 \cdot 10^{-3}\right)\left(4 \cdot 10^{-1} + 5 \cdot 10^{-2}\right) \\ &= 4(10^{-2}) + 5(10^{-3}) + 8(10^{-3}) + 10(10^{-4}) + 32(10^{-4}) + 40(10^{-5}) \\ &= \text{some arithmetic} = 0.0576 \end{aligned}$$

The main point here is to look at the term with the smallest exponent. Here, that term is the 10^{-5} term, which came from the product of the smallest terms of each factor: 10^{-3} times 10^{-2} in this example. Because the exponents add together when multiplying, we get $10^{-3} \cdot 10^{-2} = 10^{-5}$. Notice that the exponent -3 corresponds to three digits to the right of the decimal, and -2 corresponds to two digits. So the -5 corresponds to five digits after the decimal.

In general, the smallest power of 10 in the product will be the product of the smallest powers of 10 in each factor. Since the exponent on the smallest power of 10 corresponds to the number of digits to the right of the decimal, and because the exponents are added when powers of 10 are multiplied, the number of digits to the right of the decimal is additive when multiplying decimal representations together.

(f) (Recognition of powers) List the squares of the numbers from 1 to 25 and the cubes of the numbers from 1 to 12.

x	x^2	x^3	x	x^2
1	1	1	13	169
2	4	8	14	196
3	9	27	15	225
4	16	64	16	256
5	25	125	17	289
6	36	216	18	324
7	49	343	19	361
8	64	512	20	400
9	81	729	21	441
10	100	1000	22	484
11	121	1331	23	529
12	144	1728	24	576
			25	625

(g) (Recognition of decimal equivalents of rational numbers) List the decimal equivalents of all the rational numbers in lowest terms having denominators at most 11. Notice any patterns?

Denom-inator						
2	$\frac{1}{2} = 0.5$					
3	$\frac{1}{3} = 0.\overline{3}$	$\frac{2}{3} = 0.\overline{6}$				
4	$\frac{1}{4} = 0.25$	$\frac{3}{4} = 0.75$				
5	$\frac{1}{5} = 0.2$	$\frac{2}{5} = 0.4$	$\frac{3}{5} = 0.6$	$\frac{4}{5} = 0.8$		
6	$\frac{1}{6} = 0.1\overline{6}$	$\frac{5}{6} = 0.8\overline{3}$				
7	$\frac{1}{7} = 0.\overline{142857}$	$\frac{2}{7} = 0.\overline{285714}$	$\frac{3}{7} = 0.\overline{428571}$	$\frac{4}{7} = 0.\overline{571428}$	$\frac{5}{7} = 0.\overline{714285}$	$\frac{6}{7} = 0.\overline{857142}$
8	$\frac{1}{8} = 0.125$	$\frac{3}{8} = 0.375$	$\frac{5}{8} = 0.625$	$\frac{7}{8} = 0.875$		
9	$\frac{1}{9} = 0.\overline{1}$	$\frac{2}{9} = 0.\overline{2}$	$\frac{4}{9} = 0.\overline{4}$	$\frac{5}{9} = 0.\overline{5}$	$\frac{7}{9} = 0.\overline{7}$	$\frac{8}{9} = 0.\overline{8}$
10	$\frac{1}{10} = 0.1$	$\frac{3}{10} = 0.3$	$\frac{7}{10} = 0.7$	$\frac{9}{10} = 0.9$		
11 (a)	$\frac{1}{11} = 0.\overline{09}$	$\frac{2}{11} = 0.\overline{18}$	$\frac{3}{11} = 0.\overline{27}$	$\frac{4}{11} = 0.\overline{36}$	$\frac{5}{11} = 0.\overline{45}$	
11 (b)	$\frac{6}{11} = 0.\overline{54}$	$\frac{7}{11} = 0.\overline{63}$	$\frac{8}{11} = 0.\overline{72}$	$\frac{9}{11} = 0.\overline{81}$	$\frac{10}{11} = 0.\overline{90}$	

There are some great patterns here. For the rational numbers with denominator 11, the two repeated digits are the product of 9 and the numerator. For the rational numbers with denominator 7, the digits 1, 4, 2, 8, 5, 7 appear cyclically in the same order. Only the starting number changes. In terms of recognizing decimal equivalents of rational numbers, knowing this table has served me well.

c. Solve real-world and mathematical problems using numerical and algebraic expressions and equations

1. How do you model real-world situations with algebraic expressions, equations, and inequalities?

   Expressions are the nouns in the language of algebra, and equations and inequalities are the sentences. They give us some information about the expressions we are studying. So if we have information about some numbers, then we can translate that information into an equation or inequality.

   As an example, suppose that you bought four children's movie tickets and the cost was $38. We can represent this using expressions and an equation. If we let P represent the price of a child's movie ticket, then the expression representing the cost of four tickets would be $4P$. The equation is therefore $4P = 38$. We will solve this below.

   Now suppose that you don't know exactly what the price of the four children's movie tickets was, but that you did know that it was less than $40. We can represent this as an inequality. Again, if P is the price of one child's ticket, then $4P$ is the price of four children's tickets. The inequality is therefore $4P < 40$. We will solve this below.

2. How do you use equations and inequalities to solve problems?

   We will be working with equations and inequalities that contain variables. That means that there is some unknown quantity in the "sentence." When you solve an equation or inequality, you are finding out the values of the variable(s) that will make the sentence a true statement. So we will create an equation or inequality in such a way that by solving it, we will get the answer we desire.

   In the former example above, we created the equation $4P = 38$. We could solve this equation for P and that would give us the price for one child's movie ticket. We would get $P = 9.5$, or the price of a child's ticket is $9.50. In the latter example, we created the inequality $4P < 40$. If we were to solve this, then it would tell us the maximum price that a single child's ticket could cost. We would get $P < 10$, or the maximum price of a child's ticket is $10. Since the information obtained is slightly different in each case, we want to create the equation or inequality that will lead us to the information we seek.

3. What are some examples?

   See section **2.3.f** for specific examples of linear and non-linear modeling problems.

d. Apply proportional relationships to model and solve real-world and mathematical problems

1. What is a proportional relationship?

   A quantity A is said to be proportional to another quantity B if there is a constant k satisfying $A = kB$. Often, the quantity B is itself a power of another quantity. For instance, if $B = x^2$, then we can say, "A is proportional to the square of x" or "A is proportional to x^2." I suppose A could also be a power, though in practice that is seldom the case.

2. What is an inversely proportional relationship?

   A quantity A is said to be inversely proportional to another quantity B if there is a constant k satisfying $A = \dfrac{k}{B}$. Often, the quantity B is itself a power of another quantity. For instance, if $B = x^3$, then we can say, "A is inversely proportional to the cube of x" or "A is inversely proportional to x^3." I suppose A could also be a power, though in practice that is seldom the case.

3. What real-world situations can be modeled using proportional relationships?

Countless real-world situations follow a proportional or inversely proportional relationship. Some proportional examples include: how much you pay for a bunch of bananas, say, is proportional to their weight (or in some stores, to their number); if you drive at a constant speed, the distance traveled is proportional to the time spent driving; the volume of a sphere is proportional to the cube of its radius; the cost of a hotel stay is proportional to the number of nights spent there.

Some inverse proportionality relationships include: the amount of time it takes to drive somewhere is inversely proportional to the speed at which you drive; the number of bananas you can buy for \$3 is inversely proportional to their cost; under constant voltage, the resistance in a circuit is inversely proportional to the current; the amount of each heir's inheritance is inversely proportional to the number of heirs (assuming each heir receives the same amount); the gravitational force between two given stars is inversely proportional to the square of the distance between them.

4. How do you model problems using proportional relationships?

The key to modeling these problems lies in converting the language of the problem to an equation, namely, the equation that is part of the definition of proportionality. For, example, the volume of a sphere is proportional to the cube of its radius. We can parse this statement like this:

the volume of a sphere	is proportional to	the cube of its radius
V	$= k \cdot$	r^3

So, $V = kr^3$. Similarly, the amount of each heir's inheritance is inversely proportional to the number of heirs. This can be seen as

the amount of each heir's inheritance	is inversely proportional to	the number of heirs
A	$= k \div$	n

So, $A = \dfrac{k}{n}$.

5. Sample Problems

   (a) The amount of grass seed needed to cover a square field is proportional to the area of the field. If G represents the amount of grass seed, and x is the length of the square field, write down an equation for this situation. (Use k to represent the constant of proportionality.)

   (b) The volume of a sphere is proportional to the cube of its radius. What happens to the volume if the radius is doubled?

   (c) At Trader Joe's market, the cost of bananas is proportional to the number of bananas you buy. What is the common term for the constant of proportionality in this case? What are its units? If six bananas cost \$1.14, the how much would five bananas cost?

(d) Suppose the leader of a family dies, leaving each heir an equal portion of the estate. Suppose each heir is scheduled to receive $300,000. Then another heir is identified and claims an equal share of the estate. With the addition of this new heir, each portion of the estate becomes $250,000. How many original heirs were there? What was the value of the original estate? (Hint: what is the meaning of the constant of proportionality in this case?)

6. Answers to Sample Problems

(a) The amount of grass seed needed to cover a square field is proportional to the area of the field. If G represents the amount of grass seed, and x is the length of the square field, write down an equation for this situation. (Use k to represent the constant of proportionality.) $G = kx^2$.

(b) The volume of a sphere is proportional to the cube of its radius. What happens to the volume if the radius is doubled? The volume is increased by a factor of 8.

To see this, we start with the equation $V = kr^3$ that we determined above. Suppose now that r is doubled to $2r$. Then the new volume, W, satisfies $W = k(2r)^3 = 8kr^3 = 8V$. So W is eight times bigger than V.

(c) At Trader Joe's market, the cost of bananas is proportional to the number of bananas you buy. What is the common term for the constant of proportionality in this case? What are its units? If six bananas cost $1.14, the how much would five bananas cost?

Since cost is proportional to the number bought, our equation becomes $C = kn$. So $k = \dfrac{C}{n}$. In other words, k is just the cost per banana, or the unit cost. (Prices of things are really just constants of proportionality.) At Trader Joe's, the units on k are "cents per banana." To solve the problem, we use the given information to find k, and then we use that information to find the total cost of five bananas. (Note $1.14 = 114$ cents.)

$$
\begin{aligned}
C &= kn \\
114 &= k(6) \\
19 &= k
\end{aligned}
$$

So the cost per banana is 19 cents. We use this to find the cost C for five bananas: $C = (19)(5) = 95$. So five bananas cost 95 cents at Trader Joe's.

(d) Suppose the leader of a family dies, leaving each heir an equal portion of the estate. Suppose each heir is scheduled to receive $300,000. Then another heir is identified and claims an equal share of the estate. With the addition of this new heir, each portion of the estate becomes $250,000. How many original heirs were there? What was the value of the original estate? (Hint: what is the meaning of the constant of proportionality in this case?)

There are two unknowns here: the total amount of the estate and the original number of heirs, n. We haven't really talked about systems of equations yet, but this problem can be solved by substitution as well. We can set up two equations:

$$
300{,}000 = \frac{k}{n} \quad \text{and} \quad 250{,}000 = \frac{k}{n+1}.
$$

Multiplying to clear denominators in each case, we get: $300{,}000n = k$ and $250{,}000(n + 1) = k$. If you analyze this first equation, you see that the amount each original heir was scheduled to receive (\$300,000) is multiplied by the number of original heirs (n) to get k. So k must be the original value of the estate. But we cannot determine it just yet.

We can however equate these two expressions for the total estate, and then solve:

$$
\begin{aligned}
300{,}000n &= 250{,}000(n + 1) \\
300{,}000n &= 250{,}000n + 250{,}000 \\
50{,}000n &= 250{,}000 \\
n &= 5.
\end{aligned}
$$

So there were five original heirs. Thus the original estate was worth five times \$300,000, or 1.5 million dollars.

e. Reason quantitatively and use units to solve problems (i.e., dimensional analysis)

1. What does it mean to reason quantitatively?

Quantitative reasoning can mean a variety of things. As opposed to qualitative reasoning, it could mean using specific numbers to draw conclusions. For instance, one of the Sample Problems above asked what would happen to the volume of a sphere if its radius were doubled. An answer like, "the volume would increase," though technically correct, would be more of a qualitative response. A better answer is more quantitative in this case, "the volume would increase by a factor of 8."

Quantitative reasoning could also be viewed as one part of more general logical thinking. For example, statistical evidence can provide support to a variety of arguments, especially those involving decisions in public policy-making. Having an awareness and understanding of quantity and relative size can go a long way towards a deeper understanding of the world around us.

2. What is dimensional analysis? How does it work?

Dimensional analysis is a tool that I first really learned about as a physics student - physicists find this tool useful. It can help you find an answer if you do not know another method, or it can serve as a check to see if your answer might be correct. The saying "You can't add apples and oranges" is part of this line of reasoning. There are a few rules as to how you can do arithmetic on real-world quantities, and how the dimensions, or units, on the answer behave. We will list some of them below, with brief explanations. Note that a "pure number", like 3 or π, is a number that has no units to it.

- You cannot add or subtract two quantities unless they have the same units. Two quantities are not equal unless they have the same units.

    It doesn't make sense to add 2 centimeters to 3 seconds. One is a length measurement, the other is time. Here is where the "apples and oranges" comment fits in. Now, if you change your view so that the units are "pieces of fruit" then yes, you can add apples and oranges because they are both pieces of fruit. It also does not make sense to say that 2 cm equals 2 seconds. These quantities cannot be compared.

- When multiplying or dividing quantities, their units multiply or divide, respectively.

  For example, the area of a rectangle is the product of its length and its width. If length and width are in feet, then the area will have units of (feet)(feet), or square feet (ft^2). Similarly, if a city is growing at a rate of 2000 people per year for 4 years, then the total growth of the city over that period would be

  $$\left(2000 \, \frac{\text{people}}{\text{year}}\right)(4 \text{ years}) = 8000 \, \frac{\text{people}}{\text{year}} \cdot \text{years} = 8000 \text{ people}.$$

- You can only raise a quantity to a pure number power, in which case its units are also raised to that power.

  It doesn't make sense to raise four kilograms to the centimeter power. Exponents must be dimensionless.

- (more advanced) The input and output values of a transcendental function (like logarithms and trigonometric functions) must be pure numbers.

  This is more advanced, and may seem to be a rule that is broken in physics, where quantities like $\cos t$, where t is time, might show up in wave theory. However, usually when terms like $\cos t$ appear, it is because of a very particular choice of units, or a mathematical simplification by ignoring a physical constant that might have a value of 1, even though it is not dimensionless. A more precise formula would involve $\cos \omega t$, where ω is the frequency, and has units of "1 over time", such as seconds^{-1}, also known as Hertz (Hz). This way, the units cancel and you can take the cosine of a pure number. (Incidentally, radian measure is also a pure number, being a ratio of two lengths. Degrees are a unit. This is another reason why mathematics teachers like to use radians rather than degrees.)

  Also, it may seem like the output of $\cos \omega t$ might be the intensity of a sound, or something else that has units. How can this be when cosine has to be a pure number? Again, a better, more precise formula would be $A \cos \omega t$, where A is the amplitude and possesses the relevant units.

  Again, this last bullet point may seem beyond the scope of basic dimensional analysis, but I include it here as a guide to where this topic leads in more advanced science and engineering coursework.

3. What are some examples of how to solve problems using dimensional analysis?

   Let's look at a few examples. First, let's calculate how many seconds there are in a week. These kinds of conversion problems are a good application of unit equivalences. Using the Factor-Label method (often taught in Chemistry), we multiply one week by successive fractions that are equal to 1 until we arrive at a quantity with the units of seconds.

   $$(1 \text{ week}) \cdot \left(\frac{7 \text{ days}}{1 \text{ week}}\right) \cdot \left(\frac{24 \text{ hours}}{1 \text{ day}}\right) \cdot \left(\frac{60 \text{ minutes}}{1 \text{ hour}}\right) \cdot \left(\frac{60 \text{ seconds}}{1 \text{ minute}}\right) = 7 \cdot 24 \cdot 60 \cdot 60 \text{ seconds},$$

   which is 604,800 seconds. Notice how all the unit labels cancel out except for seconds.

As a different kind of example, suppose you drove a total of m miles and it took you h hours. Find your average speed for the trip. I'll give you four choices: $m + h, mh, \dfrac{m}{h}, \dfrac{h}{m}$. Which one is correct?

Well, using dimensional analysis, we can rule out $m + h$ as impossible. What would its units be? You can't add miles to hours. The second option, mh, is possible, but its units would be (miles)(hours), which are not units of speed. The third option, $\dfrac{m}{h}$, has units of $\dfrac{\text{miles}}{\text{hours}}$, or miles per hour, which are certainly units of speed. This might be the right answer. The fourth option, $\dfrac{h}{m}$, has units of hours per mile, which would describe how many hours it took to drive one mile. While this is certainly related to speed (inversely related, in fact), it does not have units of speed in the way we usually measure speed. So the third option, $\dfrac{m}{h}$, must be the correct one.

Notice that we didn't have to actually know the formula that rate times time equals distance. We only had to know that speed in this situation would be measured in miles per hour. Even in the absence of four choices, students might have come up with $\dfrac{m}{h}$ on their own. While this is the correct answer in this case, it is worth noting that just because the units are correct, does not necessarily mean that the formula is correct: $\dfrac{2m}{h}$ and $\dfrac{m}{2h}$ also have the correct units, but give the wrong answer. However, dimensional analysis can often be used to determine if you have an incorrect answer.

As a second example, let's consider the formula for the height of a projectile as a function of time: $h = -\frac{1}{2}gt^2 + v_0 t + h_0$. If the height is in feet and time is in seconds, find the dimensions of g, v_0, and h_0.

So, since h has units of feet, and since h is a sum of three terms, each of these terms must have units of feet. So $-\frac{1}{2}gt^2, v_0 t$, and h_0 all have units of feet. Since $v_0 t$ has units of feet and t has units of seconds, v_0 must be in feet per second in order to have the dimension of seconds cancel out when v_0 and t are multiplied together. (So this means v_0 must be a velocity of some sort.) Finally, $-\frac{1}{2}gt^2$ also has units of feet. So, g has units of feet divided by seconds squared, or feet per second per second. (Thus g describes a change in a velocity over time, also known as acceleration.)

Notice that if we were having trouble remembering where the acceleration and velocity pieces go in this formula, dimensional analysis can help us sort it out.

4. Sample Problems

   (a) The speed limit on a local highway is 65 miles per hour. How many feet per second is that?

   (b) A lighthouse rotates once every 53 seconds. How many times will it rotate in an eight-hour period?

   (c) Suppose a student comes to you with the following expression that will give the radius of the earth (in km): $2t/27$, where t is the length of one day, in seconds. The student says the numbers agree. The student claims to have discovered some new physics. What do you tell the student?

5. Answers to Sample Problems

   (a) The speed limit on a local highway is 65 miles per hour. How many feet per second is that? 95.33 feet per second

   $$\left(\frac{65 \text{ miles}}{1 \text{ hr}}\right) \cdot \left(\frac{1 \text{ hr}}{60 \text{ min}}\right) \cdot \left(\frac{1 \text{ min}}{60 \text{ sec}}\right) \cdot \left(\frac{5280 \text{ ft}}{1 \text{ mile}}\right) = \frac{65 \cdot 5280 \text{ ft}}{60 \cdot 60 \text{ sec}},$$

   which is 95.33 feet per second.

   (b) A lighthouse rotates once every 53 seconds. How many times will it rotate in an eight-hour period? 543.

   $$\left(\frac{1 \text{ rot}}{53 \text{ sec}}\right) \cdot \left(\frac{60 \text{ sec}}{1 \text{ min}}\right) \cdot \left(\frac{60 \text{ min}}{1 \text{ hr}}\right) (8 \text{ hrs}) = \frac{60 \cdot 60 \cdot 8 \text{rot}}{53} \approx 543.39 \text{ rot}.$$

   The lighthouse makes 543 complete rotations in an eight-hour period (plus a little more).

   (c) Suppose a student comes to you with the following expression that will give the radius of the earth (in km): $2t/27$, where t is the length of one day, in seconds. The student says the numbers agree. The student claims to have discovered some new physics. What do you tell the student?

   The student is just relating some numbers. Yes, the numbers are pretty close. There are 86,400 seconds in a day, and so $2(86,400)/27 = 6400$, which is approximately the radius of the earth in kilometers. But the units are not compatible. The formula given by the student has units of time, not length. So it doesn't make sense as is.

   But the student can alter their formula to make the units correct. By saying $R = \frac{(2 \text{ km})t}{27 \text{ sec}}$, then at least the units work out, but now the true physics question is: what is the significance of 2 km and 27 seconds? Why should those numbers be important? Physics is more than just a collection of formulas that describe the universe on many different scales. A formula must be generalizable in its applicability in order to rise to the level of a powerful physical formula.

f. Perform operations on complex numbers and represent complex numbers and their operations on the complex plane

1. What is the definition of a real number? ...of an imaginary number? ...of a complex number?

   A real number can be thought of as any point on the number line. (See section **a.** above.) Sometimes people point out that real numbers satisfy $x^2 \geq 0$.

   An imaginary number is one satisfying $x^2 \leq 0$. If we let $\mathbf{i}^2 = -1$, then imaginary numbers can be written as $b\mathbf{i}$, where b is real. [There is sometimes a debate on whether 0 is imaginary or not. I choose to think of 0 as $0\mathbf{i}$ in this case, making it imaginary. It's also real. No one said that numbers had to be either real or imaginary, but not both.]

   A complex number can be expressed as the sum of a real number and an imaginary number. So, any complex number can be written as $a + b\mathbf{i}$, where a and b are real numbers.

2. How can you add, subtract or multiply complex numbers?

Complex numbers follow the usual rules of operations and algebra, only we have to remember that $i^2 = -1$. Let's consider $w = 2 - 3i$ and $z = 5 + 4i$. Then

$$
\begin{aligned}
w + z &= (2 - 3i) + (5 + 4i) = 2 + 5 + (-3i + 4i) = 7 + i \\
w - z &= (2 - 3i) - (5 + 4i) = 2 - 5 + (-3i - 4i) = -3 - 7i \\
wz &= (2 - 3i)(5 + 4i) = 10 + 8i - 15i - 12i^2 = 10 - 7i - 12(-1) = 22 - 7i.
\end{aligned}
$$

Notice that multiples of i are like terms.

3. How do you divide complex numbers?

Before we talk about division, let's recall that the *complex conjugate* of $a+bi$ is $a-bi$. This will come in handy in order to write a quotient of complex numbers in $a + bi$ form. In particular, we will multiply a quotient by a fraction equal to 1 (namely, the conjugate of the denominator divided by itself) and then simplify our answer. Using the same w and z from above,

$$
\frac{w}{z} = \frac{2 - 3i}{5 + 4i} \left(\frac{5 - 4i}{5 - 4i} \right) = \frac{(2 - 3i)(5 - 4i)}{(5 + 4i)(5 - 4i)} = \frac{10 - 8i - 15i + 12i^2}{25 + 20i - 20i - 16i^2} = \frac{-2 - 23i}{41},
$$

which can be written in $a + bi$ form as $\dfrac{w}{z} = -\dfrac{2}{41} - \dfrac{23}{41}i$.

4. How do you find roots of complex numbers?

Finding complex roots requires trigonometry and an understanding of DeMoivre's Theorem. See details in the Trigonometry section in the study guide for CSET III, subsection **5.1.e**.

5. What is the complex plane?

The complex plane is a way of visualizing complex numbers on a two-dimensional Cartesian plane. The x-axis is called the "real" axis and the y-axis is called the "imaginary" axis. Complex numbers then correspond to points on the complex plane. The number $-2i$ corresponds to the point $(0, -2)$, while $3 + 3i$ corresponds to $(3, 3)$. Real numbers (with imaginary part equal to 0) lie on the real axis. See the picture below.

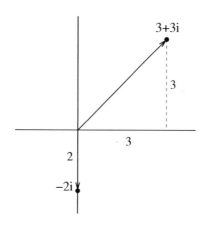

6. How do you represent addition or subtraction on the complex plane?

Addition on the complex plane can be thought of in the language of vectors. Please see section **2.4.a** (below) for more information about how vectors add and subtract.

Essentially, one adds vectors componentwise. In complex numbers, this means that one adds the real parts and imaginary parts separately. Geometrically, one adds vectors by placing the tail of one vector at the head of another. Subtraction is similar, except that we think of subtraction as adding the additive inverse. So, we add a vector that points in the opposite direction to the vector being subtracted.

In the picture, we have demonstrated $v + w$ and $v - w$, where $v = 1 - 2\mathbf{i}$ and $w = 3 + 3\mathbf{i}$. Algebraically, we get $v + w = 4 + \mathbf{i}$ and $v - w = -2 - 5\mathbf{i}$.

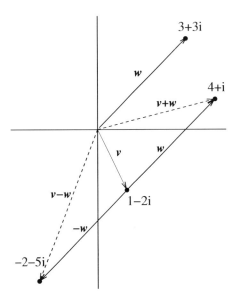

7. How do you represent multiplication on the complex plane?

Please see the Trigonometry subsection **5.1.e** for information on the polar form of complex numbers. For now, we will just say that because of trigonometry, we can write complex numbers either in $a + b\mathbf{i}$ form, or in so-called polar form, as $re^{i\theta}$. In polar form, r is the distance to the origin, and θ is the angle between the positive real axis and the line segment having one endpoint at the origin and the other at the complex number in question.

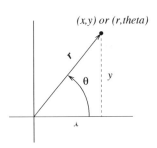

The first form is better for addition and subtraction of complex numbers graphically, because the real and imaginary parts correspond to horizontal and vertical displacements, respectively.

The second form is better for multiplication of complex numbers graphically, because it relies on geometric properties of the line segments corresponding to the complex numbers. Consider the equation:

$$(r_1 e^{i\theta_1})(r_2 e^{i\theta_2}) = (r_1 r_2)e^{i(\theta_1 + \theta_2)},$$

From here, we see that the line segment corresponding to the product has the following properties:

- Its length is the product of the lengths corresponding to the factors.

- Its angle is the sum of the angles corresponding to the factors.

So, to multiply two complex numbers graphically, one multiplies their line segment lengths and adds their angles. The result is a line segment that identifies the product. Using the same v and w as before, we show vw. Algebraically, we get $vw = (1 - 2i)(3 + 3i) = 3 - 6i + 3i - 6i^2 = 9 - 3i$. Using polar form we get

$$vw = (\sqrt{5}e^{i\alpha})(3\sqrt{2}e^{i\theta}) = 3\sqrt{10}e^{i(\alpha + \theta)}.$$

Note that $\theta = \frac{\pi}{4}$, but that $\alpha \approx 5.176$ radians.

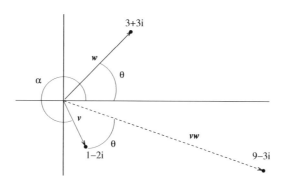

8. How do you represent division on the complex plane?

If we use the polar representation of a complex number, then it is relatively easy to perform division.

$$\frac{r_1 e^{i\theta_1}}{r_2 e^{i\theta_2}} = \left(\frac{r_1}{r_2}\right)e^{i(\theta_1 - \theta_2)}.$$

So, the line segment corresponding to the quotient has the following properties:

- Its length is a quotient: the length corresponding to the dividend divided by the length corresponding to the divisor.

- Its angle is a difference: the angle corresponding to the dividend minus the angle corresponding to the divisor.

Notice that these properties are the inverse of the properties under multiplication. So, to divide two complex numbers graphically, one divides their line segment lengths and subtracts their angles. The result is a line segment that identifies the product. Using the same v and w as before, we show $\dfrac{v}{w}$. Geometrically,

$$\frac{v}{w} = \frac{\sqrt{5}e^{i\alpha}}{3\sqrt{2}e^{i\theta}} = \frac{\sqrt{10}}{6}e^{i(\alpha-\theta)},$$

while algebraically,

$$\frac{v}{w} = \frac{1-2\mathbf{i}}{3+3\mathbf{i}} = \left(\frac{1-2\mathbf{i}}{3+3\mathbf{i}}\right)\cdot\left(\frac{3-3\mathbf{i}}{3-3\mathbf{i}}\right) = \frac{-3-9\mathbf{i}}{18} = -\frac{1}{6} - \frac{1}{2}\mathbf{i}.$$

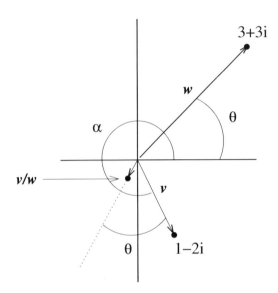

9. Sample Problems

(a) Is the length of the line segment corresponding to $\dfrac{1}{z}$ the reciprocal of the length of the line segment corresponding to z? If so, why? Is the angle of the line segment corresponding to $\dfrac{1}{z}$ the negative of the angle of the line segment corresponding to z? If so, why?

(b) For this problem, let $w = 3 - \mathbf{i}$, $v = -1 - 5\mathbf{i}$, and $z = 5 + 5\mathbf{i}$. Calculate the following:

   i. $w + v$

   ii. wv

   iii. $3w - 2\mathbf{i}z$

   iv. z^2

   v. $w\overline{w}$ (where $\overline{w}$ denotes the complex conjugate of w)

   vi. $\dfrac{v}{w}$

   vii. r and θ if $z = re^{i\theta}$

(c) Let z be a complex number. Show that $z + \overline{z}$ and $z\overline{z}$ are always real.

10. Answers to Sample Problems

(a) Is the length of the line segment corresponding to $\dfrac{1}{z}$ the reciprocal of the length of the line segment corresponding to z? If so, why? Is the angle of the line segment corresponding to $\dfrac{1}{z}$ the negative of the angle of the line segment corresponding to z? If so, why? Yes and yes. As to why these conditions are correct, we can derive them directly.

If $z = re^{i\theta}$, then $\dfrac{1}{z} = \dfrac{1}{re^{i\theta}} = \dfrac{1}{r}e^{-i\theta}$. So the length is $\dfrac{1}{r}$ and the angle is $-\theta$.

(b) For this problem, let $w = 3 - \mathbf{i}$, $v = -1 - 5\mathbf{i}$, and $z = 5 + 5\mathbf{i}$. Calculate the following:

     i. $w + v = 2 - 6\mathbf{i}$

     ii. $wv = -8 - 14\mathbf{i}$

     iii. $3w - 2\mathbf{i}z = 19 - 13\mathbf{i}$

     iv. $z^2 = 50\mathbf{i}$

     v. $w\overline{w} = 10$ (where $\overline{w}$ denotes the complex conjugate of w)

     vi. $\dfrac{v}{w} = \dfrac{2 - 16\mathbf{i}}{10} = \dfrac{1}{5} - \dfrac{8}{5}\mathbf{i}$

     vii. r and θ if $z = re^{i\theta}$; $r = 5\sqrt{2}, \theta = \dfrac{\pi}{4}$

(c) Let z be a complex number. Show that $z + \overline{z}$ and $z\overline{z}$ are always real. Let $z = a + b\mathbf{i}$. Then $\overline{z} = a - b\mathbf{i}$. So

$$z + \overline{z} = (a + b\mathbf{i}) + (a - b\mathbf{i}) = 2a; \quad z\overline{z} = (a + b\mathbf{i})(a - b\mathbf{i}) = a^2 - b^2\mathbf{i}^2 = a^2 + b^2$$

There are no terms involving $\mathbf{i}$ in the final answers. So $z + \overline{z}$ and $z\overline{z}$ are real.

1.2 Number Theory

a. Prove and use basic properties of natural numbers (e.g., properties of divisibility)

1. What are the natural numbers?

$$\mathbb{N} = \{1, 2, 3, 4, 5, \ldots\}$$

   (Often, computer science books include zero in the natural numbers, but most mathematics books do not.) In higher mathematics, the natural numbers are built out of other objects, like sets. Then, the natural numbers are used to define the integers, which are then used to define the rational numbers, which are then used to define the real numbers, which are then used to define the complex numbers. See **1.1.a** and **1.1.f** for more details.

2. What are some axioms of the natural numbers?

   (Remember, axioms do not need to be proved.)

   The natural numbers are closed under addition and multiplication, which are commutative and associate operations in which multiplication distributes over addition. Also, the natural numbers are well ordered, which means that if a and b are natural numbers, then either $a \leq b$ or $b \leq a$. It also means that there is a smallest element.

3. What is division in the natural numbers (or integers)?

   There is a Division Algorithm in the integers that says the following. If a and b are natural numbers, then there exist *unique* integers q and r (called the *quotient* and *remainder*) satisfying

   (a) $a = qb + r$, and

   (b) $0 \leq r < b$.

   Usually, $a \geq b$, although that is not technically necessary. Also, a could be any integer and division would still work.

4. What is divisibility in the natural numbers (or integers)?

   Let a and b be natural numbers [respectively, integers], with $b \neq 0$. We say a is **divisible** by b, or b **divides** a, or $b|a$, if there exists a natural number [resp., integer] k satisfying $a = bk$. In other words, the remainder is zero when a is divided by b.

5. What are some properties of divisibility?

   Let $a, b, c \in \mathbb{N}$.

   (a) $a|a$.

   (b) If $a|b$ and $b|c$, then $a|c$.

   (c) If $a|b$, then $a|bc$.

   (d) If $c|a$ and $c|b$, then $c|a + b$.

6. Sample Problems

   (a) Let $a, b \in \mathbb{N}$. Prove that the geometric mean of a and b is less than or equal to the arithmetic mean of a and b; that is, $\sqrt{ab} \leq \frac{a+b}{2}$.

   (b) Let $a, b \in \mathbb{N}$. Prove that $\sqrt{ab} = \frac{a+b}{2}$ if and only if $a = b$.

   (c) Prove that a number is divisible by 4 if the number formed by its last two digits is divisible by 4.

   (d) Prove that a number is divisible by 3 if the sum of its digits is divisible by 3. (You may assume the number has three digits, although the property is true in general.)

   (e) Prove that there are an infinite number of Pythagorean triples.

7. Answers to Sample Problems

   (a) Let $a, b \in \mathbb{N}$. Prove that the geometric mean of a and b is less than or equal to the arithmetic mean of a and b; that is, $\sqrt{ab} \leq \frac{a+b}{2}$.

   Since $a - b$ is a real number, $(a - b)^2 \geq 0$. So,

   $$
   \begin{aligned}
   a^2 - 2ab + b^2 &\geq 0 \\
   a^2 + 2ab + b^2 &\geq 4ab \\
   (a + b)^2 &\geq 4ab \\
   a + b &\geq 2\sqrt{ab},
   \end{aligned}
   $$

   where the last step follows because $ab > 0$. Dividing both sides by 2 gives the final result.

   (b) Let $a, b \in \mathbb{N}$. Prove that $\sqrt{ab} = \frac{a+b}{2}$ if and only if $a = b$.

   Multiplying both sides by 2 and then squaring both sides, we get $4ab = a^2 + 2ab + b^2$, or $0 = a^2 - 2ab + b^2 = (a - b)^2$. Thus $a - b$ must equal zero, that is, $a = b$.

   (c) Prove that a number is divisible by 4 if the number formed by its last two digits is divisible by 4.

   Since 100 is divisible by 4, we know that any number times 100 is also divisible by 4. (See properties of divisibility, above.) So we can disregard the digits in the hundreds place and higher, since they will not affect whether the overall number is divisible by 4. Only the tens and ones digits matter. As an example, consider $3424 = 34(100) + 24$. We know that 4 divides 100, and thus $34(100)$ as well. So, 3424 is divisible by 4 if and only if 24 is divisible by 4, which it is. So 3424 is divisible by 4.

   (d) Prove that a number is divisible by 3 if the sum of its digits is divisible by 3. (You may assume the number has three digits, although the property is true in general.)

   Let h, t, and u be the hundreds, tens, and ones digits of the number n. Then

   $$n = 100h + 10t + u = (h + t + u) + 99h + 9t.$$

   Suppose that the digit sum of n is divisible by 3. Then $h + t + u = 3k$ for some integer k. Then $n = 3k + 99h + 9t = 3(k + 33h + 3t)$. Clearly, n is divisible by 3. As an aside, notice that a similar argument shows that n is divisible by 9 if its digit sum is divisible by 9.

(e) Prove that there are an infinite number of Pythagorean triples.

The easy way to prove this is to prove that $(3, 4, 5)$ is a Pythagorean triple first [$3^2 + 4^2 = 9 + 16 = 25 = 5^2$]. Then we can show that $(3k, 4k, 5k)$ is another Pythagorean triple for any value of k. Indeed,

$$(3k)^2 + (4k)^2 = 9k^2 + 16k^2 = 25k^2 = (5k)^2.$$

So, $(6, 8, 10)$, $(9, 12, 15)$, etc. belong to an infinite chain of Pythagorean triples.

The harder way is to show that there are an infinite number of Pythagorean triples *no two of which are multiples of each other*. Let's look at the difference between consecutive squares.

$$(n + 1)^2 - n^2 = n^2 + 2n + 1 - n^2 = 2n + 1$$

This means that every positive odd number, because it can be written as $2n + 1$, is the difference between two consecutive squares. For example, $4^2 - 3^2 = 16 - 9 = 7$. So $7 = 2(3) + 1$ is a difference of two consecutive squares. But 7 is not itself a perfect square, which means we do not get a Pythagorean triple in this case. However, $9 = 2(4) + 1$ is an odd number and a perfect square. In fact, $5^2 - 4^2 = 25 - 16 = 9 = 3^2$, which gives us the Pythagorean triple $(3, 4, 5)$. The next odd square is $25 = 2(12) + 1$. So $13^2 - 12^2 = 169 - 144 = 25 = 5^2$, giving $(5, 12, 13)$ as a Pythagorean triple. The next one in this sequence is $(7, 24, 25)$. Since there are an infinite number of odd perfect squares, we will get an infinite number of Pythagorean triples, no two of which are multiples of each other.

b. Use the Principle of Mathematical Induction to prove results in number theory

1. What is Mathematical Induction?

If you have a sequence of statements $(S_1, S_2, S_3, \dots)$ that satisfy the following properties: (1) that S_1 is true, and (2) that if S_k is true, then it follows that S_{k+1} is also true for all $k \in \mathbb{N}$, then the Principle of Mathematical Induction says that every statement in the sequence is true.

2. What is Complete Induction?

If you have a sequence of statements $(S_1, S_2, S_3, \dots)$ that satisfy the following properties: (1) that S_1 is true, and (2) that if S_j is true for all $j \leq k$, then it follows that S_{k+1} is also true for all $k \in \mathbb{N}$, then the Principle of Complete Induction says that every statement in the sequence is true.

The difference here is that in Complete Induction, you are allowed to assume that all the previous statements are true, rather than just the immediate predecessor. This can be very useful if one statement depends on several preceding statements.

3. How does one prove a result by induction?

To prove a result by induction, one must prove the two parts of the principle. First, one must prove that S_1 is true. Second, one must prove that *if* S_k is true, for some value of k, then S_{k+1} must also be true.

4. Sample Problems (Prove the following statements.)

(a) $\displaystyle\sum_{i=1}^{n} i = \frac{n(n+1)}{2}$ for all $n \in \mathbb{N}$.

(b) The number $n^3 - n$ is divisible by 6 for any natural number n.

(c) $13|(14^n - 1)$ for all $n \in \mathbb{N}$.

(d) $\displaystyle\sum_{i=1}^{n} i^2 = \frac{n(n+1)(2n+1)}{6}$ for all $n \in \mathbb{N}$.

(e) The sum of the even integers from 2 to $2n$ is $n(n+1)$.

(f) $\displaystyle\sum_{i=0}^{n} 2^i = 2^{n+1} - 1$ for all $n \in \mathbb{N}$.

5. Answers to Sample Problems

(a) $\displaystyle\sum_{i=1}^{n} i = \frac{n(n+1)}{2}$ for all $n \in \mathbb{N}$.

Proof: First, we must show that $\displaystyle\sum_{i=1}^{1} i = \frac{1(1+1)}{2}$. But $\displaystyle\sum_{i=1}^{1} i = 1 = \frac{1(2)}{2}$. So the statement S_1 is true.

Aside: What is the general statement, S_n?

ANS: S_n is the statement we are asked to prove at the beginning, namely

$$\sum_{i=1}^{n} i = \frac{n(n+1)}{2} \text{ for all } n \in \mathbb{N}.$$

Second, we need to show that if S_k is true for some k, then S_{k+1} is also true. So, we assume that S_k is true for some k. That is, $\displaystyle\sum_{i=1}^{k} i = \frac{k(k+1)}{2}$. This will come in handy later. Now we must prove that S_{k+1} is true under this assumption. We will start by looking at the sum of i as i ranges from 1 to $k+1$ and we will algebraically manipulate it to fit the desired formula.

$$\begin{aligned}
\sum_{i=1}^{k+1} i &= \left(\sum_{i=1}^{k} i\right) + (k+1) \\
&= \frac{k(k+1)}{2} + (k+1) \\
&= (k+1)\left(\frac{k}{2} + 1\right) \\
&= \frac{(k+1)(k+2)}{2},
\end{aligned}$$

which exactly proves that S_{k+1} is true. Therefore, the Principle of Mathematical Induction implies that S_n is true for all n, namely, that $\sum_{i=1}^{n} i = \dfrac{n(n+1)}{2}$. $\square$

(b) The number $n^3 - n$ is divisible by 6 for any natural number n.

Proof: S_1 says that $1^3 - 1$ is divisible by 6. That is true, because $1^3 - 1 = 0 = 6(0)$. Now assume that $k^3 - k$ is divisible by 6, which means that $k^3 - k = 6m$ for some integer m. Consider

$$(k+1)^3 - (k+1) = k^3 + 3k^2 + 3k + 1 - k - 1 = (k^3 - k) + 3k(k+1) = 6m + 3k(k+1),$$

where we used the assumption that $k^3 - k$ is divisible by 6. Notice that for any k, either k or $k+1$ must be even, which means that $3k(k+1)$ is also divisible by 6. Thus, $(k+1)^3 - (k+1)$ is divisible by 6. Therefore, by the Principle of Mathematical Induction, $n^3 - n$ is divisible by 6 for all n. $\square$

(c) $13 | (14^n - 1)$ for all $n \in \mathbb{N}$.

Proof: Clearly, $14^1 - 1 = 13$ is divisible by 13. Let's now assume that $14^k - 1$ is divisible by 13. So, $14^k - 1 = 13m$ for some integer m. Then

$$14^{k+1} - 1 = 14(14^k) - 1 = (13+1)(14^k) - 1 = 13(14^k) + (14^k - 1) = 13(14^k) + 13m.$$

Since each term is divisible by 13, then $14^{k+1} - 1$ is also divisible by 13. Therefore, the Principle of Mathematical Induction says that $13 | (14^n - 1)$ for all $n \in \mathbb{N}$. $\square$

(d) $\sum_{i=1}^{n} i^2 = \dfrac{n(n+1)(2n+1)}{6}$ for all $n \in \mathbb{N}$.

Proof: When $n = 1$, both sides are equal to 1. So assume that $\sum_{i=1}^{k} i^2 = \dfrac{k(k+1)(2k+1)}{6}$ for some $k \in \mathbb{N}$. Then

$$
\begin{aligned}
\sum_{i=1}^{k+1} i^2 &= \left(\sum_{i=1}^{k} i^2 \right) + (k+1)^2 \\
&= \frac{k(k+1)(2k+1)}{6} + (k+1)^2 \\
&= \left(\frac{k+1}{6} \right) [k(2k+1) + 6(k+1)] \\
&= \left(\frac{k+1}{6} \right) (2k^2 + 7k + 6) \\
&= \frac{(k+1)(k+2)(2k+3)}{6} = \frac{(k+1)((k+1)+1)(2(k+1)+1)}{6},
\end{aligned}
$$

which is exactly the formula we wanted. Therefore, the Principle of Mathematical Induction says that $\sum_{i=1}^{n} i^2 = \dfrac{n(n+1)(2n+1)}{6}$ for all $n \in \mathbb{N}$. $\square$

(e) The sum of the even integers from 2 to $2n$ is $n(n+1)$.

This is the same proof as problem (a), above, except with both sides multiplied by 2.

(f) $\displaystyle\sum_{i=0}^{n} 2^i = 2^{n+1} - 1$ for all $n \in \mathbb{N}$.

Proof: Let $n = 1$. Then $\displaystyle\sum_{i=0}^{1} 2^i = 2^0 + 2^1 = 3 = 2^2 - 1$. So the statement is true when $n = 1$. Assume the statement is true for some $k \in \mathbb{N}$. That means that $\displaystyle\sum_{i=0}^{k} 2^i = 2^{k+1} - 1$. Then

$$
\begin{aligned}
\sum_{i=0}^{k+1} 2^i &= \left(\sum_{i=0}^{k} 2^i\right) + 2^{k+1} \\
&= (2^{k+1} - 1) + 2^{k+1} \\
&= 2(2^{k+1}) - 1 = 2^{k+2} - 1,
\end{aligned}
$$

which is exactly the formula we wanted. Therefore the Principle of Mathematical Induction says that $\displaystyle\sum_{i=0}^{n} 2^i = 2^{n+1} - 1$ for all $n \in \mathbb{N}$.

c. Apply the Euclidean Algorithm

1. What is the Euclidean Algorithm?

   The Euclidean Algorithm is a procedure that returns the greatest common factor (or greatest common divisor, GCD) of two given natural numbers. The input is two natural numbers a and b, with $a \geq b$. The output is the largest natural number which is a factor of both numbers.

2. How does the Euclidean Algorithm work?

   The Euclidean Algorithm (GCD) is a recursive algorithm that can be summarized as follows:

   To find the greatest common factor of a and b (where $a \geq b$), first divide a by b to find q and r satisfying $a = qb + r$ and $0 \leq r < b$. If $r = 0$, then $GCD(a, b) = b$. If $r \neq 0$, then $GCD(a, b) = GCD(b, r)$.

   Example: Find $GCD(15, 6)$.

   ANS: Since $15 = 2(6) + 3$, then $r \neq 0$. So $GCD(15, 6) = GCD(6, 3)$. We repeat the algorithm. Since $6 = 2(3) + 0$, $GCD(6, 3) = 3$. Thus $GCD(15, 6) = 3$.

3. Why does the Euclidean Algorithm work?

   Since $b > r$ at each step, meaning the next remainder $r' < r$, and so on, we have a descending chain of natural numbers: $b, r, r', \ldots$. But in the natural numbers, such a chain has to be finite. There are only a finite number of natural number solutions to $x < b$ for any value of b. Therefore the algorithm will eventually stop.

The algorithm stops at the right answer because the common factors of a and b are exactly the same as the common factors of b and r. This is because $a = qb + r$, and thus $r = a - qb$. If d is a factor of a and b, then d is a factor of $a - qb = r$ as well. Conversely, if d is a factor of b and r, then d is a factor of $qb + r = a$. Since no common factors are gained or lost, the greatest common factor of the original two numbers is preserved through every step of the algorithm.

4. What is an application of Euclidean Algorithm?

   USEFUL FACT: The greatest common factor of a and b is the smallest natural number that can be written as $as + bt$, where s and t are suitably chosen integers. (The integers s and t are not unique, but you can find suitable values via the Euclidean Algorithm.)

5. Sample Problems

   (a) Find the greatest common factor of 123 and 24.

   (b) Find the greatest common factor of 55 and 34.

   (c) Find the greatest common factor of 91 and 35.

   (d) Show that the greatest common factor of $7n + 4$ and $5n + 3$ is 1 for all $n \in \mathbb{N}$.

6. Answers to Sample Problems

   (a) Find the greatest common factor of 123 and 24. 3
       Since $123 = 5(24) + 3$, $GCD(123, 24) = GCD(24, 3)$. Since $24 = 8(3)$, $GCD(24, 3) = 3$.

   (b) Find the greatest common factor of 55 and 34. 1
       $55 = 1(34) + 21; 34 = 1(21) + 13; 21 = 1(13) + 8; 13 = 1(8) + 5; 8 = 1(5) + 3;$
       $5 = 1(3) + 2; 3 = 1(2) + 1; 2 = 2(1) + 0.$

   (c) Find the greatest common factor of 91 and 35. 7
       $91 = 2(35) + 21; 35 = 1(21) + 14; 21 = 1(14) + 7; 14 = 2(7) + 0.$

   (d) Show that the greatest common factor of $7n + 4$ and $5n + 3$ is 1 for all $n \in \mathbb{N}$.
       $7n + 4 = 1(5n + 3) + (2n + 1); 5n + 3 = 2(2n + 1) + n + 1;$
       $2n + 1 = 2(n + 1) - 1; n + 1 = -(n + 1)(-1) + 0.$
       Or, $-5(7n + 4) + 7(5n + 3) = 1$, which means 1 is the greatest common factor. (See USEFUL FACT, above.)

d. Apply the Fundamental Theorem of Arithmetic (e.g., find the greatest common factor and the least common multiple; show that every fraction is equivalent to a unique fraction where the numerator and denominator are relatively prime; prove that the square root of any number, not a perfect square number, is irrational)

1. What is the Fundamental Theorem of Arithmetic?

   The Fundamental Theorem of Arithmetic states that if n is a natural number, then n can be expressed as a product of prime numbers. Moreover, there is only one way to do so, up to a permutation of the prime factors of n. (Here, we allow a "product" to consist of only one prime, or of no primes so that we can say that EVERY natural number, including 1, is a "product" of primes.)

2. What is a prime number?

   The number $n \in \mathbb{N}$ is **prime** if $n > 1$ and the only positive divisors of n are 1 and n. As examples, 7 is prime but 9 is not, because 9 has 3 as a divisor.

3. Why is the Fundamental Theorem of Arithmetic true?

   The first sentence can be proved using Complete Induction. The second sentence can be proved by using the following Helpful Fact.

   Helpful Fact: Let p be a prime. If $p|ab$, then $p|a$ or $p|b$.

   Proof: (of Helpful Fact) Suppose $p|ab$ but p does not divide a. Then the greatest common factor of p and a must be 1, because there are no other factors of p. By the USEFUL FACT, above, there must be integers s and t satisfying $1 = as + pt$. Multiplying both sides by b, we get $b = bas + bpt$. Notice that $p|bas$ (because $p|ab$) and clearly $p|bpt$. Therefore, $p|b$. $\square$

4. How does one find the greatest common factor and the least common multiple, using the Fundamental Theorem of Arithmetic?

   Here, one can find the unique prime factorization of two numbers and use that information to determine the greatest common factor and the least common multiple. As an example, consider 12 and 18. We know $12 = 2^2 \cdot 3$ and $18 = 2 \cdot 3^2$. Both share a single factor of 2 and a single factor of 3. So, $2 \cdot 3 = 6$ is the greatest common factor. For the least common multiple, notice that we need factors of at least 2^2 and 3^2 in order to have both 12 and 18 as a factor. So, the least common multiple is $2^2 3^2 = 36$.

5. How can fractions be uniquely represented as a ratio of relatively prime integers? (What does relatively prime mean?)

   The numbers a and b are *relatively prime* if they have no common factors. This happens when $GCD(a, b) = 1$. If you are given a fraction, you can use the Fundamental Theorem of Arithmetic to write the numerator and denominator uniquely as products of primes. Then you can cancel any common factors between them. The resulting numerator and denominator will have no common factors, which makes them relatively prime.

6. What are some proofs that $\sqrt{2}$ is irrational?

   *** For a quick review of Proof by Contradiction, see the Miscellaneous Topics at the end of this book.

   (a) Euclid's proof

      (by contradiction) Assume that $\sqrt{2} = \frac{a}{b}$ and that a and b are relatively prime integers. Then $2b^2 = a^2$. Thus a^2 is even, which means that a has to be even. (The square of an odd number is odd.) So, $a = 2c$ for some integer c. Then $2b^2 = 4c^2$, which means $b^2 = 2c^2$. Thus b^2 is even, which means that b has to be even. But this is impossible, because a and b were chosen to be relatively prime; they can't both be even. Therefore, it must be impossible to write $\sqrt{2}$ as $\frac{a}{b}$, which means $\sqrt{2}$ is irrational.

   (b) Another proof

(by contradiction) Assume that $\sqrt{2} = \frac{a}{b}$. Then $2b^2 = a^2$. By the Fundamental Theorem of Arithmetic, the number on the left hand side of this equation must have an odd number of prime factors, and the number on the right hand side must have an even number of prime factors. This is impossible, because there is only one way to write a number (like $2b^2$) as a product of primes. Therefore, it must be impossible to write $\sqrt{2}$ as $\frac{a}{b}$, which means $\sqrt{2}$ is irrational.

7. Sample Problems

   (a) Consider $y = mx + b$, where m and b are rational numbers. Must there be a point on this line that has integer coordinates?

   (b) Consider $y = ax^2 + bx + c$, where a, b, and c are rational numbers. Must there be a point on this parabola that has integer coordinates?

   (c) Prove that $\sqrt{5}$ is irrational.

   (d) Prove or disprove: If x^2 is rational, then x is rational.

   (e) Prove or disprove: If x^2 is irrational, then x is irrational.

   (f) If $n = 2^2 3^3 x^5 y z^2$ and $m = 2^3 3^2 x^3 y^2$, then find the greatest common factor of n and m, and the least common multiple of n and m.

   (g) Show that if (x, y, z) is a Pythagorean triple, and if f is a common factor of x, y, and z, then $(\frac{x}{f}, \frac{y}{f}, \frac{z}{f})$ is also a Pythagorean triple.

   (h) How many natural number solutions are there to $x + y = 12$? ... to $x + y = n \in \mathbb{N}$?

   (i) How many natural number solutions are there to $xy = 12$? ... to $xy = n \in \mathbb{N}$?

8. Answers to Sample Problems

   (a) Consider $y = mx + b$, where m and b are rational numbers. Must there be a point on this line that has integer coordinates?

   Not necessarily. For example, if $y = \frac{1}{3}x + \frac{1}{2}$, no matter what integer you plug in for x, y will not come out to an exact integer.

   (b) Consider $y = ax^2 + bx + c$, where a, b, and c are rational numbers. Must there be a point on this parabola that has integer coordinates?

   Not necessarily. The example given in the previous problem (with $a = 0$) still works. Also, if $a = b = c = \frac{1}{2}$, then for any integer x, y is equal to an integer plus $\frac{1}{2}$.

   (c) Prove that $\sqrt{5}$ is irrational. We can mimic the proof given above that $\sqrt{2}$ is irrational.
   Proof: Assume that $\sqrt{5} = \frac{a}{b}$. Then $5b^2 = a^2$. By the Fundamental Theorem of Arithmetic, the number on the left hand side of this equation must have an odd number of prime factors, and the number on the right hand side must have an even number of prime factors. This is impossible, because there is only one way to write a number (like $5b^2$) as a product of primes. Therefore, it must be impossible to write $\sqrt{5}$ as $\frac{a}{b}$, which means $\sqrt{5}$ is irrational.

(d) Prove or disprove: If x^2 is rational, then x is rational.

FALSE. Suppose $x^2 = 2$, which is rational. Then $x = \pm\sqrt{2}$, which was proven to be irrational. Thus the statement is false.

(e) Prove or disprove: If x^2 is irrational, then x is irrational.

Proof: Assume that x is rational. Then $x = \frac{p}{q}$ for some integers p and q, with $q \neq 0$. Then $x^2 = \frac{p^2}{q^2}$, which is clearly rational. Therefore, by indirect reasoning (contrapositive), we have shown that if x^2 is irrational, then x must be irrational too.

(f) If $n = 2^2 3^3 x^5 y z^2$ and $m = 2^3 3^2 x^3 y^2$, then find the greatest common factor of n and m, and the least common multiple of n and m.

The greatest common factor of n and m is $2^2 3^2 x^3 y$ and their least common multiple is $2^3 3^3 x^5 y^2 z^2$.

(g) Show that if (x, y, z) is a Pythagorean triple, and if f is a common factor of x, y, and z, then $\left(\frac{x}{f}, \frac{y}{f}, \frac{z}{f}\right)$ is also a Pythagorean triple.

$$\left(\frac{x}{f}\right)^2 + \left(\frac{y}{f}\right)^2 = \frac{x^2 + y^2}{f^2} = \frac{z^2}{f^2} = \left(\frac{z}{f}\right)^2$$

(h) How many natural number solutions are there to $x + y = 12$? ...to $x + y = n \in \mathbb{N}$? For the first equation, x can be any number between 1 and 11. So there are 11 solutions. (Some of these are essentially the same, like $1 + 11$ and $11 + 1$, but we ignore that similarity here because the solutions have distinct x-values.) For the second equation, then, there are $n - 1$ solutions.

(i) How many natural number solutions are there to $xy = 12$? ...to $xy = n \in \mathbb{N}$? For the first equation, there are 6 solutions, one for each factor of 12: $1, 2, 3, 4, 6, 12$. (Again, solutions are different if they have distinct x-values.) For the second equation, the answer is the number of factors of n. If n is prime, for example, then the answer is 2.

2.1 Algebraic Structures

a. Demonstrate knowledge of why the real and complex numbers are each a field, and that particular rings are not fields (e.g., integers, polynomial rings, matrix rings)

1. What is a field? What are some examples?

    A field is a set F together with two operations (called $+$ and $\times$) satisfying the following properties. Suppose that a, b, and c are elements of F.

    (a) F is closed under $+$ and $\times$

    This means that $a + b$ and $a \times b$, also called ab, are elements of F. [The element $a \times b$ is often written ab. We will follow this conventional notation below.]

    (b) $+$ and $\times$ are associative

    This means that $(a + b) + c = a + (b + c)$ and $(ab)c = a(bc)$.

    (c) $+$ and $\times$ are commutative

    This means that $a + b = b + a$ and $ab = ba$.

    (d) $+$ and $\times$ have identity elements 0 and 1 in F, respectively

    This means that $a + 0 = a$ and $b \cdot 1 = b$.

    (e) every element has an additive inverse in F

    This means that for every a in F, there is an element $-a$ **in** F satisfying $a + (-a) = 0$.

    (f) every non-zero element has a multiplicative inverse in F

    If $b \neq 0$, then there is $\frac{1}{b}$ **in** F satisfying $b(\frac{1}{b}) = 1$.

    (g) $\times$ distributes over $+$

    This means that $a(b + c) = ab + ac$.

    The most common fields we use are the rational numbers, the real numbers, and the complex numbers.

2. What is a ring? What are some examples?

    A ring is a set R together with two operations (called $+$ and $\times$) satisfying the following properties.

    (a) R is closed under $+$ and $\times$

    (b) $+$ and $\times$ are associative

    (c) $+$ is commutative

    (d) $+$ and $\times$ have identity elements 0 and 1 in R, respectively

    (e) every element has an additive inverse in R

    (f) $\times$ distributes over $+$

There are two key differences between the definition of a ring and the definition of a field: (1) rings do not necessarily have a commutative multiplication, and (2) rings do not necessarily contain multiplicative inverses. Notice that every field is a ring, but that there are rings which are not fields.

The most common rings we use (in addition to the fields listed above) are the integers, the set of square matrices of a given size (like all 2 by 2 matrices, for instance), and the set of polynomials with coefficients in another ring.

3. What are some non-examples of fields and rings?

The following common rings are not fields: integers, the set of square matrices of a given size (like all 2 by 2 matrices, for instance), and the set of polynomials with coefficients in another ring.

The natural numbers are not a ring. The set of all quadratic polynomials is not a ring. See Sample Problems, below.

4. Sample Problems

   (a) Give an example of a ring that is not a field.

   (b) Why are the integers not a field?

   (c) Why are the natural numbers not a ring?

   (d) Why is the set of all quadratic polynomials not a ring?

   (e) Write the multiplicative inverse of $3 - 2i$ in $a + bi$ form.

   (f) Show that the set of 2 by 2 matrices with integer entries forms a non-commutative ring.

   (g) Prove that the set of 2 by 2 invertible matrices with complex number entries is NOT a field.

   (h) Write the multiplicative inverse of $x + yi$ in $a + bi$ form.

   (i) What is the smallest field that contains 0 and 1?

   (j) Using the field properties listed above, prove that $(a + b)c = ac + bc$.

   (k) Let F be the field of rational functions $\dfrac{p(x)}{q(x)}$, where $p(x)$ and $q(x)$ are any polynomials with real coefficients and $q(x) \neq 0$.

      i. Show that F contains a multiplicative identity element.

      ii. Show that F is closed under multiplication.

      iii. Show that F is closed under addition.

      iv. Show that every non-zero element of F is invertible.

5. Answers to Sample Problems

   (a) Give an example of a ring that is not a field. Examples include: the integers, polynomials, and the set of all square matrices of a given size.

(b) Why are the integers not a field? Because not every integer has a multiplicative inverse *that is an integer.* For instance, the multiplicative inverse of 3 is $\frac{1}{3}$, which is not an integer.

(c) Why are the natural numbers not a ring? Because they do not contain an additive identity (although you might see a textbook which includes 0 in the natural numbers). Also, the additive inverses of natural numbers are not natural numbers. For instance, the additive inverse of 3 is -3, which is not a natural number.

(d) Why is the set of all quadratic polynomials not a ring? The set of quadratic polynomials is not closed under multiplication. For instance, if you multiply $x^2 + 1$ by $x^2 - 1$, you obtain $x^4 - 1$, which is not quadratic.

(e) Write the multiplicative inverse of $3 - 2i$ in $a + bi$ form.

$$\frac{1}{3-2i} \cdot \frac{3+2i}{3+2i} = \frac{3+2i}{9-4i^2} = \frac{3+2i}{9+4} = \frac{3}{13} + \frac{2}{13}i.$$

(f) Show that the set of 2 by 2 matrices with integer entries forms a non-commutative ring. We will show a few of the properties directly and leave the rest to the reader. To see the closure under addition, we technically should show that the sum

$$\begin{bmatrix} a & b \\ c & d \end{bmatrix} + \begin{bmatrix} a' & b' \\ c' & d' \end{bmatrix} = \begin{bmatrix} a+a' & b+b' \\ c+c' & d+d' \end{bmatrix}$$

is again a two by two matrix of integers. But since the integers are closed under addition, each entry of the new matrix is an integer. Hence the set of 2 by 2 matrices of integers is closed under addition. We will show multiplication as well (in part to remind the reader about how to multiply matrices).

$$\begin{bmatrix} a & b \\ c & d \end{bmatrix} \cdot \begin{bmatrix} a' & b' \\ c' & d' \end{bmatrix} = \begin{bmatrix} aa'+bc' & ab'+bd' \\ ca'+dc' & cb'+dd' \end{bmatrix}$$

Since the set of integers is closed under multiplication and addition, each entry in the product matrix is again an integer. Hence the set of 2 by 2 matrices with integer entries is closed under matrix multiplication.

We now check that matrix addition is commutative. Since

$$\begin{bmatrix} a & b \\ c & d \end{bmatrix} + \begin{bmatrix} a' & b' \\ c' & d' \end{bmatrix} = \begin{bmatrix} a+a' & b+b' \\ c+c' & d+d' \end{bmatrix} = \begin{bmatrix} a' & b' \\ c' & d' \end{bmatrix} + \begin{bmatrix} a & b \\ c & d \end{bmatrix},$$

it certainly follows that matrix addition is commutative.

Most of the other properties involve straightforward checks, under two conditions. First, the additive identity element of this ring is the *zero matrix,* $\begin{bmatrix} 0 & 0 \\ 0 & 0 \end{bmatrix}$, while the multiplicative identity element is the *identity matrix,* $\begin{bmatrix} 1 & 0 \\ 0 & 1 \end{bmatrix}$.

To show that this ring is not commutative, we need to give an example of two matrices that do not commute: $\begin{bmatrix} 0 & 1 \\ 0 & 0 \end{bmatrix} \cdot \begin{bmatrix} 0 & 0 \\ 1 & 0 \end{bmatrix} = \begin{bmatrix} 1 & 0 \\ 0 & 0 \end{bmatrix}$, whereas

$$\begin{bmatrix} 0 & 0 \\ 1 & 0 \end{bmatrix} \cdot \begin{bmatrix} 0 & 1 \\ 0 & 0 \end{bmatrix} = \begin{bmatrix} 0 & 0 \\ 0 & 1 \end{bmatrix}$$

Since these answers are different, then certainly the two matrices $\begin{bmatrix} 0 & 1 \\ 0 & 0 \end{bmatrix}$ and $\begin{bmatrix} 0 & 0 \\ 1 & 0 \end{bmatrix}$ do not commute. Hence the ring of 2 by 2 matrices with integer entries is NOT commutative.

(g) Prove that the set of 2 by 2 invertible matrices with complex number entries is NOT a field. We will show that this set of matrices is not closed under addition. Recall that $1 = 1 + 0i$ is a complex number. We have

$$\begin{bmatrix} 1 & 0 \\ 0 & 1 \end{bmatrix} + \begin{bmatrix} -1 & 0 \\ 0 & -1 \end{bmatrix} = \begin{bmatrix} 0 & 0 \\ 0 & 0 \end{bmatrix},$$

which is clearly not an invertible matrix, even though each matrix summand is invertible. Another reason is that the additive identity, the zero matrix, is not invertible and is therefore not an element of the set of 2 by 2 invertible matrices with complex number entries. Hence the set of 2 by 2 invertible matrices with complex number entries is not a field.

(h) Write the multiplicative inverse of $x + yi$ in $a + bi$ form.

$$\frac{1}{x + yi} \cdot \frac{x - yi}{x - yi} = \frac{x - yi}{x^2 - i^2 y^2} = \frac{x - yi}{x^2 + y^2} = \frac{x}{x^2 + y^2} - \frac{y}{x^2 + y^2}i.$$

(i) What is the smallest field that contains 0 and 1? Since any field must be closed under addition and must contain additive inverses, we know that all positive and negative integers must lie in this field. Moreover, since fields must contain multiplicative inverses of all nonzero elements, we must have the numbers $\frac{1}{2}$, $\frac{1}{3}$, etc. in the field. Then, using closure under addition and multiplication, we can obtain any rational number. It turns out that the rational numbers form a field. Thus, the rational numbers are the smallest field containing zero and one (under usual operations). [If you want to use operations mod 2 ($1+1 = 0$), then you can make a field containing only 0 and 1!]

(j) Using the field properties listed above, prove that $(a + b)c = ac + bc$. We have $(a + b)c = c(a + b) = ca + cb = ac + bc$, where we have used the commutativity of multiplication and the distributive property in the way it was originally stated above.

(k) Let F be the field of rational functions $\dfrac{p(x)}{q(x)}$, where $p(x)$ and $q(x)$ are any polynomials with real coefficients and $q(x) \neq 0$.

  i. Show that F contains a multiplicative identity element. The element $1 = \frac{1}{1}$ is an element of F, because 1 is a (degree zero) polynomial.

  ii. Show that F is closed under multiplication.

$$\frac{p(x)}{q(x)} \cdot \frac{a(x)}{b(x)} = \frac{p(x)a(x)}{q(x)b(x)}$$

  Polynomials are closed under multiplication. Since $q(x)$ and $b(x)$ are not 0, then $q(x)b(x) \neq 0$. So the product of two elements of F is another element of F.

iii. Show that F is closed under addition.

$$\frac{p(x)}{q(x)} + \frac{a(x)}{b(x)} = \frac{p(x)b(x) + q(x)a(x)}{q(x)b(x)}$$

Again, since polynomials are closed under multiplication and addition, and since the denominator is not zero, the sum of two elements of F is again an element of F.

iv. Show that every non-zero element of F is invertible. If $\frac{p(x)}{q(x)} \neq 0$, then $p(x) \neq 0$. So that means that $\frac{q(x)}{p(x)}$ is an element of F. Multiplying, we get

$$\frac{p(x)}{q(x)} \cdot \frac{q(x)}{p(x)} = \frac{p(x)q(x)}{p(x)q(x)} = 1.$$

Hence, every non-zero element of F is invertible.

b. Apply basic properties of real and complex numbers in constructing mathematical arguments (e.g., if $a < b$ and $c < 0$, then $ac > bc$)

1. What are some basic properties of real and complex numbers?

   The field properties are the most basic properties of real and complex numbers. In addition, for the real numbers there are properties of ordering, like the Trichotomy Axiom (mentioned below), and the following. Fill in the blanks.

   (a) If $a < b$ and $c < d$, then $a + c$ _____ $b + d$.
   (b) If $a < b$ and $c > 0$, then ac _____ bc.
   (c) If $a < b$ and $c < 0$, then ac _____ bc.
   (d) If $a \leq b$ and $b \leq a$, then a _____ b.
   (e) If $a < b$ and $b < c$, then a _____ c.
   (f) (Trichotomy) If a and b are real numbers, then exactly one of the following is true: $a < b$, $a > b$, or a _____ b.

   ANS: $<$, $<$, $>$, $=$, $<$, $=$.

   There are also properties of equality. List as many as you can:

   ANS: Reflexive, Symmetric, and Transitive Properties of Equality, Additive Property of Equality, Multiplicative Property of Equality

2. What is the definition of a rational number? ...of a complex number?

   A rational number can be expressed as the ratio of two integers. So, any rational number can be written as $\frac{p}{q}$, where p and q are integers, and $q \neq 0$.

A complex number can be expressed as the sum of a real number and an imaginary number. So, any complex number can be written as $a+bi$, where a and b are real numbers and $i^2 = -1$.

What is an imaginary number?

ANS: An imaginary number is one satisfying $x^2 \leq 0$. [There is sometimes a debate on whether 0 is imaginary or not. I choose to think of 0 as $0i$ in this case, making it imaginary. It's also real. No one said that numbers had to be either real or imaginary, but not both.]

3. Sample Problems

   (a) What is proved by the following?

   Suppose that $\sqrt{2} = \frac{p}{q}$, where $\frac{p}{q}$ is written in lowest terms; i.e., p and q are integers that have no common factors other than 1. Then $2 = \frac{p^2}{q^2}$. Since p and q have no common factors, we must have $q = 1$ or else $\frac{p^2}{q^2}$ would not be an integer. So $q = 1$ and $p^2 = 2$. But this is impossible because there is no integer p with $p^2 = 2$. □

   (b) Show on a number line that if $a > b > 0$, then $-a < -b$.

   (c) Let a and b be integers with $b \neq 0$. Consider the following statement: If $\frac{a}{b} < 1$, then $a < b$.

      i. List some values for a and b that make the statement true.

      ii. List some values for a and b that make the statement false.

      iii. What is a condition on a and/or b that will make the statement necessarily true?

4. Answers to Sample Problems

   (a) What is proved by the following?

   Suppose that $\sqrt{2} = \frac{p}{q}$, where $\frac{p}{q}$ is written in lowest terms; i.e., p and q are integers that have no common factors other than 1. Then $2 = \frac{p^2}{q^2}$. Since p and q have no common factors, we must have $q = 1$ or else $\frac{p^2}{q^2}$ would not be an integer. So $q = 1$ and $p^2 = 2$. But this is impossible because there is no integer p with $p^2 = 2$. □

   This is a proof (by contradiction) that $\sqrt{2}$ is irrational. The proof started by assuming that $\sqrt{2}$ was rational and deduced a contradiction to that assumption. Hence $\sqrt{2}$ must be irrational.

   (b) Show on a number line that if $a > b > 0$, then $-a < -b$. We are told that $a > b > 0$. On a number line, this looks like:

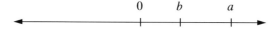

   So, if we put in $-a$ and $-b$ as well, we get:

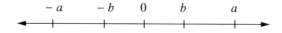

Clearly, $-a$ is to the left of $-b$, and thus $-a < -b$.

(c) Let a and b be integers with $b \neq 0$. Consider the following statement: If $\frac{a}{b} < 1$, then $a < b$.

    i. List some values for a and b that make the statement true. Answers may vary, although b must be greater than zero.

    ii. List some values for a and b that make the statement false. Answers may vary, although b must be less than zero.

    iii. What is a condition on a and/or b that will make the statement necessarily true? If b is positive, then one can use the Multiplicative Property of Inequality to deduce that the statement must be true. Conversely, if $b < 0$, then the statement is false.

c. Demonstrate knowledge that the rational numbers and real numbers can be ordered and that the complex numbers cannot be ordered, but that any polynomial equation with real coefficients can be solved in the complex field

1. What does it mean to be "ordered?"

   A set is "totally ordered" (or just "ordered") if, given any two elements a and b in the set, either $a \leq b$ or $b \leq a$. Notice that because of the Trichotomy Axiom of real numbers, we know that if x and y are real numbers, either (i) $x < y$, (ii) $x > y$, or (iii) $x = y$. Thus, the real numbers, and any subset of the real numbers, is ordered.

2. Why can't the complex numbers be ordered?

   This question is misleading. The complex numbers can indeed be ordered, but not in a meaningful way. We will examine some of the consequences of trying to order the complex numbers in the sample problems.

3. Fundamental Theorem of Algebra

   See **2.2 Polynomial Equations and Inequalities**, section **a** (below) for more information on the Fundamental Theorem of Algebra, which states that if $f(x)$ is a polynomial with real coefficients, then $f(x)$ can be factored into linear and quadratic factors, each of which has real coefficients. Moreover, $f(x)$ can be factored entirely into linear factors if you allow your factors to have complex coefficients.

   [Mathematicians say: Every complex polynomial has a root in $\mathbb{C}$. A fancy way to say this is to say that $\mathbb{C}$ is an "algebraically closed" field.]

4. Sample Problems

   (a) Which of the following sets is an ordered field: complex numbers, rational numbers, integers, or natural numbers?

   (b) List three reasons why the set of 2 by 2 matrices with real number entries do not form an ordered field.

   (c) What is the maximum number of complex solutions to $x^{17} - 573x^9 + 54x^8 - 167x + 2 = 0$?

(d) One way to order the complex numbers is as follows: $(a + bi) \lll (c + di)$ if (1) $a < c$ or (2) $a = c$ and $b < d$. In other words, compare the real parts to determine which is bigger. If they are the same, then move to the imaginary parts.

   i. Which is bigger, 2 or 20?

   ii. Which is bigger, $1 + 2i$ or $1 + 20i$?

   iii. Which is bigger, $2 + i$ or $-100 - 100i$?

   iv. Which is bigger, $100i$ or 1?

   v. What might be a disadvantage to this ordering?

(e) Another way to order the complex numbers is by their magnitudes. The magnitude of $a + bi$ is $\sqrt{a^2 + b^2}$, which is a real number. So, $(a + bi) \lll (c + di)$ if $\sqrt{a^2 + b^2} < \sqrt{c^2 + d^2}$.

   i. Which is bigger, 2 or 20?

   ii. Which is bigger, -2 or -20?

   iii. Which is bigger, 5 or $3 + 4i$?

   iv. Which is bigger, $1 + i$ or $1 - i$?

   v. What might be a disadvantage to this ordering?

5. Answers to Sample Problems

   (a) Which of the following sets is an ordered field: complex numbers, rational numbers, integers, or natural numbers? The rational numbers, integers, and natural numbers are all ordered via $<$, because they are subsets of the (ordered) real numbers.

   (b) List three reasons why the set of 2 by 2 matrices with real number entries do not form an ordered field. It's certainly hard to order them (in a meaningful way), but the set of 2 by 2 real matrices do not even form a field. Indeed, matrices like $\begin{bmatrix} 1 & 0 \\ 0 & 0 \end{bmatrix}$ do not even have a multiplicative inverse.

   (c) What is the maximum number of complex solutions to $x^{17} - 573x^9 + 54x^8 - 167x + 2 = 0$? Seventeen. The only time there may be fewer than 17 complex roots is if some of the roots have a multiplicity greater than one (like double roots, triple roots, etc.).

   (d) One way to order the complex numbers is as follows: $(a + bi) \lll (c + di)$ if (1) $a < c$ or (2) $a = c$ and $b < d$. In other words, compare the real parts to determine which is bigger. If they are the same, then move to the imaginary parts.

      i. Which is bigger, 2 or 20? ANS: 20

      ii. Which is bigger, $1 + 2i$ or $1 + 20i$? ANS: $1 + 20i$

      iii. Which is bigger, $2 + i$ or $-100 - 100i$? ANS: $2 + i$

      iv. Which is bigger, $100i$ or 1? ANS: 1

      v. What might be a disadvantage to this ordering? One disadvantage is that complex numbers with large imaginary parts but small real parts might be considered smaller than numbers that have small imaginary parts and only slightly bigger real parts. This method seems to give undue importance to the real part of a complex number.

(e) Another way to order the complex numbers is by their magnitudes. The magnitude of $a + bi$ is $\sqrt{a^2 + b^2}$, which is a real number. So, $(a+bi) \lll (c+di)$ if $\sqrt{a^2 + b^2} < \sqrt{c^2 + d^2}$.

    i. Which is bigger, 2 or 20? ANS: 20

    ii. Which is bigger, -2 or -20? ANS: -20

    iii. Which is bigger, 5 or $3 + 4i$? ANS: same magnitude

    iv. Which is bigger, $1 + i$ or $1 - i$? ANS: same magnitude

    v. What might be a disadvantage to this ordering? One disadvantage is that it is not consistent with the ordering of real numbers. ($-20 \ggg -2$, for instance.) Another disadvantage is that sometimes very different-looking complex numbers have the same magnitude. However, even though it may have drawbacks, this way of measuring the "size" of a complex number is very commonly used because it contains useful geometric information.

d. Identify and translate between equivalent forms of algebraic expressions and equations using a variety of techniques (e.g., factoring, applying properties of operations)

e. Justify the steps in manipulating algebraic expressions and solving algebraic equations and inequalities

We will treat these two standards together since they both address the techniques for manipulating expressions, equations, and inequalities, as well as the justifications for those techniques.

1. What are some of the techniques for translating between equivalent expressions? What are the justifications for these techniques?

An expression represents a number. When simplifying an expression (which involves translating between equivalent expressions), we have to make sure that we do not change the number represented by the expression. Here are some techniques which do not change the value of an expression, along with a short description, an example, and a brief justification for each.

- *Gathering like terms.* This can be thought of as a specific type of factoring, below. As an example, $3x - 2x + 4x$ can be rewritten as $5x$. This is justified by the distributive property (in reverse):
$$3x - 2x + 4x = (3 - 2 + 4)x = 5x.$$

- *Multiplying out.* This can be useful on its own or as part of other techniques. For example, when working with complex numbers, one might have the expression $(2 - 3\mathbf{i})(2 + 3\mathbf{i})$, which can be rewritten as $4 - 9\mathbf{i}^2$, or 13, when multiplied out. This can also be applied to separating fractions over the same denominator, as in rewriting $\dfrac{x^2 - 5}{x}$ as $\dfrac{x^2}{x} - \dfrac{5}{x}$, or $x - \dfrac{5}{x}$. (We can think of this as distributing $\dfrac{1}{x}$ over the numerator.) This is again justified via the distributive property.

- *Factoring.* In addition to gathering like terms, sometimes factoring can help transform an expression into a more useful format. For instance, $x^2 - 5x + 6$ can be factored as $(x - 2)(x - 3)$, which can tell us what values of x will make the expression equal to 0.

Factoring is also a form of the distributive property (in reverse):

$$\begin{aligned} x^2 - 5x + 6 &= x^2 - 2x - 3x + 6 \\ &= x(x-2) - 3(x-2) \\ &= (x-2)(x-3). \end{aligned}$$

- *Adding 0.* This is often a useful trick. For example, when completing the square on a quadratic expression, we can write $x^2 + 4x - 3$ as $x^2 + 4x + 4 - 4 - 3$, which is also $(x+2)^2 - 7$. Note that we added 0 by adding 4 and subtracting 4. The fact that adding 0 doesn't change the value of a number is because 0 is the additive identity.

- *Multiplying by 1.* This is often useful as well. For example, when rationalizing a denominator, such as $\dfrac{1}{2 + \sqrt{5}}$, we often multiply by a suitable form of 1.

$$\left(\frac{1}{2 + \sqrt{5}} \right) \left(\frac{2 - \sqrt{5}}{2 - \sqrt{5}} \right) \quad \text{which is also} \quad \frac{2 - \sqrt{5}}{4 - 5} \quad \text{or} \quad \sqrt{5} - 2.$$

  This technique is also often used to get a common denominator between two rational expressions. The fact that multiplying by 1 doesn't change the value of a number is because 1 is the multiplicative identity.

- *Canceling common factors in a rational expression.* This is essentially reducing a rational expression to its lowest terms. For instance, $\dfrac{2x^2 - 16x}{4x^3}$ can be reduced to $\dfrac{x - 8}{2x^2}$ by canceling the common factor of $2x$ that appears in the numerator and denominator. This can be justified by unraveling the meaning of a rational number. There are many equivalent forms of a rational number (like $\frac{1}{2}, \frac{2}{4}, \frac{3}{6}$, etc.) and so we are interested in the form that is in lowest terms (or at least lower terms).

  WARNING! There is a caveat here in that there can be a subtle difference between the simplified version and the original version in terms of the domain of acceptable values for x. In the above example, neither expression is defined when $x = 0$, so the second expression is equivalent to the first. However, if we write $\dfrac{(x-2)(x-3)}{x-2}$ as $x - 3$, then we have exchanged an expression where x cannot equal 2 for an expression in which x could equal 2. The expressions are equivalent, provided $x \neq 2$.

2. What are some of the techniques for translating between equivalent equations?

   An equation is a statement that two expressions denote the same number. Because we have two expressions, we have more techniques available to transform to equivalent equations. In addition to the above techniques for transforming each expression in the equation, we can also utilize the following. As before, each will be briefly explained, along with an example. Justifications will come later.

   - *Performing the same invertible (i.e. reversible) operation to both sides.* There are a variety of operations that are reversible: addition (or subtraction) of any number, multiplication (or division) by any non-zero number, extracting roots of both sides. If we are dealing with real numbers, then raising both sides to an odd power is reversible. Also, we can exponentiate both sides as powers of the same base b ($b > 0, b \neq 1$). This includes techniques like clearing denominators or raising a base to both sides of the equation, techniques which can not be done with expressions alone because they would change the value of the original expression. For example, to solve $\frac{1}{x} + 2 = \frac{5}{x}$, one can multiply both sides of the equation by x (provided $x \neq 0$ – see non-invertible operations, below) to obtain $1 + 2x = 5$, or $x = 2$. Likewise, to solve $\log x = 3$, we can transform to $10^{\log x} = 10^3$, or $x = 1000$.

- *Performing the same non-invertible (i.e. non-reversible) operation to both sides.* Here, we can still transform the equation into a new equation, but we might lose information along the way, and we might introduce new solutions that are not solutions of the original equation, called *extraneous* solutions. We have to know that when multiplying (or dividing) by a variable that might equal zero, or by raising both sides to an even power (like squaring), that we might introduce extraneous solutions. This is just further reason always to check your answers. Let's look at some examples.

  First, consider $\frac{2}{x} = 3$. We can solve this equation by multiplying both sides by x to obtain $2 = 3x$. Now we divide both sides by 3 (or multiply both sides by $\frac{1}{3}$) to get $x = \frac{2}{3}$. We check this in the original equation: $\frac{2}{\frac{2}{3}} = 2 \cdot \frac{3}{2} = 3$, which is correct.

  Second, let's try $\sqrt{x - 5} = 6$. Squaring both sides, we obtain $x - 5 = 36$ and so $x = 41$. Checking this is the original equation, we get $\sqrt{41 - 5} = \sqrt{36} = 6$.

  Note that we did not obtain any extraneous solutions in the first two examples because we checked our answers and they satisfied the original equations.

3. Why do extraneous solutions arise?

   Extraneous solutions can arise whenever your algebraic step is not reversible. For instance, $4 = -4$ is a FALSE equation, but the transformed equation from squaring both sides ($16 = 16$) is true. That's essentially how extraneous solutions can arise. Squaring both sides of an equation is not a reversible step. Neither is multiplying both sides by zero. One normally wouldn't multiply both sides of an equation by zero on purpose, but when variables are involved, students sometimes forget to check if they have inadvertently introduced extraneous solutions.

4. What are some examples of extraneous solutions?

   Let's do some examples in which extraneous solutions arise. First, consider the equation $\sqrt{4 - 3x^2} = x$. Squaring both sides, we get $4 - 3x^2 = x^2$, which simplifies to $4 = 4x^2$ or $x^2 = 1$. There are two solutions: $x = 1$ or $x = -1$ (often written $x = \pm 1$).

   If we check these values in the original equation, it's clear that $x = 1$ is a valid solution, but $x = -1$ is extraneous:

$$\sqrt{4 - 3(-1)^2} = \sqrt{4 - 3} = \sqrt{1} = 1 \neq -1.$$

   Squaring both sides of the original equation introduced an extraneous solution.

As a second example, consider $\dfrac{2x}{x-2} = 3 + \dfrac{4}{x-2}$. To clear the denominators, we will multiply both sides by $x-2$. So we get

$$
\begin{aligned}
2x &= 3(x-2) + 4 \\
2x &= 3x - 6 + 4 \\
2x &= 3x - 2 \\
2 &= x.
\end{aligned}
$$

So $x = 2$. But if we try to check this value in the original equation, we get a denominator of zero. So $x = 2$ is an extraneous solution and there is no solution to the original equation. Here, we introduced the extraneous solution when we multiplied both sides by $x - 2$. This step is only reversible if $x - 2 \neq 0$, i.e., if $x \neq 2$. If $x = 2$, it can sometimes still be done, but it destroys your chances of finding any other solutions. It's like trying to solve $x + 1 = 2$ by multiplying both sides by zero. You just get $0 = 0$, which is true, but you have lost any other information from the original equation.

5. What are some of the techniques for translating between equivalent inequalities?

An inequality is a statement that compares two expressions, and says that one is larger than (or larger than or equal to) the other. Again, we can transform any expression into an equivalent expression using the above rules. We can also transform both sides of an inequality by adding or subtracting the same number from both sides. We can also multiply or divide by a positive number without changing the direction of the inequality. But when we multiply or divide both sides of an inequality by a negative number, then we need to reverse the direction of the inequality sign. These properties can be found in section **b** above.

6. What are the justifications for these techniques?

Solving equations and inequalities with variables is what most people think of when they think of algebra. There are rules to how equations and inequalities can be manipulated, and students sometimes focus too much on the rules and lose sight of why the rules are true.

When working with equalities, most algebraic steps are based on what it means for two things to be exactly the same. If you think of numbers, a number can only equal itself - it cannot equal a different number. So $4 = 4$ is true, but $4 = 2$ is false. If two things are equal to begin with, and we transform both things in the exact same way, then the two transformed things must still be equal. This is clear. If you start with a true equality, like $4 = 4$, and you add ten to both sides, then the result (i.e. $14 = 14$) must still be a true equality. That explains the vast majority of algebraic manipulations of equations.

Inequalities are similar, but there are some transformations that will change the direction of the inequality (namely, multiplying or dividing by a negative number), and so one must be careful. If you start with a true inequality, like $4 > 2$, and you subtract 10 from both sides, you still get a true inequality: $-6 > -8$. But if you now multiply both sides of this inequality by -1, then you must remember to change the direction of the inequality. Namely, $-6 > -8$, but $6 < 8$. (This can be visualized on a number line. See Sample Problems in section **b** above.

Understanding that we are simply maintaining relationships of equality or inequality through-out the algebraic steps will help students understand why algebra leads toward a correct solution.

7. Sample Problems

   (a) Solve the following equations and inequalities. Identify any extraneous solutions, if they arise.

      i. $2x - 5 = 16$.

      ii. $2x - 5 > 16$.

      iii. $bx - c = 16$.

      iv. $\dfrac{x}{x-2} = 2$.

      v. $\dfrac{x}{x-1} = M$.

      vi. $\dfrac{x}{x-2} \leq 2$. (Careful!)

      vii. $\dfrac{x}{x+3} = 3 - \dfrac{3}{x+3}$.

      viii. $\sqrt{x} + \sqrt{x+3} = 3$.

      ix. $\sqrt{x^2 + 2x + 1} = x + 1$ (Careful!)

   (b) Explain why the solution to $3x - 5 = 4$ is $x = 3$ by showing each step. List all the properties you use.

   (c) Explain why the solution to $-3x - 5 < 4$ is $x > -3$ by showing each step. List all the properties you use.

   (d) Using various ring properties and properties of equality, give reasons for the proof of the Multiplication Property of Zero: If x is in a ring, then $0x = 0$.

      - $0 + 0 = 0$
      - $(0 + 0)x = 0x$
      - $0x + 0x = 0x$
      - $0x + 0x = 0x + 0$
      - $0x = 0$.

8. Answers to Sample Problems

   (a) Solve the following equations and inequalities. Identify any extraneous solutions, if they arise.

      i. $2x - 5 = 16$. $x = \dfrac{21}{2} = 10.5$

      ii. $2x - 5 > 16$. $x > \dfrac{21}{2} = 10.5$

      iii. $bx - c = 16$. $x = \dfrac{16 + c}{b}$, assuming $b \neq 0$.

      iv. $\dfrac{x}{x-2} = 2$. $x = 4$

v. $\dfrac{x}{x-1} = M$. $x = \dfrac{M}{M-1}$, assuming $M \neq 1$.

Here's one solution:

$$\begin{aligned}
\frac{x}{x-1} &= M \\
x &= M(x-1) = Mx - M \\
x - Mx &= -M \\
x(1-M) &= -M \\
x &= \frac{-M}{1-M} = \frac{M}{M-1}.
\end{aligned}$$

vi. $\dfrac{x}{x-2} \leq 2$. (Careful!) $x \geq 4$ or $x < 2$.

To see this, let's rewrite the left hand side by finding quotient and remainder polynomials first. It will simplify things a little bit by getting the variable x in only one location.

$$2 \geq \frac{x}{x-2} = \frac{x-2+2}{x-2} = 1 + \frac{2}{x-2},$$

and so $1 \geq \frac{2}{x-2}$. Now we need to multiply by $x-2$ but whether or not we change the direction of the inequality depends on the value of x. So let's look at two cases: $x - 2 < 0$ (i.e., $x < 2$) and $x - 2 > 0$ (i.e., $x > 2$). (Notice that if $x = 2$ we have an undefined fraction.)

Case 1: $x - 2 < 0$. Multiplying by $x - 2$, we get $x - 2 \leq 2$. Since $x - 2$ is negative in this case, it is certainly less than 2. Every value of x in this case solves the inequality.

Case 2: $x - 2 > 0$. Multiplying by $x - 2$, we get $x - 2 \geq 2$, or $x \geq 4$. So not every value of x in this case will work. We also have to restrict x to be at least 4.

Putting the two cases together, we get that $x < 2$ or $x \geq 4$.

vii. $\dfrac{x}{x+3} = 3 - \dfrac{3}{x+3}$. The "solution" $x = -3$ is extraneous; there are no solutions.

viii. $\sqrt{x} + \sqrt{x+3} = 3$. $x = 1$.

ix. $\sqrt{x^2 + 2x + 1} = x + 1$ (Careful!) This looks like an identity once you square both sides. It is tempting to state that the equation is true for all values of x. But it's not. Try $x = -2$ for instance. $\sqrt{4 - 4 + 1} = 1 \neq -2 + 1$. The equation is only true if the right-hand side is not negative. That is, $x + 1 \geq 0$, or $x \geq -1$. To reiterate: this equation is true for all values of x that are greater than or equal to -1.

(b) Explain why the solution to $3x - 5 = 4$ is $x = 3$ by showing each step. List all the properties you use.

A quick word about the following list. Each stated reason is explaining the algebraic reasoning behind the transition from the previous line to the current line. So, in the third step, "Arithmetic" refers to the transition from $4 + 5$ to 9 on the right hand side. It does not refer to the equation $(3x - 5) + 5 = 9$. The only exception to this pattern is the first "Given."

$$3x - 5 = 4 \qquad \text{Given}$$
$$(3x - 5) + 5 = 4 + 5 \qquad \text{Additive Property of Equality}$$
$$(3x - 5) + 5 = 9 \qquad \text{Arithmetic}$$
$$(3x + (-5)) + 5 = 9 \qquad \text{Definition of Subtraction}$$
$$3x + ((-5) + 5) = 9 \qquad \text{Associative Property of Addition}$$
$$3x + 0 = 9 \qquad \text{Additive Inverse}$$
$$3x = 9 \qquad \text{Additive Identity}$$
$$\frac{1}{3}(3x) = \frac{1}{3}(9) \qquad \text{Multiplicative Property of Equality}$$
$$\frac{1}{3}(3x) = 3 \qquad \text{Arithmetic}$$
$$\left(\frac{1}{3} \cdot 3\right)x = 3 \qquad \text{Associative Property of Multiplication}$$
$$1x = 3 \qquad \text{Multiplicative Inverse}$$
$$x = 3 \qquad \text{Multiplicative Identity}$$

(c) Explain why the solution to $-3x - 5 < 4$ is $x > -3$ by showing each step. List all the properties you use.

$$-3x - 5 < 4 \qquad \text{Given}$$
$$(-3x - 5) + 5 < 4 + 5 \qquad \text{Additive Property of Inequality}$$
$$(-3x - 5) + 5 < 9 \qquad \text{Arithmetic}$$
$$(-3x + (-5)) + 5 < 9 \qquad \text{Definition of Subtraction}$$
$$-3x + ((-5) + 5) < 9 \qquad \text{Associative Property of Addition}$$
$$-3x + 0 < 9 \qquad \text{Additive Inverse}$$
$$-3x < 9 \qquad \text{Additive Identity}$$
$$-\frac{1}{3}(-3x) > -\frac{1}{3}(9) \qquad \text{Multiplicative Property of Inequality}$$
$$-\frac{1}{3}(-3x) > -3 \qquad \text{Arithmetic}$$
$$\left(-\frac{1}{3} \cdot -3\right)x > -3 \qquad \text{Associative Property of Multiplication}$$
$$1x > -3 \qquad \text{Multiplicative Inverse}$$
$$x > -3 \qquad \text{Multiplicative Identity}$$

(d) Using various ring properties and properties of equality, give reasons for the proof of the Multiplication Property of Zero: If x is in a ring, then $0x = 0$.

- $0 + 0 = 0$ Additive Identity (anything plus 0 equals itself)
- $(0 + 0)x = 0x$ Multiplicative Property of Equality (i.e., multiply both sides by x)
- $0x + 0x = 0x$ Distributive Property

- $0x + 0x = 0x + 0$ Additive Identity
- $0x = 0$.   Additive Property of Equality (in reverse) (i.e., cancel $0x$ from both sides)

f. Represent situations and solve problems using algebraic equations and inequalities

See sections **1.1.c** and **2.3.f** for theoretical underpinnings and practical examples.

2.2 Polynomial Equations and Inequalities

a. Analyze and solve polynomial equations with real coefficients using:

- **the Fundamental Theorem of Algebra**

- **the Rational Root Theorem for polynomials with integer coefficients**

- **the Conjugate Roots Theorem for polynomial equations with real coefficients**

- **the Binomial Theorem**

1. What is the Fundamental Theorem of Algebra?

   The Fundamental Theorem of Algebra says that if $f(x)$ is a polynomial with real coefficients, then $f(x)$ can be factored into linear and quadratic factors, each of which has real coefficients. Moreover, $f(x)$ can be factored entirely into linear factors if you allow your factors to have complex coefficients.

2. How do you use the Fundamental Theorem of Algebra to analyze polynomial equations?

   The main way to use the Fundamental Theorem of Algebra is when determining the number of roots a polynomial has. For example, a polynomial of degree n has at most n roots. Combined with the the following theorems, we can often say more.

   Example: Say f has real coefficients and degree 5. If $2 - i$ is a root of f, then how many real roots can f have? The answer is that f has either one or three real roots. The reason for this is that because f has real coefficients, the Conjugate Roots Theorem says that $2 + i$ is also a root. This accounts for 2 of the roots of f, leaving 3 more complex roots, some of which might (also) be real. Since the complex nonreal roots have to come in conjugate pairs, there are either zero or two more complex nonreal roots. Hence the number of real roots must be three or one. (This includes the multiplicity of a double or triple root, which would count as two or three roots, respectively.)

3. What is the Rational Root Theorem for polynomials with integer coefficients?

   If $f(x) = a_n x^n + a_{n-1} x^{n-1} + \ldots + a_1 x + a_0$, with each a_i an integer, then the Rational Root Theorem says that the only possible rational roots are of the form $\pm \frac{p}{q}$, where p is a divisor of a_0 and q is a divisor of a_n.

   Proof: Suppose $\frac{p}{q}$ is a root of f. Then

   $$0 = f(p/q) = a_n (p/q)^n + a_{n-1}(p/q)^{n-1} + \ldots + a_1(p/q) + a_0.$$

   Multiply by q^n to clear denominators. Then

   $$0 = a_n p^n + a_{n-1} p^{n-1} q + \ldots + a_1 p q^{n-1} + a_0 q^n.$$

   So $-a_0 q^n = a_n p^n + a_{n-1} p^{n-1} q + \ldots + a_1 p q^{n-1} = p(a_n p^{n-1} + a_{n-1} p^{n-2} q + \ldots + a_1 q^{n-1})$, which is clearly divisible by p. If we assume that $\frac{p}{q}$ is in lowest terms, then p has no factors in common with q^n. So p must be a divisor of a_0. Similarly, $-a_n p^n = q(a_{n-1}p^{n-1}+\ldots+a_1 pq^{n-2}+a_0 q^{n-1})$, which is divisible by q. Thus, a_n must be divisible by q.   □

Alternate Explanation: Factor $f(x)$ into factors with integer coefficients. If $\pm\frac{p}{q}$ is a root, then $(qx \mp p)$ is a factor. [See Factor Theorem, below.] So, when you multiply out all the factors, q will be a factor of the leading coefficient, a_n, and p will be a factor of the constant term, a_0. [To check this, try multiplying $(2x - 3)$ by any polynomial with integer coefficients. Then notice that the leading term is divisible by 2 and the constant term is divisible by 3.]

Example: List all possible rational roots of $g(x) = 2x^3 + 9x^2 + 7x - 6$.

ANS: Any rational root must be a factor of 6 divided by a factor of 2. The possibilities are: $\pm1, \pm2, \pm3, \pm6, \pm\frac{1}{2}, \pm\frac{3}{2}$.

4. What is the Conjugate Roots Theorem for polynomial equations with real coefficients?

If $f(x)$ is a polynomial with *real* coefficients, and if $f(a + bi) = 0$, then the Conjugate Roots Theorem says that $f(a - bi) = 0$.

Proof: Since $f(x)$ has real coefficients, $f(x) = \overline{f}(x)$, where $\overline{f}(x)$ is the polynomial obtained by taking the complex conjugate of every coefficient of f. So

$$0 = \overline{f(a + bi)} = \overline{\overline{f}(a + bi)} = \overline{f}(\overline{a + bi}) = f(\overline{a + bi}) = f(a - bi). \quad \square$$

Example: Factor $g(x) = x^4 - 5x^3 + 9x^2 - 5x$ if you know that $g(2 + i) = 0$.

ANS: Since $2 + i$ is a root, the Conjugate Roots Theorem says that $2 - i$ is also a root. This means that $(x - (2 + i))$ and $(x - (2 - i))$ are factors of $g(x)$. So

$$
\begin{aligned}
(x - (2 + i))(x - (2 - i)) &= x^2 - (2 + i)x - (2 - i)x + (2 + i)(2 - i) \\
&= x^2 - 4x + 5
\end{aligned}
$$

is also a factor of $g(x)$. Notice that x is a factor as well. So, using long division, (or trial and error, or noticing that 1 is a root), we obtain

$$g(x) = x^4 - 5x^3 + 9x^2 - 5x = x(x - 1)(x^2 - 4x + 5).$$

5. What is the Conjugate Roots Theorem for polynomial equations with rational coefficients?

If $f(x)$ is a polynomial with *rational* coefficients, and if $f(a + b\sqrt{n}) = 0$ (with $\sqrt{n}$ irrational), then the Conjugate Roots Theorem says that $f(a - b\sqrt{n}) = 0$.

Proof: Abstract Algebra. Since f has rational coefficients, f doesn't change when you switch the irrational $\sqrt{n}$ with $-\sqrt{n}$. The proof then is similar to the one using complex conjugation, given above.

Example: Suppose $f(x)$ is quadratic with $f(5 - \sqrt{5}) = 0$. Find a possible formula for $f(x)$.

ANS: Let's find such an f with rational coefficients, which means that we can require $f(5 + \sqrt{5}) = 0$ also. The simplest quadratic is thus

$$
\begin{aligned}
f(x) &= (x - (5 - \sqrt{5}))(x - (5 + \sqrt{5})) \\
&= x^2 - (5 - \sqrt{5})x - (5 + \sqrt{5})x + (5 - \sqrt{5})(5 + \sqrt{5}) \\
&= x^2 - 10x + 20.
\end{aligned}
$$

6. What is the Binomial Theorem?

$$(x+y)^n = \sum_{k=0}^{n} \binom{n}{k} x^{n-k} y^k,$$

where $\binom{n}{k} = \dfrac{n!}{k!(n-k)!}$ and is read "n choose k." It is also the number of ways to choose k objects from a set of n objects.

The Binomial Theorem can be proved by mathematical induction.

Proof: We start by checking that the formula is true for $n = 1$.

$$\sum_{k=0}^{1} \binom{1}{k} x^{1-k} y^k = \binom{1}{0} x^1 y^0 + \binom{1}{1} x^0 y^1 = 1x + 1y = (x+y)^1.$$

Now we show that whenever the formula is true for some value of n then it is also true for $n+1$. (Via induction, this will imply that the formula is true for any value of n.)

$$\begin{aligned} (x+y)^{n+1} &= (x+y)(x+y)^n \\ &= (x+y)\left(\sum_{k=0}^{n} \binom{n}{k} x^{n-k} y^k \right) \\ &= \sum_{k=0}^{n} \binom{n}{k} x^{n-k+1} y^k + \sum_{k=0}^{n} \binom{n}{k} x^{n-k} y^{k+1} \end{aligned}$$

We need to re-index the second summation in order to combine like terms correctly. Let $\ell = k+1$ so that the summation is from $\ell = 1$ to $\ell = n+1$. Then

$$(x+y)^{n+1} = \sum_{k=0}^{n} \binom{n}{k} x^{n-k+1} y^k + \sum_{\ell=1}^{n+1} \binom{n}{\ell-1} x^{n-(\ell-1)} y^\ell$$

Notice that we can combine the middle terms ($1 \le k, \ell \le n$) and notice that we have like terms now, if we match up k in the first sum with ℓ in the second, but that the first and last terms need to be separated out.

$$\begin{aligned} (x+y)^{n+1} &= x^{n+1} + \left(\sum_{k=1}^{n} \left[\binom{n}{k} + \binom{n}{k-1} \right] x^{n-k+1} y^k \right) + y^{n+1} \\ &= \sum_{k=0}^{n+1} \binom{n+1}{k} x^{n+1-k} y^k, \end{aligned}$$

which is exactly what we wanted to show. $\square$

Notice that we used an identity of the binomial coefficients, namely

$$\binom{n}{k} + \binom{n}{k-1} = \binom{n+1}{k}.$$

You can verify this identity in the Sample Problems.

Example: Expand $(x + 2)^5$.

$$(x + 2)^5 = \sum_{k=0}^{5} \binom{5}{k} x^{5-k} 2^k$$

$$= \binom{5}{0} x^5 2^0 + \binom{5}{1} x^4 2^1 + \ldots + \binom{5}{5} x^0 2^5$$

$$= x^5 + 5x^4(2) + 10x^3(4) + 10x^2(8) + 5x(16) + 1(32)$$

$$= x^5 + 10x^4 + 40x^3 + 80x^2 + 80x + 32.$$

7. Sample Problems

   (a) Let $2x^4 - x^3 - 20x^2 + 13x + 30 = 0$.

      i. List all possible rational roots.
      ii. Find all rational roots.
      iii. Find all roots.

   (b) Let $6x^4 + 7x^3 + 6x^2 - 1 = 0$.

      i. List all possible rational roots.
      ii. Find all rational roots.
      iii. Find all roots.

   (c) Factor $x^3 - x - 6$ if you know that one root is $-1 + i\sqrt{2}$.

   (d) Find the coefficient of x^4 in $(x - 3)^6$.

   (e) Find the fifth term in the expansion of $(2x - y)^9$.

   (f) Explain why the number of ways to choose k objects from a group of n is the same as the number of ways to choose $n - k$ objects from a group of n.

   (g) Suppose $f(x)$ is a quartic polynomial with integer coefficients. If $f(1 + i) = 0$ and $f(2 - \sqrt{3}) = 0$, then find a possible formula for $f(x)$.

   (h) How many real roots can $x^5 - 3x^2 + x + 1$ have? Be specific.

   (i) Find a possible formula for a polynomial $f(x)$ that satisfies: $f(-2) = f(3) = f(5) = 0$ and $f(0) = 15$.

   (j) If $x^2 - 5x + 6$ is a divisor of the polynomial $f(x)$, then what is the minimum degree of f? What is $f(2)$? What is $f(3)$? Suppose $f(4) = 0$. Find a formula for $f(x)$.

   (k) Verify that $\binom{n}{k} + \binom{n}{k-1} = \binom{n+1}{k}$.

8. Answers to Sample Problems

   (a) Let $2x^4 - x^3 - 20x^2 + 13x + 30 = 0$.

      i. List all possible rational roots. $\pm 1, \pm 2, \pm 3, \pm 5, \pm 6, \pm 10, \pm 15, \pm 30, \pm\frac{1}{2}, \pm\frac{3}{2}, \pm\frac{5}{2}, \pm\frac{15}{2}$.

     ii. Find all rational roots.

$$2x^4 - x^3 - 20x^2 + 13x + 30 = (x+1)(2x^3 - 3x^2 - 17x + 30) = (x+1)(x-2)(x+3)(2x-5)$$

     So, the rational roots are $-1, 2, -3, \frac{5}{2}$.

     iii. Find all roots. $-1, 2, -3, \frac{5}{2}$. We know the list is complete because the polynomial has degree 4.

(b) Let $6x^4 + 7x^3 + 6x^2 - 1 = 0$.

     i. List all possible rational roots. $\pm 1, \pm\frac{1}{2}, \pm\frac{1}{3}, \pm\frac{1}{6}$.

     ii. Find all rational roots.

$$6x^4 + 7x^3 + 6x^2 - 1 = (2x+1)(3x-1)(x^2+x+1)$$

     So, the rational roots are $-\frac{1}{2}$ and $\frac{1}{3}$.

     iii. Find all roots. $-\frac{1}{2}, \frac{1}{3}, \frac{-1\pm i\sqrt{3}}{2}$. The other roots can be found by completing the square or the Quadratic Formula. (See the next section.)

(c) Factor $x^3 - x - 6$ if you know that one root is $-1 + i\sqrt{2}$. Since the coefficients are real, we know that another root is $-1 - i\sqrt{2}$. Hence

$$(x-(-1+i\sqrt{2}))(x-(-1-i\sqrt{2})) = (x+1-i\sqrt{2})(x+1+i\sqrt{2}) = (x+1)^2+2 = x^2+2x+3$$

is a factor of $x^3 - x - 6$. So $x^3 - x - 6 = (x^2+2x+3)(x-2)$ by long division, or by guess and check, or by looking at the leading coefficient and constant term and deducing the linear factor.

(d) Find the coefficient of x^4 in $(x-3)^6$. 135. The $k=2$ term is:

$$\binom{6}{2} x^{6-2}(-3)^2 = 15x^4(9) = 135x^4.$$

(e) Find the fifth term in the expansion of $(2x-y)^9$. The first term corresponds to $k=0$ in the summation. So the fifth term corresponds to $k=4$.

$$\binom{9}{4} (2x)^5(-y)^4 = \frac{(9)(8)(7)(6)(5!)}{(4)(3)(2)(1)(5!)}(32x^5)(y^4) = 4032x^5y^4.$$

(f) Explain why the number of ways to choose k objects from a group of n is the same as the number of ways to choose $n-k$ objects from a group of n. If you choose k objects to include in your subgroup, then you could also think of that as simultaneously choosing $n-k$ objects to exclude from your subgroup. Each way to choose a few is also a way to exclude all the rest. Mathematically, this means $\binom{n}{k} = \binom{n}{n-k}$.

(g) Suppose $f(x)$ is a quartic polynomial with integer coefficients. If $f(1+i) = 0$ and $f(2-\sqrt{3}) = 0$, then find a possible formula for $f(x)$. Since f has rational coefficients, we can employ both forms of the Conjugate Roots Theorem, implying that f has four roots. One possible formula for f is thus:

$$f(x) = (x-(1+i))(x-(1-i))(x-(2-\sqrt{3}))(x-(2+\sqrt{3})),$$

which equals $(x^2 - 2x + 2)(x^2 - 4x + 1) = x^4 - 6x^3 + 11x^2 - 10x + 2.$

(h) How many real roots can $x^5 - 3x^2 + x + 1$ have? Be specific. This polynomial could have 1, 3, or 5 real roots. However, we can use synthetic substitution (or long division) to see that 1 is a double root. Thus the polynomial must have 3 or 5 real roots.

(i) Find a possible formula for a polynomial $f(x)$ that satisfies: $f(-2) = f(3) = f(5) = 0$ and $f(0) = 15$. We know that f must have factors $(x + 2)$, $(x - 3)$, and $(x - 5)$. So we could guess $f(x) = (x + 2)(x - 3)(x - 5)$, but this satisfies $f(0) = 30$, which is not what we want. So, we could multiply our guess by $\frac{1}{2}$, which doesn't change the roots. Thus a correct answer is

$$f(x) = \frac{1}{2}(x + 2)(x - 3)(x - 5) = \frac{1}{2}(x^3 - 6x^2 - x + 30) = \frac{1}{2}x^3 - 3x^2 - \frac{1}{2}x + 15.$$

(j) If $x^2 - 5x + 6$ is a divisor of the polynomial $f(x)$, then what is the minimum degree of f? What is $f(2)$? What is $f(3)$? Suppose $f(4) = 0$. Find a formula for $f(x)$. The minimum degree of f would be 2. Since $2^2 - 5(2) + 6 = 0$, $f(2) = 0$. Similarly, $f(3) = 0$. If we also know that $f(4) = 0$, then f must have a factor of $(x - 4)$ as well, bringing its minimum degree up to 3. One possible formula for $f(x)$ is

$$(x^2 - 5x + 6)(x - 4) = x^3 - 9x^2 + 26x - 24.$$

(k) Verify that $\binom{n}{k} + \binom{n}{k-1} = \binom{n+1}{k}$. We will write out the choose functions and then get a common denominator.

$$
\begin{aligned}
\binom{n}{k} + \binom{n}{k-1} &= \frac{n!}{k!(n-k)!} + \frac{n!}{(k-1)!(n-(k-1))!} \\
&= \frac{n!(n-k+1)}{k!(n-k)!(n-k+1)} + \frac{n!(k)}{(k-1)!(n-k+1)!(k)} \\
&= \frac{n!(n-k+1) + n!(k)}{k!(n-k+1)!} \\
&= \frac{n!(n+1)}{k!(n+1-k)!} = \frac{(n+1)!}{k!(n+1-k)!} = \binom{n+1}{k}
\end{aligned}
$$

Another way to justify it is using counting and the choice function. Let's say that there are $n + 1$ people in a group, and you are one of them. Suppose they need a committee of k people from this group. There are $\binom{n+1}{k}$ ways to choose that committee.

Now let's count the same number of committees, but let's consider if you are on the committee or not. How many committees are you on? Well, since you are one of the people, there are only n people left in the group, and there are only $k - 1$ seats left on the committee. So there are $\binom{n}{k-1}$ committees that have you as a member. How many committees do not have you on them? Well, if you are not on the committee, then there are n people left in the group, and k seats left on the committee. So there are $\binom{n}{k}$ committees that you are not on. Adding these two together gives the total number of committees.

b. Prove and use the Factor Theorem and the quadratic formula for real and complex quadratic polynomials

1. What is the Factor Theorem? How do you prove it?

    The Factor Theorem says that $(x - b)$ is a factor of $f(x)$ if and only if $f(b) = 0$.

    Proof: The Factor Theorem is just a special case of the Remainder Theorem, which says that if $f(x)$ is divided by $(x - b)$, then the remainder is $f(b)$. To see this, recall that if you divide $f(x)$ by $(x - b)$, you get a quotient polynomial $q(x)$ and a remainder polynomial $r(x)$ with the degree of $r(x)$ smaller than the degree of $(x - b)$. So $r(x)$ must be a constant, say r. Hence we have

    $$f(x) = (x - b)q(x) + r.$$

    Letting $x = b$ gives the Remainder Theorem: $f(b) = r$. Therefore, $f(b) = 0$ if and only if the remainder is zero, i.e., exactly when $(x - b)$ is a factor of $f(x)$.   □

    Example: Find the roots of $f(x) = x^5 + 8x^4 + 19x^3 + 8x^2 - 20x - 16$.

    ANS: Using the Remainder Theorem (and synthetic substitution), we notice that both 1 and -1 are roots, which shortens the calculations:

x	1	8	19	8	-20	-16	
1	1	9	28	36	16	0	root
-1	1	8	20	16	0		root
-1	1	7	13	3			(not a double root)
-2	1	6	8	0			root
-2	1	4	0				double root
-4	1	0					root

    (You can also try plugging in 1, -1, -2, and -4 into the polynomial to obtain zero. Review synthetic substitution if you wish to use it.) The roots are : 1, -1, -2, and -4, where -2 is a double root. This also means that

    $$f(x) = x^5 + 8x^4 + 19x^3 + 8x^2 - 20x - 16 = (x - 1)(x + 1)(x + 2)^2(x + 4).$$

2. What is the Quadratic Formula for real and complex quadratic polynomials?

    If $ax^2 + bx + c = 0$ with $a \neq 0$, then $x = \dfrac{-b \pm \sqrt{b^2 - 4ac}}{2a}$.

    This formula will be derived as a sample problem. A Cubic Formula and a Quartic Formula also exist, but there is no Quintic Formula!

3. Sample Problems

    (a) Solve the following quadratic equations.

        i. $2x^2 = 20$.
        ii. $3(x + 4)^2 = 12$.
        iii. $x^2 - 6 = 5x$.
        iv. $x^2 + 6 = 5x$.

v. $x^2 + 6x = 5$.

vi. $3x^2 + 6x = 5$.

(b) Use the quadratic formula to solve the following. Leave constants in your answer, if necessary. If the answers are complex, write them in $a + bi$ form.

i. $x^2 + bx + 1 = 0$.

ii. $x^2 - x + 1 = 0$.

iii. $-\frac{1}{2}At^2 + Vt + S = 0$.

(c) Let $f(x) = x^2 - bx + (b - 1)$. Find $f(1)$. Explain how the Factor Theorem allows you to factor $f(x)$. Then, factor $f(x)$.

(d) Show that in $x^2 + bx + c = 0$, the sum of the two roots is $-b$ and the product of the two roots is c.

(e) Solve $z^2 - iz + 2 = 0$.

(f) Solve $x^2 + 3x = -5$.

(g) Derive the Quadratic Formula. [Hint: Complete the Square.]

4. Answers to Sample Problems

(a) Solve the following quadratic equations.

i. $2x^2 = 20$. $x = \pm\sqrt{10}$ (I used inspection.)

ii. $3(x + 4)^2 = 12$. $x = -4 \pm 2$, i.e. $x = -2$ or $x = -6$. (I used inspection.)

iii. $x^2 - 6 = 5x$. $x = 6$ or $x = -1$. (I factored.)

iv. $x^2 + 6 = 5x$. $x = 2$ or $x = 3$. (I factored.)

v. $x^2 + 6x = 5$. $x = -3 \pm \sqrt{14}$. (I completed the square.)

vi. $3x^2 + 6x = 5$. $x = -1 \pm \sqrt{\frac{8}{3}}$. (I completed the square.)

(b) Use the quadratic formula to solve the following. Leave constants in your answer, if necessary. If the answers are complex, write them in $a + bi$ form.

i. $x^2 + bx + 1 = 0$. $x = \dfrac{-b \pm \sqrt{b^2 - 4}}{2}$

ii. $x^2 - x + 1 = 0$. $x = \dfrac{1 \pm \sqrt{-3}}{2} = \dfrac{1}{2} \pm i\dfrac{\sqrt{3}}{2}$

iii. $-\frac{1}{2}At^2 + Vt + S = 0$. $x = \dfrac{V \pm \sqrt{V^2 + 2AS}}{A}$

(c) Let $f(x) = x^2 - bx + (b - 1)$. Find $f(1)$. Explain how the Factor Theorem allows you to factor $f(x)$. Then, factor $f(x)$.

$f(1) = 1 - b + (b - 1) = 0$. The Factor Theorem implies that $(x - 1)$ is thus a factor of $f(x)$. So

$$x^2 - bx + (b - 1) = (x - 1)(x - (b - 1)).$$

(d) Show that in $x^2 + bx + c = 0$, the sum of the two roots is $-b$ and the product of the two roots is c. The roots are $x = \frac{-b \pm \sqrt{b^2 - 4c}}{2}$. So,

$$\frac{-b + \sqrt{b^2 - 4c}}{2} + \frac{-b - \sqrt{b^2 - 4c}}{2} = \frac{-2b}{2} = -b,$$

and

$$\left(\frac{-b + \sqrt{b^2 - 4c}}{2}\right)\left(\frac{-b - \sqrt{b^2 - 4c}}{2}\right) = \frac{(-b + \sqrt{b^2 - 4c})(-b - \sqrt{b^2 - 4c})}{4}$$

$$= \frac{(-b)^2 - (b^2 - 4c)}{4} = \frac{4c}{4} = c.$$

(e) Solve $z^2 - iz + 2 = 0$. Using the Quadratic Formula, we get

$$z = \frac{i \pm \sqrt{-1 - 4(2)}}{2} = \frac{i \pm \sqrt{-9}}{2} = \frac{i \pm 3i}{2} = 2i, -i.$$

(f) Solve $x^2 + 3x = -5$. First, we set $x^2 + 3x + 5 = 0$ and use the Quadratic Formula.

$$x = \frac{-3 \pm \sqrt{9 - 4(5)}}{2} = \frac{-3 \pm \sqrt{-11}}{2} = \frac{-3 \pm i\sqrt{11}}{2}.$$

(g) Derive the Quadratic Formula. [Hint: Complete the Square.]

$$ax^2 + bx + c = 0 \qquad \text{Given } (a \neq 0)$$

$$x^2 + \frac{b}{a}x = -\frac{c}{a} \qquad \text{Divide by } a \neq 0 \text{ and rearrange terms}$$

$$x^2 + \frac{b}{a}x + \frac{b^2}{4a^2} = -\frac{c}{a} + \frac{b^2}{4a^2} \qquad \text{Complete the square}$$

$$\left(x + \frac{b}{2a}\right)^2 = \frac{b^2 - 4ac}{4a^2} \qquad \text{Factor, obtain common denominator}$$

$$\left(x + \frac{b}{2a}\right) = \pm\frac{\sqrt{b^2 - 4ac}}{2a} \qquad \text{Take square root of each side}$$

$$x = -\frac{b}{2a} \pm \frac{\sqrt{b^2 - 4ac}}{2a} \qquad \text{Rearrange terms}$$

and thus $x = \frac{-b \pm \sqrt{b^2 - 4ac}}{2a}$.

c. Solve polynomial inequalities

1. How do you solve linear inequalities in one variable?

(For more information on linear inequalities with two variables and their graphs, see section **2.3.c.**)

When solving a linear inequality in one variable, one should be able to isolate the variable on one side, and a number on the other, by using standard properties of algebra. See the example in section **2.1.e** above.

2. How do you solve quadratic inequalities in one variable?

Let's compare two examples and then talk about general methods. First, consider $x^2 + 6 > -5x$. By adding $5x$ to both sides, we get $x^2 + 5x + 6 > 0$, or $(x+2)(x+3) > 0$. Now we look at this inequality as saying that a product of two numbers is greater than zero. So either both of these numbers are positive, or both are negative. A quick table will tell us the values of x for which either of these situations holds. Note that the factor $(x+2)$ changes sign at -2, while $(x+3)$ changes sign at -3.

Factor	$x < -3$	$-3 < x < -2$	$-2 < x$
$x + 2$	neg	neg	pos
$x + 3$	neg	pos	pos
$(x+2)(x+3)$	pos	neg	pos

So the solution is $x < -3$ or $x > -2$.

As a second example, consider $x^2 + 6 \leq -2x$. This can be transformed to $x^2 + 2x + 6 \leq 0$. The left-hand side cannot be factored here. So we need to complete the square instead to get more information. Rewriting, we see

$$x^2 + 2x + 6 \leq 0 \implies x^2 + 2x + 1 + 5 \leq 0 \implies (x+1)^2 + 5 \leq 0,$$

which can be rewritten as $(x+1)^2 \leq -5$. Since it is a square of a real number, $(x+1)^2 \geq 0$. So the given inequality has no solutions. (Note that if we had reversed the original inequality to $\geq$, then any value of x would be a solution.)

There are a variety of methods, but I usually try to move all terms to one side of the inequality through addition/subtraction, and then try to factor that side first. If it factors, then you can consider the individual factors and look at the signs of each to determine the answer. If it doesn't factor, then try completing the square to determine more information.

3. How do you solve other polynomial inequalities in one variable?

The previous two methods, factoring and completing the square, can be generalized to some extent. Certainly making a chart of the signs of various factors can be used to determine the sign of their product (or quotient). Completing the square can be used for some polynomials with even highest powers, but that is usually only in very specific instances. See the Sample Problems for higher order polynomial inequalities.

4. Sample Problems

Solve the following inequalities.

(a) $3x + 5 > x - 7$

(b) $4x + 5 \geq x^2 - 7$

(c) $x^2 + 6x > -4$

(d) $(x - a)(x - b) \geq 0$, where $a > b$.

(e) $(3x + 5)(x - 7)(x + 1) < 0$

(f) $x^3 < 1$

(g) $x^4 < 1$

(h) $x^4 - 2x^2 > -2$.

5. Answers to Sample Problems

   Solve the following inequalities.

   (a) $3x + 5 > x - 7$. $x > -6$

   (b) $4x + 5 \geq x^2 - 7$. $-2 \leq x \leq 6$

   (c) $x^2 + 6x > -4$. $x > -3 + \sqrt{5}$ or $x < -3 - \sqrt{5}$
       Adding 9 to both sides will complete the square: $(x + 3)^2 > 5$, so $x + 3 > \sqrt{5}$ or $x + 3 < -\sqrt{5}$. The answer follows from these.

   (d) $(x - a)(x - b) \geq 0$, where $a > b$. $x < b$ or $x > a$.

   (e) $(3x + 5)(x - 7)(x + 1) < 0$. $x < -\frac{5}{3}$ or $-1 < x < 7$.

   (f) $x^3 < 1$. $x < 1$. If you factor $x^3 - 1$, the quadratic factor $x^2 + x + 1$ is always positive. The other factor $x - 1$ determines the sign.

   (g) $x^4 < 1$. $-1 < x < 1$. If you factor $x^4 - 1$, there is a quadratic factor $x^2 + 1$ which is always positive. The other factors, $x + 1$ and $x - 1$, determine the sign.

   (h) $x^4 - 2x^2 > -2$. True for all real x. To see this, add 1 to both sides to complete the square on the left: $(x^2 - 1)^2 > -1$. Since the left-hand side is a perfect square, it will always be at least zero, and so certainly it will always be greater than -1. The inequality holds for all x.

2.3 Functions

a. Analyze general properties of functions (i.e., domain and range, one-to-one, onto, inverses, composition, and differences between relations and functions) and apply arithmetic operations on functions

1. What is a relation?

   A relation from a set A to a set B is a set of ordered pairs (x, y), where $x \in A$ and $y \in B$.

2. What is a function? What are domain and range?

   A function f from A to B is a relation from A to B that satisfies the following: for every element $x \in A$, there is a unique element $y \in B$ with the property that $(x, y) \in f$. [We say that $y = f(x)$.] In other words, for all $x \in A$, $f(x)$ exists and is unique (meaning there is only one choice for $f(x)$).

   The set A is called the *domain* of f. The set B is called a *codomain* of f. It is not the same thing as the *range* of f. The range of f is $\{f(x) : x \in A\} \subseteq B$.

   Example: $f : \mathbb{R} \to \mathbb{R}$ given by $f(x) = x^2$. The domain of f is $\mathbb{R}$, but the range of f is $[0, \infty)$, the set of non-negative real numbers.

3. What is a one-to-one function?

   A function $f : A \to B$ is one-to-one if, for all $b \in B$, there is at most one $x \in A$ satisfying $f(x) = b$.

   (a) "Blob" Picture: If f is one-to-one, then each element in the domain maps to a unique element in the range.

   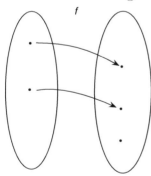

   one-to-one, but not onto

   (b) Graphs and horizontal lines: If f is one-to-one, then each horizontal line intersects the graph at most once. (Ex: $f(x) = \sqrt{x}$.)

   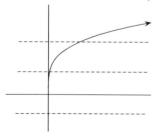

4. What is an onto function?

A function $f : A \to B$ is onto if, for all $b \in B$, there is at least one $x \in A$ satisfying $f(x) = b$.

(a) "Blob" Picture: If f is onto, then each element in the codomain has at least one element mapping to it.

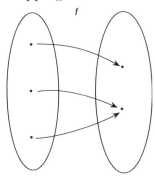

onto, but not one-to-one

(b) Graphs and horizontal lines: If f is onto, then each horizontal line intersects the graph at least once. (Ex: $f(x) = x^3 - x$.)

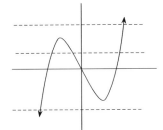

5. How do you make new functions from old functions? How do you apply arithmetic operations on functions?

There are many ways to build new functions from old ones, including the usual arithmetic operations of addition, subtraction, multiplication, and division. These methods include:

(a) shifts (translations)

To shift the graph of $y = f(x)$ up [resp. down] by k units, you _____ [resp. _____] k to the _____ of the function f. The new graph is $y =$ _____ [resp. _____].

ANS: add, [subtract], output (or y-value), $f(x) + k$, $[f(x) - k]$.

To shift the graph of $y = f(x)$ right [resp. left] by k units, you _____ [resp. _____] k to the _____ of the function f. The new graph is $y =$ _____ [resp. _____].

ANS: subtract, [add], input (or x-value), $f(x - k)$, $[f(x + k)]$.

(b) stretches and smushes (dilations & compressions)

To stretch the graph of $y = f(x)$ vertically by a factor of d units, you _____ the _____ of the function f by d. The new graph is $y =$ _____.

ANS: multiply, output, $df(x)$.

To stretch the graph of $y = f(x)$ horizontally by a factor of d units, you _____ the _____ of the function f by d. The new graph is $y =$ _____.

ANS: divide, input, $f(\frac{x}{d})$.

(c) reflections

To reflect the graph of $y = f(x)$ over the x-axis, you _____ the _____ of the function f by -1. The new graph is $y =$ _____.

ANS: multiply, output, $-f(x)$.

To reflect the graph of $y = f(x)$ over the y-axis, you _____ the _____ of the function f by -1. The new graph is $y =$ _____.

ANS: multiply (or divide!), input, $f(-x)$.

(d) sum, difference, product, quotient

You can add functions f and g to get a new function: $f + g$. The new function is defined by:

$$(f + g)(x) = f(x) + g(x).$$

The other operations are similar, except that there is one restriction when you divide two functions. What is it?

ANS: You are not allowed to divide by zero. If $g(a) = 0$, then a cannot be in the domain of $(f/g)(x) = \frac{f(x)}{g(x)}$.

(e) composition

In addition to addition, subtraction, multiplication, and division, you can compose two functions to obtain a new one. That is, if $f : A \to B$ and $g : B \to C$, then you can compose them to get a new function $h : A \to C$ defined by $h(x) = g(f(x))$. We say $h = g \circ f$.

Example: $f(x) = x^2$ and $g(x) = x + 3$. Then $(g \circ f)(x) = x^2 + 3$ and $(f \circ g)(x) = (x + 3)^2 = x^2 + 6x + 9$. Notice that $f \circ g$ can be different from $g \circ f$.

(f) inverse functions

Also, if a function $f : A \to \mathrm{range}(f)$ is one-to-one, then you can define a new function $f^{-1} : \mathrm{range}(f) \to A$ according to:

$$f^{-1}(b) = x \quad \Longleftrightarrow \quad f(x) = b.$$

The roles of domain and range are swapped.

Example: $f(x) = \dfrac{3x - 5}{7}$. Find f^{-1}.

ANS: The usual algorithm involves switching x and y and then solving for y. That is, instead of $y = \frac{3x-5}{7}$, we start with $x = \frac{3y-5}{7}$, which means $7x = 3y - 5$, or $y = \frac{7x+5}{3}$. So $f^{-1}(x) = \dfrac{7x + 5}{3}$.

The graph of f^{-1} can be obtained from the graph of f by reflecting over the line $y = x$ (which essentially switches y and x, thus swapping the domain and the range).

(g) identity function ($f(x) = x$)

The identity function is a boring function in one sense, but it plays a necessary role both in inverse functions and in function composition. How so?

ANS: The composition of a function and its inverse should be the identity function (because the inverse function "undoes" whatever the original function does). Also, the composition of any function g with the identity function is equal to the function g. (The identity function is "inert" under composition.)

6. Sample Problems

(a) If $f(x) = 2x^2 - 8$ and if $g(x) = \sqrt{x}$, then what is the domain of $g(f(x))$?

(b) Let $f = \{(1,1), (2,3), (2,4), (3,1)\}$ and let $g = \{(4,3), (3,3), (2,1), (1,4)\}$

    i. Which set is a function?

    ii. What is the domain of that function? ... range ... ?

    iii. Is that function one-to-one? Explain.

    iv. Is that function onto the set $\{1,3,4\}$? Explain.

(c) Fill in the table below. If there is not enough information, put a question mark.

x	1	2	3	4	5
$f(x)$	5	4	3	2	1
$g(x)$	3	5	2	1	4
$(f+g)(x)$					
$(g/f)(x)$					
$(g \circ f)(x)$					
$(f \circ g)(x)$					
$g^{-1}(x)$					

(d) If $f(x) = 3x - 5$, then find $f(f(2))$ and $f^{-1}(2)$.

(e) Sketch the graph of $y = f(x) = |x|$ on the domain $[-2, 2]$. Then sketch the following graphs, labeling the vertex and the endpoints.

    i. $y = f(x) - 3$

    ii. $y = f(x - 3)$

    iii. $y = 3f(x)$

    iv. $y = f(3x)$

    v. $y = -f(x)$

    vi. $y = f(-x)$

(f) Find formulas for the following (separate) transformations of $f(x) = x^3 - x$.

    i. Shift f to the right 4 units and then up 2 units.

    ii. Stretch f horizontally by a factor of 5 and then reflect in the y-axis.

    iii. Shift f to the left 3 units, then reflect in the x-axis, and then compress vertically by a factor of 2.

(g) Give an example of functions f and g where $f \neq g$, neither function is the identity, but $f \circ g = g \circ f$.

(h) Find $f^{-1}(x)$ if $f(x) = \frac{5x-2}{3}$. Verify that $f(f^{-1}(x)) = x$ and that $f^{-1}(f(x)) = x$.

7. Answers to Sample Problems

(a) If $f(x) = 2x^2 - 8$ and if $g(x) = \sqrt{x}$, then what is the domain of $g(f(x))$? First, note that $g(f(x)) = \sqrt{2x^2 - 8}$. Its domain is $(-\infty, -2] \cup [2, \infty)$.

(b) Let $f = \{(1,1), (2,3), (2,4), (3,1)\}$ and let $g = \{(4,3), (3,3), (2,1), (1,4)\}$

    i. Which set is a function? g. f is not a function.

    ii. What is the domain of that function? $\{4,3,2,1\}$ range? $\{1,3,4\}$.

    iii. Is that function one-to-one? Explain. NO. $g(4) = g(3) = 3$. Two elements of the domain map to the same element of the range, which means that g is not one-to-one.

    iv. Is that function onto the set $\{1,3,4\}$? Explain. YES. Since g maps to 1, 3, and 4, we say that g is onto the set $\{1,3,4\}$.

(c) Fill in the table below. If there is not enough information, put a question mark.

x	1	2	3	4	5
$f(x)$	5	4	3	2	1
$g(x)$	3	5	2	1	4
$(f+g)(x)$	8	9	5	3	5
$(g/f)(x)$	3/5	5/4	2/3	1/2	4
$(g \circ f)(x)$	4	1	2	5	3
$(f \circ g)(x)$	3	1	4	5	2
$g^{-1}(x)$	4	3	1	5	2

(d) If $f(x) = 3x - 5$, then find $f(f(2))$ and $f^{-1}(2)$. Since $f(2) = 1$, $f(f(2)) = f(1) = -2$. We can find the inverse function directly or use the definition:

$$y = f^{-1}(2) \Leftrightarrow f(y) = 2.$$

So we need to solve $2 = f(y) = 3y - 5$, or $y = f^{-1}(2) = \frac{7}{3}$.

(e) Sketch the graph of $y = f(x) = |x|$ on the domain $[-2, 2]$. Then sketch the following graphs, labeling the vertex and the endpoints. Labels have been left off of the answers, but for the original graph, the vertex is at $(0,0)$, and the endpoints are $(-2,2)$ and $(2,2)$.

    i. $y = f(x) - 3 = |x| - 3$, vertex: $(0,-3)$, endpts: $(-2,-1)$ and $(2,-1)$

    ii. $y = f(x-3) = |x-3|$, vertex: $(3,0)$, endpts: $(1,2)$ and $(5,2)$

    iii. $y = 3f(x) = 3|x|$, vertex: $(0,0)$, endpts: $(-2,6)$ and $(2,6)$

    iv. $y = f(3x) = |3x|$, vertex: $(0,0)$, endpts: $(-\frac{2}{3},2)$ and $(\frac{2}{3},2)$

v. $y = -f(x) = -|x|$, vertex: $(0, 0)$, endpts: $(-2, -2)$ and $(2, -2)$

vi. $y = f(-x) = |-x| = |x|$ (same as original graph)

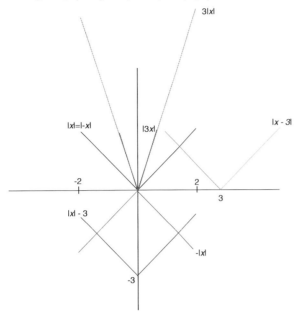

(f) Find formulas for the following (separate) transformations of $f(x) = x^3 - x$.

   i. Shift f to the right 4 units and then up 2 units. $(x - 4)^3 - (x - 4) + 2$

   ii. Stretch f horizontally by a factor of 5 and then reflect in the y-axis. $-(\frac{x}{5})^3 + \frac{x}{5}$

   iii. Shift f to the left 3 units, then reflect in the x-axis, and then compress vertically by a factor of 2. $\frac{1}{2}[(-x + 3)^3 - (-x + 3)]$

(g) Give an example of functions f and g where $f \neq g$, neither function is the identity, but $f \circ g = g \circ f$. There are many answers. For example, $f(x) = x + 3$ and $g(x) = x - 5$. Also, $f(x) = px$ and $g(x) = qx$, where p and q are any real numbers with $p \neq q$.

(h) Find $f^{-1}(x)$ if $f(x) = \frac{5x - 2}{3}$. Verify that $f(f^{-1}(x)) = x$ and that $f^{-1}(f(x)) = x$.

$$f^{-1}(x) = \frac{3x + 2}{5}.$$

$$f(f^{-1}(x)) = f\left(\frac{3x + 2}{5}\right)$$

$$= \frac{5\left(\frac{3x+2}{5}\right) - 2}{3} = \frac{3x + 2 - 2}{3} = x.$$

$$f^{-1}(f(x)) = f^{-1}\left(\frac{5x - 2}{3}\right)$$

$$= \frac{3\left(\frac{5x-2}{3}\right) + 2}{5} = \frac{5x - 2 + 2}{5} = x.$$

b. Analyze properties of linear functions (e.g., slope, intercepts) using a variety of representations

1. What is a linear equation?

Let's begin with what is called the Standard Form of a linear equation: $Ax + By = C$, where A, B, and C are real numbers (and A and B are not both equal to zero). Any linear equation can be put into this form, and any equation in this form is a linear equation.

Another common form is as a linear *function*, which is often written $y = mx + b$. Any linear function can be put into Standard Form, but there are some linear equations that are not linear functions (e.g., if $B = 0$ in the Standard Form).

2. What does the graph of a linear equation look like?

One nice feature of the Standard Form of a linear equation is that the graph of its solution set is a straight line on the xy-plane. Conversely, any line on the xy-plane is the solution set to some linear equation.

Linear function graphs are also straight lines, but not every straight line is the graph of a linear function (e.g., vertical lines are not graphs of functions).

3. What are the important features of a linear equation, and how do they relate to its graph?

Probably the most important feature mathematically is the ratio of changes in y to changes in x, called the *slope* of the line. It shows up on the graph as the ratio of the "rise" to the "run" of the line. In Standard Form, the slope is $-\frac{A}{B}$, if $B \neq 0$. When $B = 0$, then the slope is not defined, and the line is vertical. See the examples below.

Also, most lines intersect the y-axis at a unique point called the y-intercept. Since it is the point where $x = 0$, it can be found by setting $x = 0$ in the Standard Form and then solving for y. Hence, $By = C$, or $y = \frac{C}{B}$ (assuming $B \neq 0$). When $B = 0$ in the Standard Form equation, then the corresponding line is vertical, and it does not have a y-intercept.

Instead, a vertical line has a constant x-coordinate. Since $B = 0$ in the Standard Form for vertical lines, we can solve for x to find the equation of the line. Hence, $Ax = C$, or $x = \frac{C}{A}$. We know that A is not zero, because we said earlier that A and B cannot both be zero in the Standard Form.

Incidentally, x-intercepts can also be looked at. Since it is the point where $y = 0$, it can be found by setting $y = 0$ in the Standard Form and then solving for x. Hence, $Ax = C$, or $x = \frac{C}{A}$ (assuming $A \neq 0$). If $A = 0$, then the corresponding line is horizontal, its slope is zero, and its equation is $y = \frac{C}{B}$.

4. What are some different forms of a linear equation?

First, we will find a formula for the slope. The slope m of the line passing through (x_1, y_1) and (x_2, y_2) is $m = \dfrac{y_2 - y_1}{x_2 - x_1}$ (assuming $x_1 \neq x_2$). If $x_1 = x_2$, then the line is vertical, and its slope is not defined.

Slope-Intercept Form: If a line has slope m and y-intercept b, then its equation is $y = mx + b$.

Point-Slope Form: If a line has slope m and passes through (h, k), then its equation is $y - k = m(x - h)$.

5. What are some examples of linear equations and their graphs?

(a) $x = 3$; $y = 4$. Here, we have one vertical and one horizontal line. To graph them, you can plot a few points. For instance, for the equation $x = 3$, there are several points that satisfy that equation: $(3,0)$, $(3,1)$, and $(3,3)$, to name just a few. Similarly, any point with a y-coordinate of 4 will satisfy the equation $y = 4$. The two graphs are given below.

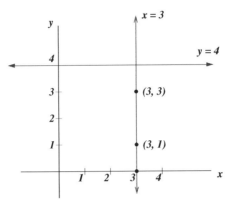

(b) $x + y = 2$; $x - 2y = 2$. Here we have one line with negative slope $m = -1$ (down to the right) and one line with positive slope $m = \frac{1}{2}$ (up to the right). To graph these lines, one can either choose an x-value and plug it in to the equation to determine its corresponding y-value, or you can put the line into Slope-Intercept Form algebraically. Then, plotting its y-intercept and its slope leads to the line. So, $x + y = 2$ becomes $y = -x + 2$, which has slope -1 and y-intercept 2. Similarly, $x - 2y = 2$ becomes $y = \frac{1}{2}x - 1$, which has slope $\frac{1}{2}$ and y-intercept -1.

The two graphs are given below.

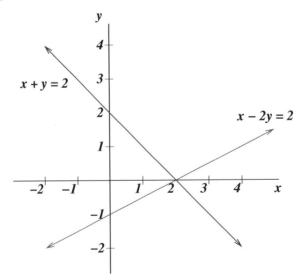

6. What are the slope criteria for parallel lines? ... for perpendicular lines?

Two distinct lines are parallel if 1) they are both vertical, or 2) they have the same slope. (Recall that slope is not defined for vertical lines.) Two lines are perpendicular if 1) one is vertical and one is horizontal, or 2) the product of their slopes is -1. Another way to say this is that their slopes are negative reciprocals of each other. (For a proof of these facts (and more), see my book *Common Core State Standards for High School Math: Geometry - What Every Math Teacher Should Know*, Createspace, 2012.)

7. Sample Problems

   (a) Graph the following: $3x + 2y = 5$, $x = -3$, and $x - y = 0$. Put each equation in Slope-Intercept Form, if possible.

   (b) Find a Point-Slope form of the line that passes through $(2, -4)$ and is parallel to $4x - 3y = 2$.

   (c) Find a line that is perpendicular to the line through $(1, -3)$ and $(4, 2)$, but passes through the point $(1, 5)$.

   (d) There is a linear equation relating a temperature on the Fahrenheit scale to its value on the Celsius scale. You know that zero degrees Celsius corresponds to 32 degrees Fahrenheit, and that 100 degrees Celsius corresponds to 212 degrees Fahrenheit. Sketch a graph of temperature Fahrenheit versus temperature Celsius. What is the slope of the graph? What is the linear formula giving Fahrenheit temperature as a function of Celsius temperature?

8. Answers to Sample Problems

   (a) Graph the following: $3x + 2y = 5$, $x = -3$, and $x - y = 0$. Put each equation in Slope-Intercept Form, if possible.

   The Slope-Intercept Form is not possible for $x = -3$ because this line is vertical and therefore does not have a defined slope. However, using algebra, $3x + 2y = 5$ can be written as $y = -\frac{3}{2}x + \frac{5}{2}$. Also, $x - y = 0$ can be written as $y = x$. The graphs are below.

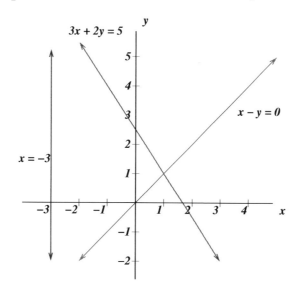

   (b) Find a Point-Slope form of the line that passes through $(2, -4)$ and is parallel to $4x - 3y = 2$. The slope of $4x - 3y = 2$ can be found by putting the equation into Slope-Intercept

Form (i.e., $y = \frac{4}{3}x - \frac{2}{3}$), or by knowing that in Standard Form, the slope is $-\frac{A}{B}$. Either route leads to a slope of $\frac{4}{3}$. So, our desired line is

$$y + 4 = \frac{4}{3}(x - 2).$$

(c) Find a line that is perpendicular to the line through $(1, -3)$ and $(4, 2)$, but passes through the point $(1, 5)$.

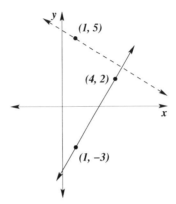

The slope through $(1, -3)$ and $(4, 2)$ is $\frac{2+3}{4-1} = \frac{5}{3}$. Since we want a line perpendicular to this one, the slope we want is $-\frac{3}{5}$. So we need a line with slope $-\frac{3}{5}$ and passing through the point $(1, 5)$. Using the Point-Slope form of the line, we get

$$y - 5 = -\frac{3}{5}(x - 1).$$

(d) There is a linear equation relating a temperature on the Fahrenheit scale to its value on the Celsius scale. You know that zero degrees Celsius corresponds to 32 degrees Fahrenheit, and that 100 degrees Celsius corresponds to 212 degrees Fahrenheit. Sketch a graph of temperature Fahrenheit versus temperature Celsius. What is the slope of the graph? What is the linear formula giving Fahrenheit temperature as a function of Celsius temperature?

We will graph Fahrenheit temperature (F) as a function of Celsius temperature (C). That means that F goes on the y-axis and C on the x-axis. The two known points we have are $(0, 32)$ and $(100, 212)$. See the graph below.

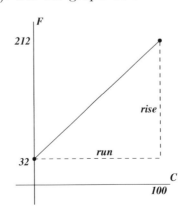

So the slope is the rise divided by the run, or $\dfrac{212 - 32}{100 - 0} = \dfrac{180}{100} = \dfrac{9}{5}$. Thus the formula is

$$F - 32 = \frac{9}{5}(C - 0) \quad \text{or} \quad F = \frac{9}{5}C + 32.$$

c. Demonstrate knowledge of why graphs of linear inequalities are half planes and be able to apply this fact

1. Why is the graph of a linear inequality a half plane?

   If you can solve the inequality for y, then it is clear that you are looking for values of y either above ($y > f(x)$) or below ($y < f(x)$) the line. If y doesn't appear in the equation, then the line must be vertical, and the inequality tells you if you are looking for points to the right ($x > a$) or to the left ($x < a$) of this line. In the following examples, the boundary lines have been labeled. Dotted boundary lines are not part of the solution set.

   Examples: $y \le 5, \quad x > -2, \quad x + 2y \ge 3$

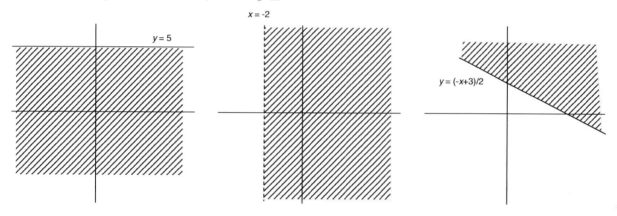

2. How do you apply linear inequalities?

   Linear programming can be used to solve optimization problems in many different fields. Usually, you are asked to maximize some quantity with respect to various linear constraints.

   Simple(x) Example: Say you have 20 days to knit hats and scarves for a friend's store. It takes you 1.5 days to knit a hat and only 1 day to knit a scarf. You plan to charge $20 per hat and $15 per scarf, but your friend says that she wants no more than 16 items from you. How many hats and how many scarves should you knit in order to maximize your revenue?

   ANS: Let x be the number of hats knitted and y the number of scarves knitted. So $x \ge 0$ and $y \ge 0$. Also, $x + y \le 16$ because your friend only wants 16 items at most. The number of days it takes to knit hats is $1.5x$, while the number of days it takes to knit scarves is y. So $1.5x + y \le 20$ since there are only 20 days to knit. If we graph all of these inequalities, we obtain a region of all the possible numbers of scarves and hats you could knit. The revenue function is $20x + 15y$, which we would like to maximize on the given region. According to the simplex method, since the revenue condition is linear, we need only check the corners of our region, which occur at any intersection point of two linear conditions.

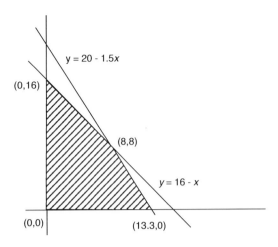

Checking, we get:

- no scarves and no hats yields 0 dollars of revenue

- 16 scarves and no hats yields $(16)(15) = 240$ dollars of revenue

- 8 scarves and 8 hats yields $8(15) + 8(20) = 280$ dollars of revenue

- 13 hats and no scarves yields $13(20) = 260$ dollars of revenue

So, to maximize revenue, you should knit eight scarves and eight hats.

3. Sample Problems

  (a) Sketch the solution to $y \leq 2x - 5$.

  (b) Sketch the solution to $2x + 3y > 6$.

  (c) Sketch all the complex numbers $a + bi$ with $a \leq 2b$.

  (d) Suppose that a company makes two kinds of puzzles: easy and hard. The company has 10 weeks to make puzzles before putting the products on the market. They can make 60 easy puzzles per week and 40 hard puzzles per week. They make \$12 profit on each easy puzzle and \$15 profit on each hard puzzle. Assuming that they can only put 500 puzzles on the market, how many of each should they make?

4. Answers to Sample Problems

  (a) Sketch the solution to $y \leq 2x - 5$.

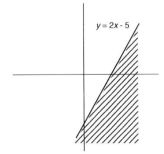

(b) Sketch the solution to $2x + 3y > 6$.

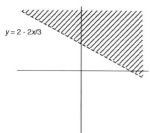

y = 2 - 2x/3

(c) Sketch all the complex numbers $a + bi$ with $a \leq 2b$.

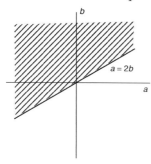

a = 2b

(d) Suppose that a company makes two kinds of puzzles: easy and hard. The company has 10 weeks to make puzzles before putting the products on the market. They can make 60 easy puzzles per week and 40 hard puzzles per week. They make $12 profit on each easy puzzle and $15 profit on each hard puzzle. Assuming that they can only put 500 puzzles on the market, how many of each should they make? 300 easy, 200 hard.

The corners of the region of interest are $(0, 0)$, $(0, 400)$, $(500, 0)$, and $(300, 200)$, where x is the number of easy puzzles made and y is the number of hard puzzles made. Checking each one, we obtain the maximum revenue at $(300, 200)$.

d. Analyze properties of polynomial, rational, radical, and absolute value functions in a variety of ways (e.g., graphing, solving problems)

1. Continuity and holes

Polynomials and absolute value functions are continuous on the entire domain of real numbers. Rational functions are continuous everywhere except when the denominator is zero. Radical functions are continuous on their domains, but are not always defined for all reals.

Examples include: $3x^3 - x$, $|x - 4|$, $\dfrac{x + 3}{x^2 - 4}$ (discontinuities at $x = \pm 2$), and $\sqrt{x - 2}$ (not defined for $x < 2$).

2. Intercepts, horizontal and vertical

Every function has exactly one vertical intercept, provided that $x = 0$ is in its domain. Functions can have several horizontal intercepts, which can be found by setting the value of the function to zero and solving for x. For example, $x^3 - 2x + 1$ has one vertical intercept at $y = 1$, and three horizontal intercepts: $\dfrac{-1 \pm \sqrt{5}}{2}$ and 1.

3. Asymptotes, horizontal and vertical

Polynomials, radicals, and absolute value functions have no asymptotes. Rational functions have horizontal asymptotes exactly when the degree of the numerator is less than or equal to the degree of the denominator. Rational functions can have vertical asymptotes or holes at the points where the denominator is zero. How can you tell which is which? (See example.)

Example: $f(x) = \dfrac{x^2 + 4x + 4}{x^2 - 4}$ versus $g(x) = \dfrac{x^2 + 2x + 1}{x^2 - 4}$

$f(x)$ can be factored and reduced to $\dfrac{x+2}{x-2}$, provided that $x \neq -2$. This means that there is a hole in the graph of f at the point $(-2, \frac{-2+2}{-2-2}) = (-2, 0)$. The function $g(x)$ cannot be reduced, which means that the $(x+2)$ factor cannot be canceled. Thus $g(x)$ has a vertical asymptotc at $x = -2$.

4. Sample Problems

   (a) Solve for x: $\sqrt{x} + \sqrt{x+3} = 3$.

   (b) Find the range of $f(x) = |2x - 5| + 3$ and sketch the graph of $y = f(x)$.

   (c) Say that $y = f(x)$ is a cubic polynomial and that $f(3) = f(1) = f(-2) = 0$. Also, say that $f(0) = 12$. Find the formula for f.

   (d) What is the [subtle] difference between $f(x) = x + 1$ and $g(x) = \dfrac{x^2 - 1}{x - 1}$? How does this show up on their graphs?

   (e) Explain why the domain of $\sqrt{x}$ is $[0, \infty)$ but the domain of $\sqrt[3]{x}$ is all real numbers.

   (f) Sketch a graph of $y = \dfrac{x^2 - 1}{x^2 - 4}$, labeling all intercepts and asymptotes.

   (g) Sketch a graph of $y = \dfrac{1}{x^2 + 1}$, labeling all intercepts and asymptotes.

   (h) Sketch $y = \sqrt{x}$. Then sketch its inverse graph and find the formula. What is the domain of f^{-1} in this case?

   (i) Explain why $f(x) = x^2$ is not invertible on its domain of all real numbers, but that it is invertible on the restricted domain $[0, \infty)$.

5. Answers to Sample Problems

   (a) Solve for x: $\sqrt{x} + \sqrt{x+3} = 3$. $x = 1$

   (b) Find the range of $f(x) = |2x - 5| + 3$ and sketch the graph of $y = f(x)$. The range is $[3, \infty)$.

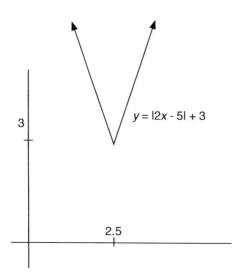

$y = |2x - 5| + 3$

3

2.5

(c) Say that $y = f(x)$ is a cubic polynomial and that $f(3) = f(1) = f(-2) = 0$. Also, say that $f(0) = 12$. Find the formula for f. $f(x) = 2(x-3)(x-1)(x+2) = 2x^3 - 4x^2 - 10x + 12$

(d) What is the [subtle] difference between $f(x) = x + 1$ and $g(x) = \dfrac{x^2 - 1}{x - 1}$? How does this show up on their graphs?

The only difference is that 1 is in the domain of f but it is not in the domain of g. Other than that, the two functions are identical. This means that the graph of $y = g(x)$ is the line $x + 1$ except that it has a hole at the point $(1, 2)$.

(e) Explain why the domain of $\sqrt{x}$ is $[0, \infty)$ but the domain of $\sqrt[3]{x}$ is all real numbers. The square root of a negative number is not real, whereas the cube root of a negative number is negative. For example, since $(-2)^3 = -8$, $\sqrt[3]{-8} = -2$.

(f) Sketch a graph of $y = \dfrac{x^2 - 1}{x^2 - 4}$, labeling all intercepts and asymptotes.

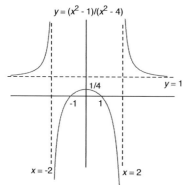

$y = (x^2 - 1)/(x^2 - 4)$

1/4

$y = 1$

-1   1

$x = -2$ $x = 2$

(g) Sketch a graph of $y = \dfrac{1}{x^2 + 1}$, labeling all intercepts and asymptotes.

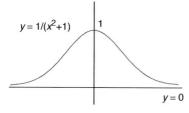

$y = 1/(x^2+1)$ 1

$y = 0$

(h) Sketch $y = \sqrt{x}$. Then sketch its inverse graph and find the formula. What is the domain of f^{-1} in this case? The domain of the inverse function is $[0, \infty)$.

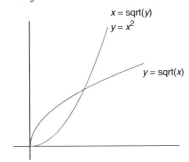

(i) Explain why $f(x) = x^2$ is not invertible on its domain of all real numbers, but that it is invertible on the restricted domain $[0, \infty)$. The function $f(x) = x^2$ is not one-to-one on its domain, $((-2)^2 = 2^2 = 4$, for instance), but it *is* one-to-one on its restricted domain. That means that f is invertible if we only consider non-negative values of x.

e. Analyze properties of exponential and logarithmic functions in a variety of ways (e.g., graphing, solving problems)

*** *For a quick review of logarithms, see the Miscellaneous Topics at the end of this book.*

1. How are exponential and logarithmic functions related?

   The exponential and logarithmic functions are inverse functions of each other. So,

   - $y = e^x \Leftrightarrow x = \ln y$,
   - $y = 10^x \Leftrightarrow x = \log y$, and in general,
   - $y = b^x \Leftrightarrow x = \log_b y$.

2. Continuity

   The basic exponential functions are continuous on the entire domain of real numbers.

   The basic logarithmic functions are continuous on their domains (positive real numbers).

3. Intercepts, horizontal and vertical

   The basic exponential functions have only one intercept, at $(0, 1)$.

   The basic logarithmic functions have only one intercept, at $(1, 0)$.

4. Asymptotes, horizontal and vertical

   Exponential functions have one horizontal asymptote, at $y = 0$. As an example, $\lim\limits_{x \to -\infty} 2^x = 0$.

   Logarithmic functions have one vertical asymptote, at $x = 0$. For example, as $x \to 0^+$, $\ln x \to -\infty$.

5. Sample Problems

   (a) Explain the domains and ranges, intercepts, and asymptotes of basic exponential and logarithmic functions in terms of inverse functions.

(b) Simplify, if possible:

    i. $e^{\ln 4}$

    ii. $\ln(e^{3x})$

    iii. $\log 200 + \log 50$

    iv. $\log_3(2) - \log_3(18)$

    v. $\log_b 1$

    vi. $\log_b 0$

    vii. $10^{\log x + \log x^2}$

(c) Solve for x: $3 - \log x = 10$.

(d) Solve for x: $\ln 2^x = \ln 3$.

(e) Suppose that the value of your \$20,000 car depreciates by 10% each year after you bought it. Find a formula for the value of your car V as a function of t, the number of years since you bought it.

(f) Suppose that you have money in a bank account earning 5% interest. Then the amount of money you have after t years is given by $A(t) = P(1.05)^t$. where P is the principal amount invested. Find the doubling time of this account. Leave logarithms in your answer.

(g) Find a formula for an exponential function that passes through the point $(0, 4)$ and the point $(1, 8)$.

(h) Sketch a rough graph of $y = 5 - e^{-x}$. [Hint: Use transformations of a basic graph.] Name a real-world process you could model with a graph of this shape.

6. Answers to Sample Problems

(a) Explain the domains and ranges, intercepts, and asymptotes of basic exponential and logarithmic functions in terms of inverse functions.

Feature	Exponential	Logarithmic
Domain	all reals	$x > 0$
Range	$y > 0$	all reals
Intercepts	$y = 1$	$x = 1$
Asymptotes	$y = 0$	$x = 0$

Notice that switching x and y (reflecting over the line $y = x$) takes the domain of one function to the range of the other and vice versa. Also, the $y = 1$ intercept of a basic exponential function switches with the $x = 1$ intercept of a basic logarithmic function. Similarly, the horizontal asymptote of a basic exponential function switches with the vertical asymptote of a basic logarithmic function.

(b) Simplify, if possible:

    i. $e^{\ln 4} = 4$

    ii. $\ln(e^{3x}) = 3x$

    iii. $\log 200 + \log 50 = \log 10{,}000 = 4$

    iv. $\log_3(2) - \log_3(18) = \log_3 \frac{1}{9} = -2$

v. $\log_b 1 = 0$

vi. $\log_b 0$ is not defined.

vii. $10^{\log x + \log x^2} = 10^{\log x^3} = x^3$

(c) Solve for x: $3 - \log x = 10$. $x = 10^{-7}$

(d) Solve for x: $\ln 2^x = \ln 3$. $2^x = 3$; $x = \log_2 3 = \frac{\ln 3}{\ln 2} = \frac{\log 3}{\log 2}$

(e) Suppose that the value of your \$20,000 car depreciates by 10% each year after you bought it. Find a formula for the value of your car V as a function of t, the number of years since you bought it. $V(t) = 20{,}000(0.9)^t$

(f) Suppose that you have money in a bank account earning 5% interest. Then the amount of money you have after t years is given by $A(t) = P(1.05)^t$. where P is the principal amount invested. Find the doubling time of this account. Leave logarithms in your answer.

If $2P = P(1.05)^t$, then $2 = (1.05)^t$, or $t = \log_{1.05} 2 = \frac{\ln 2}{\ln 1.05} = \frac{\log 2}{\log 1.05}$.

(g) Find a formula for an exponential function that passes through the point $(0, 4)$ and the point $(1, 8)$. $y = 4 \cdot 2^x$

(h) Sketch a rough graph of $y = 5 - e^{-x}$. [Hint: Use transformations of a basic graph.] Name a real-world process you could model with a graph of this shape.

Using transformations: you can start with $y = e^x$, flip it over the y-axis to get $y = e^{-x}$, then flip it over the x-axis to get $y = -e^{-x}$. Finally, shift it up five units.

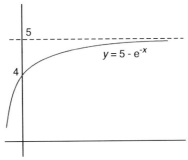

One possible process is heating an object. As the object sits in an oven (at a constant temperature), the object's temperature exponentially approaches the temperature of the oven. There are other valid answers.

f. Model and solve problems using nonlinear functions

There are similarities between this section and **1.1.c** and **2.1.f**. We will include a linear example here just to keep most of the modeling problems in one place.

1. What are some linear and quadratic examples of modeling and solving problems?

We will begin with a linear example to help set the stage. Assume that your cell phone contract costs \$20 a month plus \$0.05 per minute for calls. We'll ignore texting and data. Suppose your bill for last month was \$42.15. We can write an equation to represent this. If we let m represent the number of minutes spent calling, then the total cost of those minutes is $0.05m$, and so the cost of your monthly bill is $20 + 0.05m$. So, our equation representing last month's bill is:

$$20 + 0.05m = 42.15.$$

Suppose that we want the bill to be at most \$40. We can write that as an inequality: $20 + 0.05m \leq 40$.

For solving the equation $20 + 0.05m = 42.15$, we subtract 20 from both sides, giving $0.05m = 22.15$. Next we divide by 0.05 (or multiply by 20), to get $m = 443$. So the total usage that month was 443 minutes.

For a quadratic example, let's turn to economics – to revenue in particular. One simple model says that the price of a product determines the quantity sold. Let's suppose that the quantity sold is $3250 - 25p$, where p is the price of the item in dollars. Now suppose that the total revenue is \$32,725. We can write an equation to represent this. Since the revenue is the total amount of money coming in, it must equal the product of the quantity sold and the price. So, our equation is

$$(3250 - 25p)p = 32{,}725 \quad \text{or} \quad 3250p - 25p^2 = 32{,}725.$$

Suppose that we want a revenue of at least \$100,000. Then we can write that as an inequality: $3250p - 25p^2 \geq 100{,}000$.

To solve this inequality, we add $-3250p + 25p^2$ to both sides. (There are other methods; I find it easier to have a positive leading coefficient on the quadratic term.) This gives

$$0 \geq 25p^2 - 3250p + 100{,}000 \quad \text{or} \quad 0 \geq p^2 - 130p + 4000 = (p - 50)(p - 80).$$

So since $0 \geq (p - 50)(p - 80)$, we need one factor to be positive and one to be negative. This happens in the region between 50 and 80. So the solution would be $50 \leq p \leq 80$. In the terms of the original problem, the revenue will exceed \$100,000 when the price is between \$50 and \$80.

2. What are some rational and exponential examples of modeling and solving problems?

The rational expression $\dfrac{k}{x^2}$ can be used to model the behavior of certain physical quantities, such as the force due to gravity between two bodies that are separated by a distance, x, where k is a nonzero constant. If you wanted to determine the value(s) of x for which this force is equal to $\dfrac{2k}{3}$, you could create the equation $\dfrac{k}{x^2} = \dfrac{2k}{3}$. If you wanted to know the values of x for which the force is greater than $2k$, you would create the inequality $\dfrac{k}{x^2} > 2k$.

To solve the equation $\dfrac{k}{x^2} = \dfrac{2k}{3}$, we can clear denominators by multiplying through by $3x^2$. This gives the new equation $3k = 2kx^2$. Since $k \neq 0$, we can divide by $2k$ to get $x^2 = \dfrac{3}{2}$.

So $x = \pm\sqrt{\dfrac{3}{2}}$. Since x represents the distance between two bodies, only the positive answer makes sense. So $x = \sqrt{\dfrac{3}{2}}$.

For an exponential example, you may recall the expression $P(1 + r)^t$ that represents the amount of money in a bank account, where P is the initial deposit, r is the annual interest rate, and t is the number of years that have passed since the initial deposit. The interest is compounded annually. How long does it take for $5000 to grow to $7500 in an account bearing 4.5% interest, compounded annually?

To solve this, we first need to set up the correct equation. Here, $P = 5000$, $r = 0.045$, and the entire expression is equal to 7500. That is,

$$5000(1.045)^t = 7500.$$

Next, we divide both sides by 5000, to get $1.045^t = \dfrac{3}{2}$. Taking a logarithm (let's use natural log) of both sides gives

$$\ln(1.045^t) = \ln \frac{3}{2} \quad \text{or} \quad t \ln 1.045 = \ln 1.5.$$

We used a property of logarithms to help simplify. So $t = \dfrac{\ln 1.5}{\ln 1.045} \approx 9.212$. So if the interest is compounded annually, it would take ten years before the bank account rose above $7500. (Nine years would not be long enough.)

If we wanted to know when the account had more than $8000 dollars, then we could solve the inequality: $5000(1.045)^t > 8000$.

3. Sample Problems

   (a) The time it takes to drive 60 miles depends on how fast you are driving. Write an equation describing this situation in terms of t, the time the journey takes, and v, the speed at which you are driving. Sketch a graph of t as a function of v.

   (b) Create an equation for P and t, where P is the population of bacteria in a Petri dish at time t. Assume the initial population is 1000 bacteria, and that the population doubles every hour. Is this linear growth or exponential growth? Explain.

   (c) The time, t, that it takes to grade papers depends on n, the number of papers you have to grade. Assuming it takes 7 minutes to prepare the answer key and then 3 minutes to grade each paper, write down an equation relating t and n. Sketch a graph of t as a function of n.

   (d) You may recall that the formula for a Celsius temperature C, is related to its equivalent Fahrenheit temperature F via: $C = \frac{5}{9}(F - 32)$. Manipulate this equation so that the Fahrenheit temperature is isolated. What does the formula tell us now?

   (e) The area, A, of a circle depends on its radius, r: $A = \pi r^2$. Solve this equation for r. What does the formula tell us now?

4. Answers to Sample Problems

   (a) The time it takes to drive 60 miles depends on how fast you are driving. Write an equation describing this situation in terms of t, the time the journey takes, and v, the speed at which you are driving. Sketch a graph of t as a function of v.

There are a few ways to reach this answer. One is to recall that "rate times time equals distance." So $vt = 60$, or $t = \dfrac{60}{v}$. Another way is to think about a few points. How long would the journey take if you drove 60mph? One hour. What if you drove 30mph? Two hours. What if you drove 120mph? Then the journey would only take half an hour. So these also satisfy $t = \dfrac{60}{v}$.

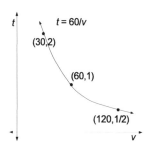

(b) Create an equation for P and t, where P is the population of bacteria in a Petri dish at time t. Assume the initial population is 1000 bacteria, and that the population doubles every hour. Is this linear growth or exponential growth? Explain.

We'll answer the second part first. This set-up is an example of exponential growth. Linear growth would increase by the same *amount* every hour, whereas exponential growth increases by the same *factor* every hour. Let's compare these two models in a table, assuming each model starts with 1000 bacteria and has 2000 bacteria after one hour.

t (in hours)	0	1	2	3
Linear	1000	2000	3000	4000
Exponential	1000	2000	4000	8000

Now let's find a formula for the exponential population, because that is the one we want. First, let's divide each entry by 1000 so we can see what is going on. Then, our population is 1, 2, 4, and 8. Notice that these are powers of 2: 2^0, 2^1, 2^2, and 2^3. In general, we get 2^t. So the population satisfies $P = 1000 \cdot 2^t$. (You could also think of it as a 100% growth rate each hour. Then we would use $r = 1$ in the interest formula, $P = 1000(1+r)^t$, to get $P = 1000(1+1)^t = 1000 \cdot 2^t$.)

(c) The time, t, that it takes to grade papers depends on n, the number of papers you have to grade. Assuming it takes 7 minutes to prepare the answer key and then 3 minutes to grade each paper, write down an equation relating t and n. Sketch a graph of t as a function of n.

$t = 7 + 3n$

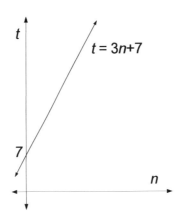

(d) You may recall that the formula for a Celsius temperature C, is related to its equivalent Fahrenheit temperature F via: $C = \frac{5}{9}(F - 32)$. Manipulate this equation so that the Fahrenheit temperature is isolated. What does the formula tell us now?

We would get $F = \frac{9}{5}C + 32$. Now the formula tells us which Fahrenheit temperature corresponds to a given Celsius temperature. In other words, if you know the temperature in degrees Celsius, then this formula is more useful in finding the equivalent Fahrenheit temperature.

(e) The area, A, of a circle depends on its radius, r: $A = \pi r^2$. Solve this equation for r. What does the formula tell us now?

We would get $r = \sqrt{\dfrac{A}{\pi}}$. This tells us the radius of a circle if we know its area. (Since the radius of a circle cannot be negative, we do not use a $\pm$ sign.)

2.4 Linear Algebra

a. Understand and apply the geometric interpretation and basic operations of vectors in two and three dimensions, including their scalar multiples

1. What is a vector?

   A vector is a mathematical object that has a magnitude and a direction. People often think of two-dimensional (2-D) vectors as arrows drawn on the plane, and three-dimensional (3-D) vectors as arrows in space. The starting point of a vector is not important to the definition. Consequently, vectors are often depicted in *standard position* (starting at the origin). The magnitude (or length) of $\vec{v}$ is often denoted $\|\vec{v}\|$.

2. What is a vector space?

   A vector space is a set (made up of elements called vectors) that is closed under an operation called vector addition (which is commutative and associative and has an identity and inverses) and under multiplication by a field of scalars (usually the real numbers) which has nice associative and distributive properties over vector addition. The main examples of vector spaces for us will be $\mathbb{R}^2$ (the Cartesian coordinate plane) and $\mathbb{R}^3$ (three-dimensional space).

3. How do you write vectors?

   There are three common main ways to write vectors:

   (a) as ordered n-tuples: $\langle 1, -2 \rangle$ or $\langle -3, 0, 4 \rangle$, [or sometimes as $(1, -2)$ or $(-3, 0, 4)$]

   (b) in terms of component vectors: $\vec{i} - 2\vec{j}$ or $-3\vec{i} + 4\vec{k}$, or

   (c) as columns: $\begin{bmatrix} 1 \\ -2 \end{bmatrix}$ or $\begin{bmatrix} -3 \\ 0 \\ 4 \end{bmatrix}$.

4. How do you add vectors? How do you multiply vectors by scalars?

   Algebraically, you can add vectors by adding their corresponding components. You can multiply a vector by a scalar by multiplying each of its components by that scalar. For example, if $\vec{v} = \langle 1, 4, -6 \rangle$ and $\vec{w} = \langle -3, 0, -2 \rangle$, then:

   $\vec{v} + \vec{w} = \langle 1 + (-3), 4 + 0, (-6) + (-2) \rangle = \langle -2, 4, -8 \rangle$,

   $2\vec{v} = \langle 2(1), 2(4), 2(-6) \rangle = \langle 2, 8, -12 \rangle$,

   and $\vec{v} - \vec{w} = \langle 1 - (-3), 4 - 0, (-6) - (-2) \rangle = \langle 4, 4, -4 \rangle$.

   Geometrically, you can add vectors by drawing one vector at the head of another. You can also multiply a vector by a scalar by scaling the vector by that amount. For example,

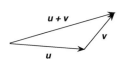
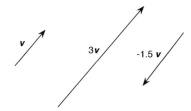

5. How do you "multiply" two vectors?

In general, you cannot multiply vectors, which is one of the ways that they are different from numbers. However, there are two specific products that are useful.

(a) Dot Product (scalar)

The dot product is defined for vectors in any dimension. The dot product of two vectors is always a scalar (and is never a vector). So it's also called the scalar product.

i. Algebraic
If $\vec{v} = \langle v_1, v_2, \ldots, v_n \rangle$ and $\vec{w} = \langle w_1, w_2, \ldots, w_n \rangle$, then

$$\vec{v} \cdot \vec{w} = v_1 w_1 + v_2 w_2 + \ldots + v_n w_n.$$

ii. Geometric
The dot product of two vectors is the product of their lengths times the cosine of the angle between them. That is,

$$\vec{v} \cdot \vec{w} = \|\vec{v}\| \|\vec{w}\| \cos \theta.$$

iii. Why is the dot product important?
The dot product is the easiest way to determine the angle between two vectors. So, it can be used to tell when two vectors are perpendicular. Also, the dot product of a vector with itself gives you the square of the length because $\theta = 0$ in this case. Physicists use the dot product to decompose a vector into its various components. For example, work is the dot product of the force vector with the displacement vector. Force that is perpendicular to the direction of motion ($\theta = 90°$) does not do any work.

(b) Cross Product (vector)

The cross product is only defined for three-dimensional vectors. The cross product of two vectors is always a vector (and is never a scalar). So it's also called the vector product.

i. Algebraic
If $\vec{v} = \langle v_1, v_2, v_3 \rangle$ and $\vec{w} = \langle w_1, w_2, w_3 \rangle$, then

$$\vec{v} \times \vec{w} = \langle v_2 w_3 - v_3 w_2, v_3 w_1 - v_1 w_3, v_1 w_2 - v_2 w_1 \rangle.$$

ii. Geometric
The cross product of two vectors is a vector whose length is the product of the two vectors' lengths times the sine of the angle between them. That is,

$$\|\vec{v} \times \vec{w}\| = \|\vec{v}\| \|\vec{w}\| \sin \theta.$$

Also, the direction of the cross product is perpendicular to the two vectors and points in a direction determined by the Right Hand Rule. Using your right hand, point your fingers in the direction of $\vec{v}$. Keeping your fingers pointing that way, rotate your hand until curling your fingers would make them point in the direction of $\vec{w}$. Now your thumb points in the direction of $\vec{v} \times \vec{w}$.

iii. Why is the cross product important?

The cross product provides a vector that is perpendicular to the plane spanned by two given vectors. Physicists use the cross product with vector quantities and vector fields. For example, torque is the cross product of a force vector with a displacement vector on which the force acts. If a force pulls directly away from a point, ($\theta = 0°$) then that point experiences zero torque from that force.

6. Sample Problems

(a) Draw a picture describing $\langle -3, 5 \rangle + \langle 3, -3 \rangle$.

(b) Draw a picture describing $3 \langle -1, 2 \rangle$.

(c) If $\vec{v}$ has magnitude 13 and points in a direction 135° counter-clockwise from the positive x-axis, then find the magnitude and direction of $2\vec{v}$ and $-3\vec{v}$.

(d) Find the magnitude and direction of $\vec{i} + \vec{j}$.

(e) Give an example showing that the two definitions of the dot product are the same.

(f) Give an example showing that the two definitions of the cross product are the same.

(g) (CSET Sample Test #11) Given any two unit vectors $\vec{a}$ and $\vec{b}$, explain why

$$-1 \leq (\vec{a} \cdot \vec{b}) \leq 1.$$

(h) Show on a graph that any vector $\vec{v} = v_1 \vec{i} + v_2 \vec{j}$ which is perpendicular to $2\vec{i} + \vec{j}$ has to satisfy $2v_1 + v_2 = 0$. [Hint: think of slopes.]

7. Answers to Sample Problems

(a) Draw a picture describing $\langle -3, 5 \rangle + \langle 3, -3 \rangle$.

(b) Draw a picture describing $3 \langle -1, 2 \rangle$.

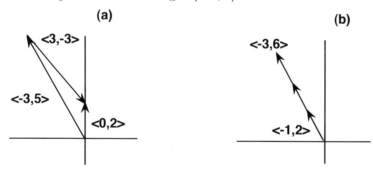

(c) If $\vec{v}$ has magnitude 13 and points in a direction 135° counter-clockwise from the positive x-axis, then find the magnitude and direction of $2\vec{v}$ and $-3\vec{v}$. $2\vec{v}$ has magnitude 26 and points 135° counter-clockwise from the positive x-axis, while $-3\vec{v}$ has magnitude 39, but points 315° counter-clockwise (or 45° clockwise) from the positive x-axis.

(d) Find the magnitude and direction of $\vec{i} + \vec{j}$. The magnitude is $\sqrt{2}$ and the direction is 45° counterclockwise from the positive x-axis.

(e) Give an example showing that the two definitions of the dot product are the same. There are many answers. Consider the example $\langle -1, 1 \rangle \cdot \langle 2, 0 \rangle$. Algebraically, the dot product is $(-1)(2) + (1)(0) = -2$. Geometrically, the magnitude of the first vector is $\sqrt{2}$ and the magnitude of the second vector is 2. The angle between them is $135°$. So the geometric version of the dot product is

$$(\sqrt{2})(2)(\cos 135°) = 2\sqrt{2}\left(-\frac{\sqrt{2}}{2}\right) = -2.$$

(f) Give an example showing that the two definitions of the cross product are the same. There are many answers. Consider the example $\langle 1, 1, 0 \rangle \times \langle 1, 0, 0 \rangle$. There is a $45°$ angle between these vectors. Algebraically, the cross product is $0\vec{i} + 0\vec{j} + (-1)\vec{k} = -\vec{k}$. Geometrically, the magnitude of the cross product is $(\sqrt{2})(1)(\sin 45°) = \sqrt{2}(\frac{\sqrt{2}}{2}) = 1$ and the direction is perpendicular to the xy-plane, in a direction given by the Right Hand Rule. Thus the geometric version of the cross product gives $-\vec{k}$ as well.

(g) (CSET Sample Test #11) Given any two unit vectors $\vec{a}$ and $\vec{b}$, explain why

$$-1 \leq (\vec{a} \cdot \vec{b}) \leq 1.$$

From the geometric version of the dot product, we know that

$$\vec{a} \cdot \vec{b} = \|\vec{a}\|\|\vec{b}\| \cos \theta,$$

where θ is the angle between $\vec{a}$ and $\vec{b}$. Since $\vec{a}$ and $\vec{b}$ are unit vectors, their magnitudes equal 1. So $\vec{a} \cdot \vec{b} = \cos \theta$, which is always between -1 and 1.

(h) Show on a graph that any vector $\vec{v} = v_1\vec{i} + v_2\vec{j}$ which is perpendicular to $2\vec{i} + \vec{j}$ has to satisfy $2v_1 + v_2 = 0$. [Hint: think of slopes.]

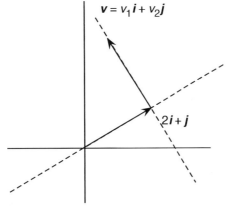

Notice that the slope of any vector $a\vec{i} + b\vec{j}$ is $\frac{\text{rise}}{\text{run}} = \frac{b}{a}$. So the slope of $2\vec{i} + \vec{j}$ is $\frac{1}{2}$. Since perpendicular lines have negative reciprocal slopes, the slope of $\vec{v}$ must be -2. So

$$-2 = \frac{v_2}{v_1} \Rightarrow -2v_1 = v_2 \Rightarrow 0 = 2v_1 + v_2.$$

b. Prove the basic properties of vectors (e.g., perpendicular vectors have zero dot product)

1. What are some basic properties of vectors?

   (a) Assume $\vec{v} \neq \vec{0} \neq \vec{w}$. Then $\vec{v} \cdot \vec{w} = 0$ if and only if $\vec{v} \perp \vec{w}$.

   Proof: From the geometric definition of the dot product (above),

   $$\vec{v} \cdot \vec{w} = \|\vec{v}\|\|\vec{w}\|\cos\theta,$$

   where θ is the angle between $\vec{v}$ and $\vec{w}$. Since the vectors have nonzero lengths, this dot product equals zero if and only if $\cos\theta = 0$. But this means $\theta = 90°$; that is, $\vec{v} \perp \vec{w}$.

   (b) Assume $\vec{v} \neq \vec{0} \neq \vec{w}$. Then $\vec{v} \times \vec{w} = \vec{0}$ if and only if $\vec{v}$ and $\vec{w}$ are parallel or anti-parallel.

   Proof: From the geometric definition of the cross product (above),

   $$\|\vec{v} \times \vec{w}\| = \|\vec{v}\|\|\vec{w}\|\sin\theta,$$

   where θ is the angle between $\vec{v}$ and $\vec{w}$. Since the vectors have nonzero lengths, this dot product equals zero if and only if $\sin\theta = 0$. But this means that either $\theta = 0°$, in which case $\vec{v}$ is parallel to $\vec{w}$, or that $\theta = 180°$, in which case $\vec{v}$ is anti-parallel to $\vec{w}$.

2. Sample Problems

   (a) Let $\vec{v} = 2\vec{i} - 3\vec{j}$ and let $\vec{w} = 7\vec{i} + \vec{j} - 3\vec{k}$. Find the following.

       i. $\vec{v} \cdot \vec{w}$

       ii. $\vec{v} \times \vec{w}$

       iii. $\|\vec{v}\|$ and $\|\vec{w}\|$

       iv. the angle between $\vec{v}$ and $\vec{w}$

   (b) Using the example above, show that $\vec{v} \times \vec{w}$ is perpendicular to $\vec{v}$ and to $\vec{w}$.

   (c) Show that $\vec{v} \times \vec{w}$ is always perpendicular to $\vec{v}$ and to $\vec{w}$.

   (d) Show that $(\vec{v} \times \vec{w}) = -(\vec{w} \times \vec{v})$.

   (e) Show that $\vec{u} \cdot (\vec{v} + \vec{w}) = \vec{u} \cdot \vec{v} + \vec{u} \cdot \vec{w}$. You can assume $\vec{u}$, $\vec{v}$, and $\vec{w}$ are two-dimensional. [The property is true in general.]

   (f) Show that $(\alpha\vec{v}) \cdot \vec{w} = \vec{v} \cdot (\alpha\vec{w}) = \alpha(\vec{v} \cdot \vec{w})$, where α is a scalar (real number). You can assume $\vec{v}$ and $\vec{w}$ are two-dimensional. [The property is true in general.]

   (g) Using the Law of Cosines [In $\triangle ABC$, $c^2 = a^2 + b^2 - 2ab\cos C$.], derive the geometric definition of the dot product. [Hint: draw a triangle of sides $\vec{v}$, $\vec{w}$, and $\vec{w} - \vec{v}$ and apply the formula for length: $\vec{v} \cdot \vec{v} = \|\vec{v}\|^2$.]

3. Answers to Sample Problems

   (a) Let $\vec{v} = 2\vec{i} - 3\vec{j}$ and let $\vec{w} = 7\vec{i} + \vec{j} - 3\vec{k}$. Find the following.

       i. $\vec{v} \cdot \vec{w} = 11$

       ii. $\vec{v} \times \vec{w} = 9\vec{i} + 6\vec{j} + 23\vec{k}$

iii. $\|\vec{v}\| = \sqrt{13}$ and $\|\vec{w}\| = \sqrt{59}$

iv. the angle between $\vec{v}$ and $\vec{w}$ is arccos $\left(\dfrac{11}{\sqrt{767}}\right) \approx 1.16$ radians, or $66.6°$.

(b) Using the example above, show that $\vec{v} \times \vec{w}$ is perpendicular to $\vec{v}$ and to $\vec{w}$. Using the dot product, $\vec{v} \cdot (\vec{v} \times \vec{w}) = 2(9) + (-3)(6) = 18 - 18 = 0$. Similarly, $\vec{w} \cdot (\vec{v} \times \vec{w}) = 7(9) + 1(6) - 3(23) = 63 + 6 - 69 = 0$.

(c) Show that $\vec{v} \times \vec{w}$ is always perpendicular to $\vec{v}$ and to $\vec{w}$. We will show one directly and leave the other part to the reader.

$$
\begin{aligned}
\vec{v} \cdot (\vec{v} \times \vec{w}) &= \langle v_1, v_2, v_3 \rangle \cdot \langle v_2 w_3 - v_3 w_2, v_3 w_1 - v_1 w_3, v_1 w_2 - v_2 w_1 \rangle \\
&= v_1(v_2 w_3 - v_3 w_2) + v_2(v_3 w_1 - v_1 w_3) + v_3(v_1 w_2 - v_2 w_1) \\
&= v_1 v_2 w_3 - v_1 v_3 w_2 + v_2 v_3 w_1 - v_1 v_2 w_3 + v_1 v_3 w_2 - v_2 v_3 w_1 \\
&= 0 + 0 + 0 = 0.
\end{aligned}
$$

Hence, $\vec{v}$ is perpendicular to $\vec{v} \times \vec{w}$. The proof that $\vec{w}$ is perpendicular to $\vec{v} \times \vec{w}$ is similar.

(d) Show that $(\vec{v} \times \vec{w}) = -(\vec{w} \times \vec{v})$.

$$
\begin{aligned}
\vec{v} \times \vec{w} &= \langle v_2 w_3 - v_3 w_2, v_3 w_1 - v_1 w_3, v_1 w_2 - v_2 w_1 \rangle \\
&= \langle -(w_2 v_3 - w_3 v_2), -(w_3 v_1 - w_1 v_3), -(w_1 v_2 - w_2 v_1) \rangle \\
&= -\langle w_2 v_3 - w_3 v_2, w_3 v_1 - w_1 v_3, w_1 v_2 - w_2 v_1 \rangle = -(\vec{w} \times \vec{v}).
\end{aligned}
$$

(e) Show that $\vec{u} \cdot (\vec{v} + \vec{w}) = \vec{u} \cdot \vec{v} + \vec{u} \cdot \vec{w}$. You can assume $\vec{u}$, $\vec{v}$, and $\vec{w}$ are two-dimensional. [The property is true in general.]

Let $\vec{u} = \langle u_1, u_2 \rangle$, $\vec{v} = \langle v_1, v_2 \rangle$, and $\vec{w} = \langle w_1, w_2 \rangle$. Then $\vec{v} + \vec{w} = \langle v_1 + w_1, v_2 + w_2 \rangle$. So,

$$
\begin{aligned}
\vec{u} \cdot (\vec{v} + \vec{w}) &= u_1(v_1 + w_1) + u_2(v_2 + w_2) \\
&= u_1 v_1 + u_1 w_1 + u_2 v_2 + u_2 w_2 \\
&= (u_1 v_1 + u_2 v_2) + (u_1 w_1 + u_2 w_2) \\
&= \vec{u} \cdot \vec{v} + \vec{u} \cdot \vec{w}.
\end{aligned}
$$

(f) Show that $(\alpha \vec{v}) \cdot \vec{w} = \vec{v} \cdot (\alpha \vec{w}) = \alpha(\vec{v} \cdot \vec{w})$, where α is a scalar (real number). You can assume $\vec{v}$ and $\vec{w}$ are two-dimensional. [The property is true in general.]

Let $\vec{v} = \langle v_1, v_2 \rangle$ and $\vec{w} = \langle w_1, w_2 \rangle$. Then $\alpha \vec{v} = \langle \alpha v_1, \alpha v_2 \rangle$.

$$
\begin{aligned}
(\alpha \vec{v}) \cdot \vec{w} &= (\alpha v_1) w_1 + (\alpha v_2) w_2 \\
&= \alpha(v_1 w_1 + v_2 w_2) = \alpha(\vec{v} \cdot \vec{w}) \\
&= v_1(\alpha w_1) + v_2(\alpha w_2) = \vec{v} \cdot (\alpha \vec{w}).
\end{aligned}
$$

(g) Using the Law of Cosines [In $\triangle ABC$, $c^2 = a^2 + b^2 - 2ab \cos C$.], derive the geometric definition of the dot product. [Hint: draw a triangle of sides $\vec{v}$, $\vec{w}$, and $\vec{w} - \vec{v}$ and apply the formula for length: $\vec{v} \cdot \vec{v} = \|\vec{v}\|^2$.]

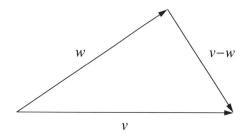

We'll begin with computing the length of the side $\vec{v} - \vec{w}$:

$$\begin{aligned}
\|\vec{v} - \vec{w}\|^2 &= (\vec{v} - \vec{w}) \cdot (\vec{v} - \vec{w}) \\
&= \vec{v} \cdot \vec{v} - 2\vec{v} \cdot \vec{w} + \vec{w} \cdot \vec{w} \\
&= \|\vec{v}\|^2 + \|\vec{w}\|^2 - 2\vec{v} \cdot \vec{w}.
\end{aligned}$$

Comparing this to the Law of Cosines, we see that the squares of the side lengths match up, giving $c^2 = a^2 + b^2 - 2\vec{v} \cdot \vec{w}$. Thus

$$-2ab\cos C = -2\vec{v} \cdot \vec{w},$$

which means $\vec{v} \cdot \vec{w} = ab\cos C = \|\vec{v}\|\|\vec{w}\|\cos C$, which is what we wanted. □

c. Understand and apply the basic properties and operations of matrices and determinants (e.g., to determine the solvability of linear systems of equations)

1. What is a matrix?

   A matrix is a rectangular array of numbers. Matrices can be very useful in solving systems of linear equations, among other applications.

2. How do you multiply matrices?

   You can multiply two matrices if the number of columns of the first matrix equals the number of rows of the second matrix. As an example,

   $$\begin{bmatrix} a & b \\ c & d \end{bmatrix} \begin{bmatrix} 1 & 2 & 3 \\ 4 & 5 & 6 \end{bmatrix} = \begin{bmatrix} a+4b & 2a+5b & 3a+6b \\ c+4d & 2c+5d & 3c+6d \end{bmatrix}.$$

   In general, if A is an m by n matrix and B is an n by p matrix, then AB is an m by p matrix and the entry of AB in row i and column j is given by:

   $$(AB)_{ij} = \sum_{k=1}^{n} A_{ik} B_{kj}.$$

3. What is the determinant of a matrix?

   The determinant of a square matrix is a specific number that encodes some of the properties of that matrix. For instance, if $\det M = 0$, then the matrix M is not invertible. If $\det M \neq 0$, then there is a matrix N satisfying $MN = NM = I$, where I means the identity matrix (1s on the diagonal, 0s elsewhere). In this case, N is also called M^{-1}, the inverse matrix of M.

For 2 by 2 matrices, the determinant is given by:

$$\det \begin{bmatrix} a & b \\ c & d \end{bmatrix} = \begin{vmatrix} a & b \\ c & d \end{vmatrix} = ad - bc.$$

Also, for 2 by 2 matrices, there is a relatively simple formula for finding the inverse matrix:

$$\begin{bmatrix} a & b \\ c & d \end{bmatrix}^{-1} = \left(\frac{1}{ad - bc} \right) \begin{bmatrix} d & -b \\ -c & a \end{bmatrix}, \text{ if } ad - bc \neq 0.$$

For 3 by 3 matrices, the determinant is given by:

$$\begin{vmatrix} a & b & c \\ d & e & f \\ g & h & i \end{vmatrix} = aei + bfg + cdh - bdi - afh - ceg.$$

One way to remember this formula involves recopying the first two columns and then looking along the diagonals of the resulting array.

$$\begin{array}{ccc|cc} a & b & c & a & b \\ d & e & f & d & e \\ g & h & i & g & h \end{array}$$

Multiplying along diagonals down and to the right, we get the terms aei, bfg, and cdh. These are the first three (positive) terms in the determinant formula. Multiplying down and to the left, we obtain the terms bdi, afh, and ceg, which are the next three (negative) terms in the determinant formula.

There is also a recursive way to find the determinant, called expansion by minors. This means that the determinant of a 3 by 3 matrix (for instance) can be written in terms of determinants of various 2 by 2 submatrices of the original matrix. The tricky part is that there is a factor of $(-1)^{r+c}$, where r is the row number and c the column number, counted from the upper left. We'll expand along the top row, although any row or column would work. Pick the first element, a, and then form a submatrix by deleting the row and column containing a. Continue throughout the row. See the example, below.

$$\begin{aligned} \begin{vmatrix} a & b & c \\ d & e & f \\ g & h & i \end{vmatrix} &= (-1)^2 a \begin{vmatrix} e & f \\ h & i \end{vmatrix} + (-1)^3 b \begin{vmatrix} d & f \\ g & i \end{vmatrix} + (-1)^4 c \begin{vmatrix} d & e \\ g & h \end{vmatrix} \\ &= a(ei - fh) - b(di - fg) + c(dh - eg) \\ &= aei + bfg + cdh - afh - bdi - ceg. \end{aligned}$$

Expansion by minors applies to larger matrices, whereas the trick of repeating the first two columns works only for 3 by 3 matrices.

4. How can you use a matrix to determine the solvability of a system of linear equations?

If you have a system of n linear equations in n variables, you can write it as $A\vec{x} = \vec{b}$, where A is the square (n by n) coefficient matrix, $\vec{x}$ is the vector of variables, and $\vec{b}$ is a column vector of right-hand sides to the equations. See Example, below. Method 1 uses row operations, which are really just manipulations of entire equations. For instance, you can multiply an equation by a constant. So, one valid row operation is to multiply the entire row by a constant.

If A is invertible (that is, if $\det A \neq 0$), then there is exactly one solution to the system, namely $\vec{x} = A^{-1}\vec{b}$. Again, see Example, below, Method 2.

If A is not invertible, then the situation is a little trickier. There might be no solutions (in which case the system of equations is *inconsistent*), or there might be an infinite number of solutions. An example of an inconsistent system is $x + y = 1; x + y = 2$. Clearly these two equations cannot simultaneously be true. An example of a system having an infinite number of solutions is $x + y = 1; 2x + 2y = 2$. This system has an entire line of solution points.

5. How can you use a matrix to solve a system of linear equations?

   Example: Solve the equations $2x + 3y = 5$ and $x - y = 5$ simultaneously.

   Method 1 (row operations):

   $$\begin{bmatrix} 2 & 3 & 5 \\ 1 & -1 & 5 \end{bmatrix} \sim \begin{bmatrix} 1 & -1 & 5 \\ 2 & 3 & 5 \end{bmatrix} \text{ (switch rows)}$$

   $$\sim \begin{bmatrix} 1 & -1 & 5 \\ 0 & 5 & -5 \end{bmatrix} \text{ (add } -2(\text{row 1}) \text{ to row 2)}$$

   $$\sim \begin{bmatrix} 1 & -1 & 5 \\ 0 & 1 & -1 \end{bmatrix} \text{ (divide row 2 by 5)}$$

   So the equations now read $x - y = 5$ and $y = -1$. We can substitute to find that $x = 4$.

   Method 2 (inverse matrices): First, rewrite the system of equations in matrix form:

   $$\begin{bmatrix} 2 & 3 \\ 1 & -1 \end{bmatrix} \begin{bmatrix} x \\ y \end{bmatrix} = \begin{bmatrix} 5 \\ 5 \end{bmatrix}.$$

   Using the formula for the inverse of a 2 by 2 matrix gives:

   $$\begin{bmatrix} 2 & 3 \\ 1 & -1 \end{bmatrix}^{-1} = \left(\frac{1}{(2)(-1) - (3)(1)} \right) \begin{bmatrix} -1 & -3 \\ -1 & 2 \end{bmatrix} = \begin{bmatrix} 1/5 & 3/5 \\ 1/5 & -2/5 \end{bmatrix}.$$

   So, we can multiply the original matrix equation on the left to obtain:

   $$\begin{bmatrix} 1/5 & 3/5 \\ 1/5 & -2/5 \end{bmatrix} \begin{bmatrix} 2 & 3 \\ 1 & -1 \end{bmatrix} \begin{bmatrix} x \\ y \end{bmatrix} = \begin{bmatrix} 1/5 & 3/5 \\ 1/5 & -2/5 \end{bmatrix} \begin{bmatrix} 5 \\ 5 \end{bmatrix},$$

   which simplifies to

   $$\begin{bmatrix} 1 & 0 \\ 0 & 1 \end{bmatrix} \begin{bmatrix} x \\ y \end{bmatrix} = \begin{bmatrix} x \\ y \end{bmatrix} = \begin{bmatrix} 4 \\ -1 \end{bmatrix}.$$

   Therefore, $(x, y) = (4, -1)$.

6. Sample Problems

   (a) Check the formula for the 2 by 2 inverse matrix by calculating AA^{-1} and $A^{-1}A$.

   (b) Give an example of 2 by 2 matrices A and B satisfying $AB \neq BA$.

   (c) Solve the following system of equations: $4x - 3y = 15$ and $6x + y = 6$.

   (d) Solve the following system of equations: $x - y = 12$ and $-3x + 3y = 3$.

   (e) Describe how to solve the following system and set up the appropriate matrix equation, but do not actually solve the system.

$$
\begin{aligned}
34x - 56y + 223z &= 217 \\
24x + 25y - 100z &= 27 \\
-30x + 29y + 231z &= -429
\end{aligned}
$$

   (f) Find the determinant of $\begin{bmatrix} 11 & 6 \\ 2 & -5 \end{bmatrix}$.

   (g) Find the determinant of $\begin{bmatrix} 4 & 3 & 7 \\ 5 & -5 & 4 \\ 0 & -9 & -8 \end{bmatrix}$.

   (h) Find B so that $AB = C$, where $A = \begin{bmatrix} 3 & 5 \\ -3 & 4 \end{bmatrix}$ and $C = \begin{bmatrix} 9 \\ 9 \end{bmatrix}$.

   (i) Using A and C above, find AC, if possible. Then find CA, if possible.

7. Answers to Sample Problems

   (a) Check the formula for the 2 by 2 inverse matrix by calculating AA^{-1} and $A^{-1}A$. We assume $ad - bc \neq 0$ so that the inverse of A is defined.

$$
\begin{bmatrix} a & b \\ c & d \end{bmatrix} \left(\frac{1}{ad - bc} \begin{bmatrix} d & -b \\ -c & a \end{bmatrix} \right) = \frac{1}{ad - bc} \begin{bmatrix} ad - bc & -ab + ba \\ cd - dc & -cb + da \end{bmatrix} = \begin{bmatrix} 1 & 0 \\ 0 & 1 \end{bmatrix},
$$

$$
\left(\frac{1}{ad - bc} \begin{bmatrix} d & -b \\ -c & a \end{bmatrix} \right) \begin{bmatrix} a & b \\ c & d \end{bmatrix} = \frac{1}{ad - bc} \begin{bmatrix} ad - bc & db - bd \\ -ca + ac & -bc + ad \end{bmatrix} = \begin{bmatrix} 1 & 0 \\ 0 & 1 \end{bmatrix}.
$$

   (b) Give an example of 2 by 2 matrices A and B satisfying $AB \neq BA$. There are many answers.

$$
\begin{bmatrix} 0 & 1 \\ 0 & 0 \end{bmatrix} \begin{bmatrix} 0 & 0 \\ 1 & 0 \end{bmatrix} = \begin{bmatrix} 1 & 0 \\ 0 & 0 \end{bmatrix}, \text{ but } \begin{bmatrix} 0 & 0 \\ 1 & 0 \end{bmatrix} \begin{bmatrix} 0 & 1 \\ 0 & 0 \end{bmatrix} = \begin{bmatrix} 0 & 0 \\ 0 & 1 \end{bmatrix}.
$$

   (c) Solve the following system of equations: $4x - 3y = 15$ and $6x + y = 6$.
       Using matrices, we get
$$
\begin{bmatrix} 4 & -3 \\ 6 & 1 \end{bmatrix} \begin{bmatrix} x \\ y \end{bmatrix} = \begin{bmatrix} 15 \\ 6 \end{bmatrix}.
$$

The inverse of the coefficient matrix is $\dfrac{1}{22}\begin{bmatrix} 1 & 3 \\ -6 & 4 \end{bmatrix}$. So, multiplying both sides (on the left) by this inverse matrix gives:

$$\frac{1}{22}\begin{bmatrix} 1 & 3 \\ -6 & 4 \end{bmatrix}\begin{bmatrix} 4 & -3 \\ 6 & 1 \end{bmatrix}\begin{bmatrix} x \\ y \end{bmatrix} = \frac{1}{22}\begin{bmatrix} 1 & 3 \\ -6 & 4 \end{bmatrix}\begin{bmatrix} 15 \\ 6 \end{bmatrix} = \frac{1}{22}\begin{bmatrix} 33 \\ -66 \end{bmatrix} = \begin{bmatrix} 1.5 \\ -3 \end{bmatrix}.$$

So $x = 1.5$ and $y = -3$.

(d) Solve the following system of equations: $x - y = 12$ and $-3x + 3y = 3$.

Dividing the second equation by -3 gives $x - y = -1$. Hence there are no solutions to this system of equations. The system is inconsistent.

(e) Describe how to solve the following system and set up the appropriate matrix equation, but do not actually solve the system.

$$\begin{aligned} 34x - 56y + 223z &= 217 \\ 24x + 25y - 100z &= 27 \\ -30x + 29y + 231z &= -429 \end{aligned}$$

We can set up a matrix equation and then use row operations or finding an inverse matrix to reduce and solve the system. The corresponding matrix equation is:

$$\begin{bmatrix} 34 & -56 & 223 \\ 24 & 25 & -100 \\ -30 & 29 & 231 \end{bmatrix}\begin{bmatrix} x \\ y \\ z \end{bmatrix} = \begin{bmatrix} 217 \\ 27 \\ -429 \end{bmatrix}.$$

(f) Find the determinant of $\begin{bmatrix} 11 & 6 \\ 2 & -5 \end{bmatrix}$. -67

(g) Find the determinant of $\begin{bmatrix} 4 & 3 & 7 \\ 5 & -5 & 4 \\ 0 & -9 & -8 \end{bmatrix}$. 109

(h) Find B so that $AB = C$, where $A = \begin{bmatrix} 3 & 5 \\ -3 & 4 \end{bmatrix}$ and $C = \begin{bmatrix} 9 \\ 9 \end{bmatrix}$. In order for AB to be a 2 by 1 matrix, we need B to be a 2 by 1 matrix. Let $B = \begin{bmatrix} x \\ y \end{bmatrix}$ and solve. Or, find A^{-1}. Then $B = A^{-1}C$. In any case,

$$B = \begin{bmatrix} -\frac{1}{3} \\ 2 \end{bmatrix}.$$

(i) Using A and C above, find AC, if possible. Then find CA, if possible. $AC = \begin{bmatrix} 72 \\ 9 \end{bmatrix}$. The product CA is not defined because C has only one column, but A has two rows.

d. Analyze the properties of proportional relationships, lines, linear equations, and their graphs, and the connections between them

1. What are some properties of proportional relationships and their graphs?

   (a) What is a proportional relationship?

   (In what follows, we revisit and expand on what was covered in section **1.1.d** on proportional relationships.)

   A proportional relationship can be described in a number of equivalent ways. One way is to describe it in terms of an equation. We say that A is proportional to B if there is some constant k satisfying $A = kB$. The number k is called the "constant of proportionality."

   Another equivalent way to describe a proportional relationship is to say that two quantities are in proportion if every time one quantity is increased by a certain constant amount, then the other quantity is also increased by another constant (possibly different) amount.

   A third way to describe it is to say that two quantities are in proportion if whenever one quantity is multiplied by a certain number, then the other quantity will also be multiplied by the same number.

   We will use the equation formulation most of the time, but there is understanding to be gained when students can switch back and forth between these representations.

   (b) What does the graph of a proportional relationship look like?

   If A is proportional to B, then we can graph that by putting A on the y-axis and B on the x-axis. The graph of $A = kB$ is a straight line that passes through the origin. The slope of this line is k. Slope was introduced in section **2.3.b**.

   (c) What are the important features of a proportional relationship, and how do they relate to its graph?

   We have touched on the important features a little bit when we talked about the different equivalent ways of describing a proportional relationship. Each of these relate to a graph of a straight line passing through the origin, and can be explained using similar triangles. For example, if we add a certain amount to the x-coordinate, then the y-coordinate will change by a constant amount that is exactly k times the change in x. In the first picture below, k is equal to 3.

   Also, if we multiply the x-coordinate by a constant, then the y-coordinate will be multiplied by the same constant. In the second picture below, we have doubled the x-coordinate.

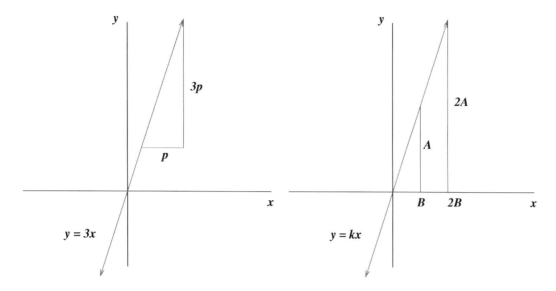

(d) What are some different kinds of proportional relationships?

I like to explain to my students that "is proportional to" means "equals a constant times". So, A is proportional to B means A equals a constant times B, or $A = kB$.

This can be expanded to sentences like A is proportional to the square of B. So $A = kB^2$. Graphing this on a set of axes of A versus B will no longer yield a straight line, but if we were to graph A versus B^2, then we would see a straight line again.

There is also a phrase "is inversely proportional to", which means "is proportional to the reciprocal of". So if A is inversely proportional to B, then A is proportional to the reciprocal of B, or $A = \dfrac{k}{B}$.

These can also be combined in statements like: A is proportional to the cube of B and inversely proportional to the square root of C. Thus $A = \dfrac{kB^3}{\sqrt{C}}$.

Again, only when comparing two quantities that are (directly) proportional does one obtain a graph that is a straight line passing through the origin.

(e) What are some examples of proportional relationships?

Example 1: Suppose you buy food in bulk. The price you pay for dried lentils is proportional to their weight. Suppose that 1.5 pounds of lentils costs \$1.20. Find the constant of proportionality and interpret it in terms of the problem.

We are given that the price is proportional to the weight. Let's keep the units on these quantities, which will allow us to determine the units on k. So,

$$1.2 \text{ dollars} = k(1.5 \text{ pounds}) \implies k = \frac{1.2 \text{ dollars}}{1.5 \text{ pounds}} = 0.8 \text{ dollars per pound.}$$

So k is the price of lentils per pound.

Example 2: When you are driving at a constant speed, say 70 miles per hour, then the distance traveled is proportional to the time that you have been driving. Find a model for this situation.

Here, we are not given any specific quantities, but we are told that we are driving at a rate of 70 miles per hour. So that means that if we drive for one hour, we would have traveled 70 miles. So, 70 miles = k(1 hour). Thus $k = 70$ miles per hour. The constant of proportionality is exactly the constant driving speed. To put it in language that is similar to what is taught in Calculus, k is the rate of change of our distance traveled with respect to time.

This is generally true when modeling a proportion problem. If A is proportional to B, and $A = kB$, then k is the (constant) rate of change of A with respect to B.

2. What are some properties of linear equations and their graphs?

See section **2.3.b** for information about linear functions, lines, and their graphs.

3. What are some connections between proportional relationships, linear equations, and their graphs?

The straight line is the graphical connection between all of these. Proportional relationships are graphed as straight lines that go through the origin. We should point out that they do not include vertical lines through the origin. They all have the property that if you multiply one of the quantities by a constant, then the other quantity will get multiplied by that same constant.

Linear equations, on the other hand, also have straight lines as graphs, but they can include vertical lines, and they can include lines that do not pass through the origin. They do not necessarily have the property that multiplying one quantity by a constant will cause the other quantity to be multiplied by the same constant, but they do share the following property with proportional relationships: that if you add a constant amount to one quantity, then the other quantity will be increased by a constant multiple of the increase to the first quantity. And this constant multiple is the same no matter what increase you start with. This constant even has a special name: either the "constant of proportionality" or the "slope."

Another way to think of it is that all proportional relationships can be graphed as lines with a defined slope, but not all linear equations describe proportional relationships.

4. Sample Problems

    (a) Determine if each of the following situations describes a proportional relationship or not.
        i. The cost of buying socks is related to the number of pairs of socks you buy.
        ii. The cost of cable TV is related to the number of channels you order.
        iii. The amount you pay to the doctor is related to the number of visits you make. (Assume you have a health plan.)

    (b) Suppose that the cost of a plane ticket were proportional to the distance traveled. If it costs \$770 to fly 1221 miles, then how much would a ticket cost to fly 555 miles?

    (c) TRUE or FALSE: Every linear function f can be thought of as expressing a proportional relationship between the change in x and the change in f. (Explain your answer.)

5. Answers to Sample Problems

(a) Determine if each of the following situations describes a proportional relationship or not.

   i. The cost of buying socks is related to the number of pairs of socks you buy. YES, proportional.

   ii. The cost of cable TV is related to the number of channels you order. NO, not proportional. (Premium channels cost more than others.)

   iii. The amount you pay to the doctor is related to the number of visits you make. (Assume you have a health plan.) NO, not proportional. (If you have a health plan, chances are you have to pay something even if you don't visit the doctor. So the graph would not pass through the origin.)

(b) Suppose that the cost of a plane ticket were proportional to the distance traveled. If it costs $770 to fly 1221 miles, then how much would a ticket cost to fly 555 miles? $350.

(c) TRUE or FALSE: Every linear function f can be thought of as expressing a proportional relationship between the change in x and the change in f. (Explain your answer.) TRUE. This is what the slope formula describes. Let $y = f(x)$. Since f is assumed to be a linear function, then we know it has a slope m. We also know that $m = \dfrac{y_2 - y_1}{x_2 - x_1} = \dfrac{\Delta y}{\Delta x}$. This means that $\Delta y = m(\Delta x)$, which describes a proportional relationship. The change in f is proportional to the change in x, and the constant of proportionality is the slope.

e. Model and solve problems using linear equations, pairs of simultaneous linear equations, and their graphs

1. What are some examples of linear models?

   We have already given an example of a linear model in section **2.3.f**. For another example, consider the act of reading a book. The number of pages read in a book depends linearly on the amount of time spent reading. (This assumes that each page has roughly the same number of words on it, is roughly at the same difficulty level, etc.) Suppose that after 40 minutes, you have read 46 pages. How much will you have read after an hour?

   To set up the model, let's use m for the number of minutes spent reading, and p for the number of pages read. This model is strictly proportional - zero pages have been read after zero minutes. So we can write $p = km$, where k is some constant. Using the given information, we get $46 = k(40)$, or $k = \dfrac{46}{40} = \dfrac{23}{20}$. So our model is $p = \dfrac{23}{20}m$.

   To determine how many pages have been read after an hour, we can set $m = 60$. Then

   $$p = \frac{23}{20}(60) = (23)(3) = 69.$$

   So 69 pages have been read after one hour.

2. How do you solve a system of linear equations?

   In section **c.** above, we saw how to solve a system of linear equations using matrices. We now talk about finding exact and approximate solutions.

- How do you find exact solutions?

  The main methods have been mentioned above: replacing one equation by its sum with a multiple of another equation, replacing one equation by a nonzero multiple of itself, switching the order of equations, and substitution. If a system can be solved exactly, it will usually be by a combination of these approaches.

- How do you find approximate solutions?

  Approximate solutions can be found by graphing, or by using technology, such as a graphing calculator or other mathematical software. Sketching the graphs of the equations that make up the system allows one to see if the individual graphs intersect. The intersection points are the solutions to the system. To use a graphing calculator or other software, consult the manual or online help features.

- What are some examples?

  We'll look at two ways to solve the system the equations: $2x + 3y = 5$ and $x - y = 5$. (Notice that these are the same systems we solved using matrices above.)

  Method 1 (manipulating equations): By looking at the left-hand sides, we see a $3y$ term in the first equation and a $-y$ term in the second equation. So let's add 3 times the second equation to the first equation. This gives

  $$2x + 3y + 3(x - y) = 5 + 3(5) \quad \text{and} \quad x - y = 5 \text{ or:}$$
  $$5x = 20 \quad \text{and} \quad x - y = 5.$$

  From here, we can divide the first equation by 5 (or multiply it by $\frac{1}{5}$). So the equations now read $x = 4$ and $x - y = 5$. We can now substitute to find that $y = -1$. The solution to the system is the single point $(4, -1)$.

  Method 2 (substitution): First, we will rewrite the second equation to solve for x, obtaining $x = y + 5$. We now substitute this expression into the first equation for x to obtain:

  $$2(y + 5) + 3y = 5 \iff 2y + 10 + 3y = 5 \iff 5y = -5.$$

  From here, we can multiply the equation by $\frac{1}{5}$ (or divide by 5) to obtain $y = -1$. Then, since $x = y + 5$, $x = 4$. Therefore, $(x, y) = (4, -1)$ is the solution.

  Next, let's solve the following system of equations: $4x - 3y = 15$ and $6x + y = 6$. As before, let's add 3 times the second equation to the first. This makes the first equation into $4x - 3y + 3(6x + y) = 15 + 3(6)$, or after simplification, $22x = 33$, which means $x = \frac{3}{2} = 1.5$. From here, we can use either equation to determine the value of y. Using the second equation, we get $6(1.5) + y = 6$, or $9 + y = 6$, from which we get $y = -3$. So $x = 1.5$ and $y = -3$.

  Next, let's solve the following system of equations: $x - y = 12$ and $-3x + 3y = 3$. Dividing the second equation by -3 (or multiplying by $-\frac{1}{3}$) gives $x - y = -1$. So our system is now $x - y = 12$ and $x - y = -1$. Hence there are no solutions to this system of equations. Such a system is called *inconsistent*. If we had tried to add 3 times the first equation to the second, we would have obtained $-3x + 3y + 3(x - y) = 3 + 3(12)$, or $0 = 39$, which is clearly not a true statement. That is a sure sign of an inconsistent system.

And as a final example, let's solve the system $x - 5y = 2$ and $-2x + 10y = -4$. Here, let's add 2 times the first equation to the second, to obtain:

$$-2x + 10y + 2(x - 5y) = -4 + 2(2),$$

or $0 = 0$. What does this mean?

It means that the second equation is a multiple of the first. Thus, we really only need one of the equations. This system has an infinite number of solutions, namely any pair (x, y) that satisfies $x - 5y = 2$ will necessarily satisfy the system. Here, the original equations are said to be *dependent* on each other.

3. What are some examples of models involving a pair of simultaneous linear equations?

We will present two examples here, and then will solve them using the techniques we just described.

Example 1: Jane buys three oranges and two apples at the store and pays $1.50. Johnny buys four oranges and three apples at the same store and pays $2.11. How much does each fruit cost?

To solve this, we first need to set up the system of equations. Let's use O for the price of an orange and A for the price of an apple. (Make sure not to confuse the letter O with zero.) Then from what Jane bought, we know $3O + 2A = 1.5$, and from what Johnny bought, we know $4O + 3A = 2.11$. So

$$
\begin{aligned}
3O + 2A &= 1.5 \\
4O + 3A &= 2.11.
\end{aligned}
$$

Let's multiply the first equation by 3 and the second equation by -2. Then we get

$$
\begin{aligned}
9O + 6A &= 4.5 \\
-8O - 6A &= -4.22.
\end{aligned}
$$

If we now add the two equations (and replace one of them with the sum), we get

$$
\begin{aligned}
9O + 6A &= 4.5 \\
O &= 0.28
\end{aligned}
$$

So one orange costs $0.28. With this information, we can go back to either initial equation to find that one apple costs $0.33.

Let's check these answers. Three oranges and two apples should cost $3(0.28) + 2(0.33) = 0.84 + 0.66 = 1.5$, while four oranges and three apples cost $4(0.28) + 3(0.33) = 1.12 + 0.99 = 2.11$. So yes, these answers are correct.

Example 2: Suppose you have a solution that is 20% bleach and a solution that is 4% bleach. You need to make 32 ounces of a solution that is 7% bleach. How much of each solution needs to be mixed together to accomplish this?

It may seem like there aren't two equations here. But there are two different amounts in question: the total amount of liquid, and the total amount of bleach in the liquid. We can model this situation with a system of linear equations. Let x be the number of ounces of the 20% bleach solution needed, and let y be the number of ounces of the 4% bleach solution needed. Then, since we need 32 ounces total, we know $x + y = 32$.

Then, since we need 32 ounces of a 7% bleach solution, we know we need $(32)(0.07) = 2.24$ ounces of bleach total. Similarly, the amount of bleach in x ounces of the 20% solution is $(0.2)x$, while the amount of bleach in y ounces of the 4% solution is $(0.04)y$. So, we know that $(0.2)x + (0.04)y = 2.24$.

Before writing the system, we will multiply the second equation by 25. (You can think of multiplying by 100 and then dividing by 4 to reduce.)

$$\begin{aligned} x + y &= 32 \\ 5x + y &= 56 \end{aligned}$$

Using the first equation to solve for y, we get $y = 32 - x$. Substituting into the second equation, we get $5x + (32 - x) = 56$, or $4x = 24$. So $x = 6$. Then $y = 32 - 6 = 26$.

Let's check. Certainly $6 + 26 = 32$ total ounces. To check the bleach, $(0.2)(6) + (0.04)(26) = 1.2 + 1.04 = 2.24$ total ounces of bleach. The answers are correct.

4. Sample Problems

   (a) Find the cost of a pound of beef and a pound of potatoes given the following information. 120 pounds of beef and 315 pounds of potatoes cost \$735 total, while 150 pounds of beef and 420 pounds of potatoes cost \$930 total. (Round to the nearest cent.)

   (b) On Monday, the M&M factory makes candies that are 33% brown, while on Tuesday, they make candies that are 25% brown. How much of each day's candies do they need to mix together to have one ton (2000 pounds) of candies that are 30% brown? (Round to the nearest pound.)

   (c) It takes Jane and Johnny 75 minutes to paint a room in their house. When Johnny's brother helps them, it only takes 55 minutes. Assuming that Johnny and his brother paint at the same rate, find how long it would take Jane to paint the room by herself, and how long it would take Johnny to paint the room by himself. (Round to the nearest minute. Hint: find each one's painting rate.)

5. Answers to Sample Problems

   (a) Find the cost of a pound of beef and a pound of potatoes given the following information. 120 pounds of beef and 315 pounds of potatoes cost \$735 total, while 150 pounds of beef and 420 pounds of potatoes cost \$930 total. (Round to the nearest cent.) Beef costs \$5 per pound, while potatoes cost $\frac{3}{7}$ of a dollar per pound, or about 43 cents per pound.

   (b) On Monday, the M&M factory makes candies that are 33% brown, while on Tuesday, they make candies that are 25% brown. How much of each day's candies do they need to mix together to have one ton (2000 pounds) of candies that are 30% brown? (Round to the nearest pound.) They should mix 1250 pounds of Monday's candies with 750 pounds of Tuesday's candies.

(c) It takes Jane and Johnny 75 minutes to paint a room in their house. When Johnny's brother helps them, it only takes 55 minutes. Assuming that Johnny and his brother paint at the same rate, find how long it would take Jane to paint the room by herself, and how long it would take Johnny to paint the room by himself. (Round to the nearest minute. Hint: find each one's painting rate.) Jane paints at a rate of $\frac{7}{825}$ rooms per minute, while Johnny paints at a rate of $\frac{4}{825}$ rooms per minute. Thus Jane paints a room in $\frac{825}{7} \approx 118$ minutes when working alone, while Johnny paints a room in $\frac{825}{4} \approx 206$ minutes when working alone.

Miscellaneous Extra Review Topics

a. Logarithms

1. What is a logarithm?

   A logarithm is an exponent. The logarithm base b of n is the exponent needed on b to obtain n. In symbols:
   $$x = \log_b n \iff b^x = n.$$

   Any simple logarithmic equation can be transformed into an exponential equation according to the formula above. One consequence of this definition is that you cannot take the logarithm of a number unless that number is positive. This is because basic exponential functions only take positive values.

   Example: Find $\log_3 \frac{1}{81}$.

   Let $x = \log_3 \frac{1}{81}$. Then $3^x = \frac{1}{81} = \frac{1}{3^4} = 3^{-4}$. So, $x = -4$. Therefore, $\log_3 \frac{1}{81} = -4$.

2. What are some bases for logarithms?

   The bases most often used are 10 and e. Logs base 10 are called "common" logs and are written "log" (with no subscript). Logs base e are called "natural" logs and are written "ln."

   Aside: By the way, $e \approx 2.718281828459045\ldots$ One reason e is so useful has to do with calculus. The slope of the graph of $y = e^x$ at any point is equal to the y-coordinate of that point. So, e^x is its own derivative. (See Derivatives, Test 3 materials.)

3. What are some properties of logarithms?

   The following properties hold for any base, b.

   (a) $x = \log_b n \iff b^x = n$ (the definition)

   (b) $\log_b(x^m) = m \log_b x$

   (c) $\log_b(xy) = \log_b x + \log_b y$

   (d) $\log_b x = \dfrac{\log x}{\log b} = \dfrac{\ln x}{\ln b} = \dfrac{\log_a x}{\log_a b}$ (for any base a) [Change of Base Formula]

   The following facts may help you solve log problems.

   (a) $\log_b 1 = 0$. (In particular, $\log 1 = \ln 1 = 0$.)

   (b) $\log_b b = 1$. (In particular, $\log 10 = \ln e = 1$.)

   (c) $\log_b 0$ is not defined.

   (d) $b^{\log_b x} = x$. (In particular, $10^{\log x} = e^{\ln x} = x$.)

   More properties can be found in the Sample Problems.

   Example: Simplify $\log 16 + \log 125 - \log 2$.

Answer: Using the properties, we can deduce that $\log_b \frac{x}{y} = \log_b x - \log_b y$. (See Sample Problems, below.) So, working backwards, we get

$$
\begin{aligned}
\log 16 + \log 125 - \log 2 &= \log \frac{(16)(125)}{(2)} \\
&= \log 1000 \\
&= \log 10^3 \\
&= 3 \log 10 \\
&= 3.
\end{aligned}
$$

4. Sample Problems

   (a) Simplify, if possible:

      i. $\log_4 64$

      ii. $\log_2 128$

      iii. $\log 0.000001$

      iv. $\ln e^{-1}$

      v. $\ln(-e)$

      vi. $\log_7 7$

      vii. $e^{\ln 4}$

      viii. $\log_2 5 - \log_2 40$

      ix. $\log_2 4^t$

      x. $e^{2 \ln w}$

      xi. $\log 10^{4x}$

      xii. $(\log e)(\ln 10)$ [Hint: Use the Change of Base Formula.]

   (b) Write as a single logarithm: $2 \ln w + 5 \ln x - \frac{1}{2} \ln y$.

   (c) Expand as a sum of logarithms of single variables: $\log_5 \left(\frac{x^7}{y^2 \sqrt[3]{z}} \right)$.

   (d) Solve for x: $\log_6 x + \log_6 (x+5) = 1$.

   (e) Why does $\log_6 x - \log_6 (x+5) = 1$ not have a real solution?

   (f) Using the log properties, show that $\log_b b^m = m$.

   (g) Using the log properties, show that $\log_b \frac{x}{y} = \log_b x - \log_b y$.

5. Answers to Sample Problems

   (a) Simplify, if possible:

      i. $\log_4 64 = 3$

      ii. $\log_2 128 = 7$

      iii. $\log 0.000001 = -6$

      iv. $\ln e^{-1} = -1$

    v. $\ln(-e)$ is not defined.

    vi. $\log_7 7 = 1$

    vii. $e^{\ln 4} = 4$

    viii. $\log_2 5 - \log_2 40 = \log_2(\frac{1}{8}) = -3$

    ix. $\log_2 4^t = \log_2(2^{2t}) = 2t$

    x. $e^{2\ln w} = e^{\ln w^2} = w^2$

    xi. $\log 10^{4x} = 4x$

    xii. $(\log e)(\ln 10) = \left(\dfrac{\ln e}{\ln 10}\right)(\ln 10) = 1$

(b) Write as a single logarithm: $2\ln w + 5\ln x - \frac{1}{2}\ln y$. $\ln\left(\dfrac{w^2 x^5}{\sqrt{y}}\right)$

(c) Expand as a sum of logarithms of single variables: $\log_5\left(\dfrac{x^7}{y^2 \sqrt[3]{z}}\right)$.

$$7\log_5 x - 2\log_5 y - \frac{1}{3}\log_5 z$$

(d) Solve for x: $\log_6 x + \log_6(x+5) = 1$. $x = 1$ ($x = -6$ is extraneous)

$$\log_6 x + \log_6(x+5) = 1 \Rightarrow \log_6(x(x+5)) = 1 \Rightarrow x(x+5) = 6 \Rightarrow$$

$$\Rightarrow x^2 + 5x - 6 = 0 \Rightarrow (x+6)(x-1) = 0 \Rightarrow x = 1 \text{ or } -6$$

Checking both of these shows that -6 is extraneous.

(e) Why does $\log_6 x - \log_6(x+5) = 1$ not have a real solution? If we proceed as in the previous problem, we get $\frac{x}{x+5} = 6$, which has $x = -6$ as a solution. But since $\log_6(-6)$ is not defined, there is no solution to the original equation.

(f) Using the log properties, show that $\log_b b^m = m$. Answers may vary.

$$\log_b b^m = m(\log_b b) = m(1) = m.$$

(g) Using the log properties, show that $\log_b \frac{x}{y} = \log_b x - \log_b y$. Answers may vary.

$$\log_b \frac{x}{y} = \log_b(xy^{-1}) = \log_b x + \log_b(y^{-1}) = \log_b x - \log_b y.$$

b. Proof by Contradiction

1. What is a proof by contradiction?

A proof by contradiction is a way to show that a statement is true by showing that it cannot be false. You assume that it is false, and then show that your assumption leads to a contradiction of some other mathematical fact or hypothesis of the problem.

Aside: This proof technique relies HEAVILY on the "Law of the Excluded Middle," which says that either a mathematical statement is true or else it is false. There is no room for any other outcome.

2. Sample Problems

    (a) Let m be an integer and let m^2 be odd. Then m is odd.

    (b) Let $r, s \in \mathbb{R}$ and let $r + s$ be irrational. Then r is irrational or s is irrational.

    (c) Let m and n be integers and let mn be odd. Then m is odd and n is odd.

    (d) Suppose that n is an integer which is not divisible by 3. Then n is not divisible by 6.

    (e) Prove that $\log_2 3$ is irrational.

3. Answers to Sample Problems

    (a) Let m be an integer and let m^2 be odd. Then m is odd.

       Proof: Suppose that m^2 is odd, but m is even. Then $m = 2k$ for some integer k. So $m^2 = 4k^2 = 2(2k^2)$, which is also even. But this contradicts our hypothesis that m^2 is odd. Therefore m must be odd. $\square$

    (b) Let $r, s \in \mathbb{R}$ and let $r + s$ be irrational. Then r is irrational or s is irrational.

       Proof: Suppose that $r + s$ is irrational, but both r and s are rational. Then there exist integers a, b, c, and d with $b \neq 0 \neq d$ such that $r = \frac{a}{b}$ and $s = \frac{c}{d}$. Then $r + s = \frac{a}{b} + \frac{c}{d} = \frac{ad+bc}{bd}$, which is clearly rational. But this contradicts our hypothesis that $r + s$ is irrational. Therefore r is irrational or s is irrational. $\square$

    (c) Let m and n be integers and let mn be odd. Then m is odd and n is odd.

       Proof: Suppose that mn is odd, but either m or n is even. Without loss of generality, say $m = 2k$ for some integer k. Then $mn = 2kn$, which is clearly even. But this contradicts our hypothesis that mn is odd. So therefore m and n must be odd. $\square$

    (d) Suppose that n is an integer which is not divisible by 3. Then n is not divisible by 6.

       Proof: Suppose that n is not divisible by 3, but that n is divisible by 6. Then there exists an integer k satisfying $n = 6k = 3(2k)$. Thus n is also divisible by 3. But this contradicts our hypothesis that n is not divisible by 3. Therefore, n must not be divisible by 6. $\square$

    (e) Prove that $\log_2 3$ is irrational.

       Proof: Suppose that $\log_2 3$ is rational. Then $\log_2 3 = \frac{p}{q}$ for some integers p and q with $q \neq 0$. Then $2^{p/q} = 3$, or, raising both sides to the q-th power, $2^p = 3^q$. According to the Fundamental Theorem of Arithmetic, the only power of 2 that is also a power of 3 is the number $1 = 2^0 = 3^0$. So $p = q = 0$. But this contradicts the fact that $q \neq 0$. Therefore, $\log_2 3$ must be irrational. $\square$

SUBTEST II

Geometry; Probability and Statistics

3.1 Plane Euclidean Geometry

a. Apply the Parallel Postulate and its implications and justify its equivalents (e.g., the Alternate Interior Angle Theorem, the angle sum of every triangle is 180 degrees)

1. Geometry Notation

   Before we begin, let's agree to some notation. Most of it is straightforward, but there are some important technicalities. There is a difference between a line segment and the length of the line segment. As a geometric object, the line segment between point A and point B will be denoted $\overline{AB}$. The length of this segment, also known as the distance from A to B, is a positive real number denoted AB. Similarly, the angle with vertex at A will be denoted $\angle A$ as a geometric object, but the measure of that angle in degrees, denoted $m\angle A$, is a number between 0 and 180.

2. What does "parallel" mean?

   This may seem like a simple question, but in geometry, two lines are "parallel" if and only if they do not intersect. There is no mention of "slope" until coordinate geometry. "Having the same slope" is a numerical, algebraic property. "Not intersecting" is a geometric property.

3. What is the Parallel Postulate? (What is Euclidean geometry?)

   Euclid's *Elements* are made up of 13 books in which Euclid presents geometry from an axiomatic point of view. In particular, he builds geometry on a foundation of five postulates, 23 definitions, and five common notions. Euclid's postulates are:

   i. To draw a straight line from any point to any point.

   ii. To produce a finite straight line continuously in a straight line.

   iii. To describe a circle with any center and radius.

   iv. That all right angles equal one another.

   v. That, if a straight line falling on two straight lines makes the interior angles on the same side less than two right angles, the two straight lines, if produced indefinitely, meet on that side on which are the angles less than the two right angles.

   (Visit http://aleph0.clarku.edu/~djoyce/java/elements/elements.html for an online version of Euclid's *Elements*.)

   The fifth postulate is often called Euclid's Parallel Postulate (but it is not *our* Parallel Postulate). Notice that it is rather bulky. In our language, we might state Euclid's Fifth Postulate as: "If two lines are cut by a transversal, and same side interior angles add up to less than 180, then the two lines will eventually intersect on the side of the transversal on which the angle sum is less than 180." In terms of the picture below, if $m\angle 1 + m\angle 4 < 180$, then k and m intersect on the left side of t.

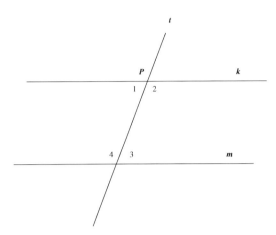

Euclidean geometry is the geometry described in Euclid's *Elements*. It is the geometry of flat planes on which the Fifth Postulate is assumed to be true. However, this is still not the Parallel Postulate as it appears in most school texts.

4. What are some implications of the Parallel Postulate?

One of the implications of Euclid's Parallel Postulate (and indeed equivalent to it) is Playfair's Postulate: "If m is a line and P is a point not on m, then there is exactly one line through P that is parallel to m." In fact, *this* is the formulation which the CSET thinks of (and what many Geometry textbooks state) as the Parallel Postulate.

> *The Parallel Postulate.* Through a given external point there is exactly one line parallel to a given line.

The following statements are equivalent to the Parallel Postulate. (This list is by no means complete.)

(a) Euclid's Fifth Postulate

(b) If two parallel lines are cut by a transversal, then alternate interior angles are congruent.

(c) The angle sum of a triangle is 180.

(d) If a line intersects one of two parallel lines, then it intersects the other.

(e) If a line is perpendicular to one of two parallel lines, then it is perpendicular to the other.

(f) Rectangles exist.

5. What is the Alternate Interior Angle Theorem? Why is it equivalent to the Parallel Postulate?

The short answer is that the Alternate Interior Angle Theorem is the second of the equivalences listed above: "If two parallel lines are cut by a transversal, then alternate interior angles are congruent." We will call this statement AIAT below. The longer answer is that the "Alternate Interior Angle Theorem" is different in different textbooks. For instance, in *Roads to Geometry*, by Wallace and West (NJ: Pearson Education, 2004), their Alternate Interior Angle Theorem is the converse statement: "If two lines are cut by a transversal so that alternate interior angles are congruent, then the two lines are parallel." It is interesting to note that THIS statement can be proved *without* using Euclid's Parallel Postulate.

Because our Alternate Interior Angle Theorem (AIAT) is equivalent to the Parallel Postulate, it is also equivalent to Euclid's Fifth Postulate (E5). This means two things:

- If E5 is true, then AIAT is true; AND

- If AIAT is true, then E5 is true.

Sample Proof: To prove the first item, we assume E5 is true. Then start with two parallel lines cut by a transversal. See figure below.

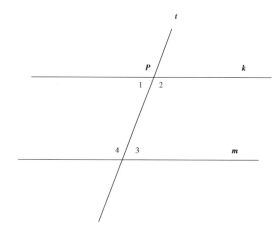

Suppose that ∠1 were smaller than ∠3. Then ∠2 would be larger than ∠4 (because of supplementary angle properties - see the next section for the definition of supplementary angles). So then the sum of ∠1 plus ∠4 would be smaller than the sum of ∠2 plus ∠3. In equations,

$$
\begin{aligned}
m\angle 1 + m\angle 4 &< m\angle 2 + m\angle 3 \\
m\angle 1 + m\angle 4 &< (180 - m\angle 1) + (180 - m\angle 4) \\
m\angle 1 + m\angle 4 &< 360 - (m\angle 1 + m\angle 4) \\
2(m\angle 1 + m\angle 4) &< 360,
\end{aligned}
$$

which means that the measure of ∠1 plus the measure of ∠4 is less than 180. Therefore, by E5, lines k and m would have to intersect on that side of t, contradicting the fact that they are parallel. So ∠1 cannot be smaller than ∠3. By a very similar argument, ∠1 cannot be larger than ∠3. So ∠1 must be congruent to ∠3. It then follows that ∠2 is congruent to ∠4.

To prove the other direction of this equivalence, see the exercises.

6. How does the fact that the angle sum of a triangle is 180 follow from the Parallel Postulate?

In the picture below, we start with a triangle. Then we draw a line through P that is parallel to the opposite side of the triangle. If we assume the Parallel Postulate, then there is only one such line, meaning that the two angles marked A are congruent by the AIAT. Similarly, the two B angles are congruent. So, the sum of A, B, and C is clearly 180. Thus the Parallel Postulate implies that the sum of angles in a triangle is 180.

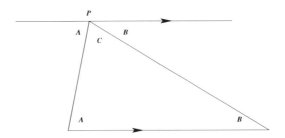

7. Sample Problems

   (a) Explain why Euclid's Fifth Postulate follows from the Alternate Interior Angle Theorem. (You may need the Exterior Angle Theorem, which says that an exterior angle of a triangle is always larger than either of the remote interior angles.)

   (b) Draw a picture of two parallel lines cut by a transversal. Label the eight angles formed.
      i. State the Alternate Interior Angle Theorem in terms of your diagram.
      ii. Create an Alternate Exterior Angle Theorem and its converse.
      iii. Create a Corresponding Angle Theorem and its converse.
      iv. Create a Same-side Interior Angle Theorem and its converse.
      v. List all equivalences among your theorems, the Alternate Interior Angle Theorem, and its converse.

   (c) If the Parallel Postulate were false, then what other statements would be false?

   (d) Explain why the Parallel Postulate implies that rectangles exist.

8. Answers to Sample Problems

   (a) Explain why Euclid's Fifth Postulate follows from the Alternate Interior Angle Theorem. (You may need the Exterior Angle Theorem, which says that an exterior angle of a triangle is always larger than either of the remote interior angles.)

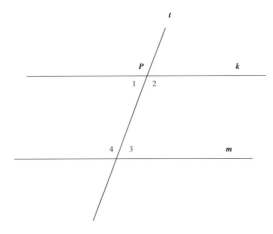

   Suppose that two lines are cut by a transversal in such a way that same-side interior angles add up to less than 180. (In the diagram above, say $m\angle 1 + m\angle 4 < 180$.) We can also conclude that either $m\angle 1 < m\angle 3$ or $m\angle 4 < m\angle 2$. Without loss of generality, let's say that $m\angle 1 < m\angle 3$.

If alternate interior angles were congruent, then $m\angle 1 + m\angle 4$ would be 180. So, the alternate interior angles are not congruent. Then by the contrapositive of AIAT, lines k and m are not parallel. Thus, the lines k and m must intersect. Suppose they intersect on the *right* side of t.

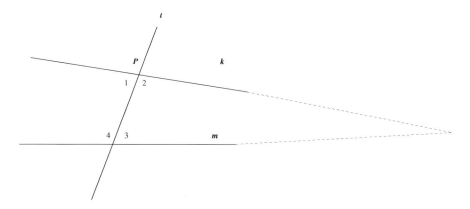

Then $\angle 1$ would be an exterior angle of the triangle formed by k, m, and t. (See section **d** below for more information on exterior angles.) Also, $\angle 3$ would be a remote interior angle in the same triangle, meaning that $m\angle 1 \geq m\angle 3$. This is a contradiction to the assumption that $m\angle 1 < m\angle 3$. So the intersection of k and m must happen on the *left* side of t, which is the side on which the same-side interior angles add up to less than 180. Therefore, if AIAT is true, then E5 is true.

(b) Draw a picture of two parallel lines cut by a transversal. Label the eight angles formed.

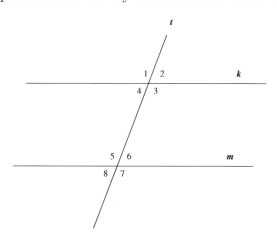

   i. State the Alternate Interior Angle Theorem in terms of your diagram.
     If $k \parallel m$, then $\angle 4 \cong \angle 6$ (or $\angle 3 \cong \angle 5$).

  ii. Create an Alternate Exterior Angle Theorem and its converse.
     Theorem: If $k \parallel m$, then $\angle 1 \cong \angle 7$ (or $\angle 2 \cong \angle 8$).
     Converse: If $\angle 1 \cong \angle 7$ (or if $\angle 2 \cong \angle 8$), then $k \parallel m$.

 iii. Create a Corresponding Angle Theorem and its converse.
     Theorem: If $k \parallel m$, then $\angle 1 \cong \angle 5$ (or $\angle 2 \cong \angle 6$, or $\angle 3 \cong \angle 7$, or $\angle 4 \cong \angle 8$).
     Converse: If $\angle 1 \cong \angle 5$ (or if $\angle 2 \cong \angle 6$, or if $\angle 3 \cong \angle 7$, or if $\angle 4 \cong \angle 8$), then $k \parallel m$.

iv. Create a Same-side Interior Angle Theorem and its converse.

Theorem: If $k \parallel m$, then $\angle 4$ and $\angle 5$ are supplementary, (or $\angle 3$ and $\angle 6$ are supplementary). (See the next section for more about supplementary angles.)

Converse: If $\angle 4$ and $\angle 5$ are supplementary, (or if $\angle 3$ and $\angle 6$ are supplementary), then $k \parallel m$.

v. List all equivalences among your theorems, the Alternate Interior Angle Theorem, and its converse.

All the converse statements are equivalent to each other, but are not equivalent to any of the theorems. All the theorems above are equivalent to each other, and the theorems are also equivalent to Euclid's Fifth Postulate and the Parallel Postulate.

(c) If the Parallel Postulate were false, then what other statements would be false?

If the Parallel Postulate were false, then every statement equivalent to it would also be false. So, triangle angle sums would not be 180, Euclid's Fifth Postulate would not be true, the Alternate Interior Angle Theorem would not be true, etc.

(d) Explain why the Parallel Postulate implies that rectangles exist.

Let k be a line and let P be a point not on k. The Parallel Postulate says that there is only one line (call it m) through P which is parallel to k. Draw line m. Let Q be another point on m. Now draw the line t through P which is perpendicular to k. Call the point of intersection (of t and k) A. By the Alternate Interior Angle Theorem (which is equivalent to the Parallel Postulate), $t \perp m$. The Parallel Postulate guarantees that there is only one line s through Q which is parallel to t. So $s \perp m$ and thus $s \perp k$ at some point B. By construction, then, $ABQP$ is a rectangle.

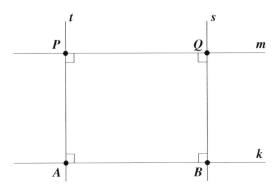

b. Demonstrate knowledge of complementary, supplementary, and vertical angles

1. What are complementary angles? What are supplementary angles?

Two angles are *complementary* if their measures add up to 90 (a right angle). Two angles are *supplementary* if their measures add up to 180 (a straight angle).

ENGLISH LANGUAGE FACT: There is a similar word, "complimentary," in the English language that has to do with being nice or flattering towards someone. Telling someone that their new haircut looks nice is an example of being complimentary. The word "complementary" is spelled differently (with an "e") and has a different meaning. Complementary and supplementary both come from the Latin word for "full".

2. What are vertical angles?

Two angles are *vertical* if they share the same vertex and if their sides lie on two intersecting lines, but they do not share a side. It's best seen in a picture - see the Sample Problems, below.

3. Sample Problems

    (a) In the picture below, identify all sets of complementary angles, supplementary angles, and vertical angles.

    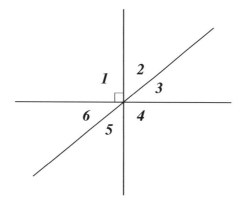

    (b) True or False. No explanations needed yet.

        i. Complementary angles are congruent.
        ii. Supplementary angles are congruent.
        iii. Vertical angles are congruent.
        iv. Complementary angles can be supplementary.
        v. Vertical angles can be complementary.
        vi. Vertical angles can be supplementary.

4. Answers to Sample Problems

    (a) In the picture below, identify all sets of complementary angles, supplementary angles, and vertical angles.

    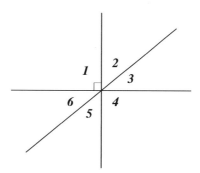

Complementary:	$\angle 2$ and $\angle 3$; $\angle 5$ and $\angle 6$; $\angle 2$ and $\angle 6$; $\angle 3$ and $\angle 5$;
Supplementary:	$\angle 1$ and $\angle 4$
Vertical:	$\angle 1$ and $\angle 4$; $\angle 2$ and $\angle 5$; $\angle 3$ and $\angle 6$

Note that even though $m\angle 1 + m\angle 2 + m\angle 3 = 180$, we can't say they are supplementary because our definition only referred to two angles.

(b) True or False. No explanations needed yet.

    i. Complementary angles are congruent. FALSE (They might be congruent, at 45 each, but since they do not have to be, the statement is false.)

    ii. Supplementary angles are congruent. FALSE (Similar as above. Congruent supplementary angles are right angles, measuring 90 each. But this is a special case. The general statement here is false.)

    iii. Vertical angles are congruent. TRUE (You can prove this using supplementary angles. See a Geometry textbook if you're not sure how to prove it.)

    iv. Complementary angles can be supplementary. FALSE (If two numbers add up to 90, then they do not add up to 180.)

    v. Vertical angles can be complementary. TRUE, if they are 45 each.

    vi. Vertical angles can be supplementary. TRUE, if they are 90 each.

c. Prove theorems, justify steps, and solve problems involving similarity and congruence

1. What does "congruent" mean? What does "similar" mean?

Two line segments are congruent ($\cong$) if they have the same length. Two angles are congruent if they have the same measure. Two polygons are congruent if you can match up their vertices in sequence so that all corresponding sides and all corresponding angles are congruent.

Two polygons are similar ($\sim$) if you can match up their vertices in sequence so that all corresponding angles are congruent, and so that all corresponding sides are in the same proportion.

2. What are the most common triangle congruence theorems?

We say $\triangle ABC \cong \triangle DEF$ if and only if $\overline{AB} \cong \overline{DE}$; $\overline{AC} \cong \overline{DF}$; $\overline{BC} \cong \overline{EF}$; $\angle A \cong \angle D$; $\angle B \cong \angle E$; and $\angle C \cong \angle F$. This is a total of six conditions.

However, in practice, you do not need to show all six. There are postulates or theorems that tell you when two triangles are congruent. They are: SAS (Side-Angle-Side), ASA, AAS, SSS, and for right triangles, HL (hypotenuse-leg).

3. What are the most common triangle similarity theorems?

We say $\triangle ABC \sim \triangle DEF$ if and only if there is a value of $k > 0$ so that $AB = kDE$; $AC = kDF$; $BC = kEF$; $\angle A \cong \angle D$; $\angle B \cong \angle E$; and $\angle C \cong \angle F$. This is also a total of six conditions.

However, in practice, you do not need to show all six. For triangles, any time their three angles are congruent, the triangles are similar. So, there is (in Euclidean geometry) an AA (Angle-Angle) Similarity Theorem. Other theorems include sss and sAs. (The lower-case "s" means that the corresponding sides are in the same proportion.) Also, there are lots of similarities available in right triangle ABC (with right angle at C) if you draw altitude $\overline{CD}$. In particular, $\triangle ABC \sim \triangle CBD \sim \triangle ACD$.

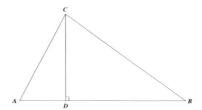

4. What does "CPCTC" mean?

   In my geometry class, this was our abbreviation for "corresponding parts of congruent triangles are congruent." It is most helpful in proofs.

5. Sample Problems

   (a) Complete the statement and then prove it: In parallelogram $ABCD$, $\triangle ABC \cong \triangle$_____.

   (b) Suppose that X is the common midpoint of $\overline{AB}$ and $\overline{CD}$. Then $\triangle AXC \cong \triangle$_____. Prove it.

   (c) The Isosceles Triangle Theorem says that if two sides of a triangle are congruent, then the angles opposite those sides are also congruent. Prove the Isosceles Triangle Theorem by drawing the angle bisector of the vertex angle.

   (d) Prove that the diagonals of a rhombus bisect their vertex angles.

   (e) True or false: Any two isosceles triangles must be similar. If true, prove it, and if false, give a counterexample.

   (f) Draw $\triangle ABC$. On $\overline{AB}$, draw point M so that $AM = 2MB$. On $\overline{AC}$, draw point N so that $AN = 2NC$. Prove that $\overline{MN} \parallel \overline{BC}$.

   (g) Draw an isosceles trapezoid and its two diagonals. The trapezoid is now divided into four triangular regions. Prove that two of these regions must be similar. Then prove that the other two regions must be congruent.

6. Answers to Sample Problems

   (a) Complete the statement and then prove it: In parallelogram $ABCD$, $\triangle ABC \cong \triangle \underline{CDA}$.

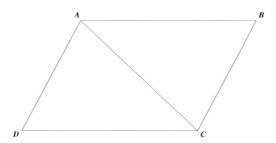

   Proof: Draw diagonal $\overline{AC}$. Since $\overline{AB} \parallel \overline{CD}$, $\angle BAC \cong \angle DCA$. Also, since $\overline{AD} \parallel \overline{BC}$, $\angle BCA \cong \angle DAC$. And of course $\overline{AC} \cong \overline{AC}$. Therefore, by ASA, $\triangle ABC \cong \triangle CDA$. □

   (b) Suppose that X is the common midpoint of $\overline{AB}$ and $\overline{CD}$. Then $\triangle AXC \cong \triangle \underline{BXD}$. Prove it.

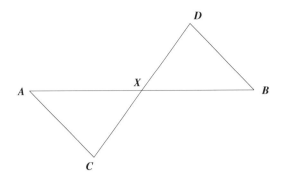

Proof: Draw $\overline{AC}$ and $\overline{BD}$. Since X is the midpoint of $\overline{AB}$, $\overline{AX} \cong \overline{XB}$. Similarly, $\overline{CX} \cong \overline{XD}$. Also, $\angle AXC \cong \angle BXD$ because they are vertical. Therefore, by SAS, $\triangle AXC \cong \triangle BXD$. □

Notice that even though we drew a picture, the proof did not rely on it. The proof only relied on properties that could be deduced from the given information. Someone else might draw a different picture, but the same proof would apply.

(c) The Isosceles Triangle Theorem says that if two sides of a triangle are congruent, then the angles opposite those sides are also congruent. Prove the Isosceles Triangle Theorem by drawing the angle bisector of the vertex angle.

Given: In $\triangle ABC$, $\overline{AB} \cong \overline{AC}$. Prove that $\angle B \cong \angle C$.

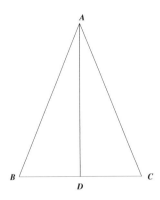

Proof: Draw $\overline{AD}$, the angle bisector of $\angle A$. This means that $\angle DAB \cong \angle DAC$. We are told that $\overline{AB} \cong \overline{AC}$, and clearly $\overline{AD} \cong \overline{AD}$. So, by SAS, $\triangle DAB \cong \triangle DAC$. Therefore, $\angle B \cong \angle C$ because CPCTC (corresponding parts of congruent triangles are congruent).

(d) Prove that the diagonals of a rhombus bisect their vertex angles.

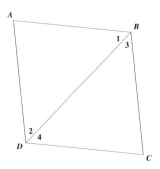

Proof: Since $ABCD$ is a rhombus, we know $\overline{AB} \cong \overline{BC} \cong \overline{CD} \cong \overline{DA}$ and clearly, $\overline{BD} \cong \overline{BD}$. Thus, by SSS, $\triangle ABD \cong \triangle CBD$. So, $\angle 1 \cong \angle 3$ and $\angle 2 \cong \angle 4$ by CPCTC. Therefore, $\overline{BD}$ bisects $\angle ABC$ and $\angle CDA$. An equivalent proof would show that the other diagonal bisects its vertex angles as well. $\square$

(e) True or false: Any two isosceles triangles must be similar. If true, prove it, and if false, give a counterexample. FALSE

Consider an isosceles triangle with a third side shorter than the other two. (See the picture used in the Isosceles Triangle proof, above.) This happens when the vertex angle is less than 60 degrees, because a vertex angle of 60 degrees would make our isosceles triangle into an equilateral triangle. Now consider the isosceles triangle with side lengths 1, 1, and $\sqrt{2}$. Then the third side is longer than the other two. (This happens to be a right triangle; its vertex angle is 90 degrees.) Since similar triangles must have congruent angles, there is no way that these two isosceles triangles can be similar.

(f) Draw $\triangle ABC$. On $\overline{AB}$, draw point M so that $AM = 2MB$. On $\overline{AC}$, draw point N so that $AN = 2NC$. Prove that $\overline{MN} \parallel \overline{BC}$.

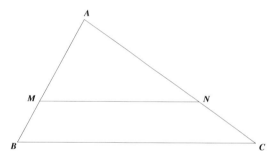

Proof: By the construction of M and N, it follows that $AM = \frac{2}{3}AB$ and $AN = \frac{2}{3}AC$. Clearly $\angle A \cong \angle A$. Thus, by sAs, $\triangle AMN \sim \triangle ABC$. Hence, $\angle AMN \cong \angle ABC$, because corresponding angles of similar triangles are congruent. Therefore, $\overline{MN} \parallel \overline{BC}$, by the converse of the Corresponding Angle Theorem. (See previous section on Parallelism for the Corresponding Angle Theorem.)

(g) Draw an isosceles trapezoid and its two diagonals. The trapezoid is now divided into four triangular regions. Prove that two of these regions must be similar. Then prove that the other two regions must be congruent.

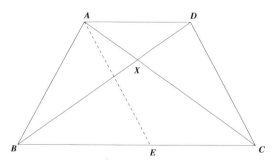

Proof: We are given isosceles trapezoid $ABCD$, in which $\overline{AD} \parallel \overline{BC}$ and $\overline{AB} \cong \overline{CD}$. By the Alternate Interior Angle Theorem, $\angle DAC \cong \angle BCA$. Also, $\angle AXD \cong \angle CXB$ because they are vertical. So, by AA, $\triangle AXD \sim \triangle CXB$. $\square$

Now, draw $\overline{AE}$ parallel to $\overline{CD}$. Thus, $AECD$ is a parallelogram, and hence, $\overline{AE} \cong \overline{CD}$. By the transitive property of congruence, $\overline{AE} \cong \overline{AB}$. This makes $\triangle AEB$ isosceles, and so by the Isosceles Triangle Theorem, $\angle ABE \cong \angle AEB$. Because they are corresponding angles, $\angle AEB \cong \angle DCB$. By transitivity, then, $\angle ABC \cong \angle DCB$. Since $\overline{BC} \cong \overline{BC}$, SAS implies that $\triangle ABC \cong \triangle DCB$. Thus, $\angle BAC \cong \angle CDB$ by CPCTC. Moreover, $\angle AXB \cong \angle DXC$ because they are vertical. Therefore, by AAS, $\triangle AXB \cong \triangle DXC$. □

d. Apply and justify properties of triangles (e.g., the Exterior Angle Theorem, concurrence theorems, trigonometric ratios, triangle inequality, Law of Sines, Law of Cosines, the Pythagorean Theorem and its converse)

1. What does the Exterior Angle Theorem say?

   The Exterior Angle Theorem says (in Euclidean geometry) that the measure of an exterior angle of a triangle is equal to the sum of the measures of the other two remote interior angles.

   Even if you did not have the Parallel Postulate, you could say that the measure of an exterior angle is greater than the measure of either remote interior angle, but you could not say that the sum of the two remote angles equals the exterior angle. That part is strictly Euclidean; it requires the Parallel Postulate.

2. What do the concurrence theorems say?

   There are several concurrence theorems for triangles. The medians of a triangle are concurrent at a point called the centroid, which also lies two thirds of the distance along each median from its vertex end. The angle bisectors of a triangle are concurrent at the incenter. The perpendicular bisectors of the sides are concurrent at the circumcenter. The three altitudes of a triangle are concurrent at the orthocenter. There are more, but these are the most common.

3. What are the standard trigonometric ratios?

   The six basic trigonometric ratios are sine, cosine, tangent, cotangent, secant, and cosecant (csc). Usually in Geometry, only sine, cosine, and tangent are used, while the others are written in terms of these three. [Incidentally, the word "cosine" is a contraction of "complement's sine." That is: $\cos(A) = \sin(90 - A)$. The other "co-" functions have a similar meaning.]

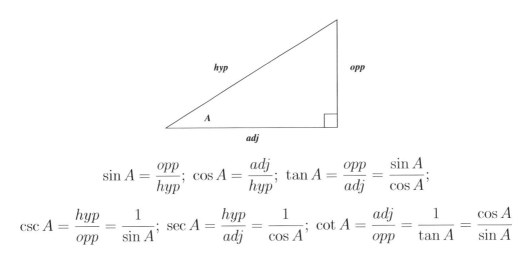

$$\sin A = \frac{opp}{hyp}; \ \cos A = \frac{adj}{hyp}; \ \tan A = \frac{opp}{adj} = \frac{\sin A}{\cos A};$$

$$\csc A = \frac{hyp}{opp} = \frac{1}{\sin A}; \ \sec A = \frac{hyp}{adj} = \frac{1}{\cos A}; \ \cot A = \frac{adj}{opp} = \frac{1}{\tan A} = \frac{\cos A}{\sin A}$$

4. What does the Triangle Inequality say?

The Triangle Inequality says that the sum of the lengths of *any* two sides of a triangle must be greater than the length of the third side.

5. What does the Law of Sines say? How do you justify it?

The Law of Sines says that in $\triangle ABC$, $\dfrac{\sin A}{a} = \dfrac{\sin B}{b} = \dfrac{\sin C}{c}$. To justify the Law of Sines, try calculating the area of the triangle three different ways (using its three different altitudes) and then set your areas equal to each other. (See area formulas, section **e** below.)

6. What does the Law of Cosines say? How do you justify it?

The Law of Cosines says that in $\triangle ABC$, $c^2 = a^2 + b^2 - 2ab(\cos C)$. To justify the Law of Cosines, we will use coordinate geometry. See section **3.2.a**.

7. What does the Pythagorean Theorem say?

If $\triangle ABC$ has a right angle at C, then $a^2 + b^2 = c^2$.

8. What does the converse of the Pythagorean Theorem say?

If $a^2 + b^2 = c^2$ in $\triangle ABC$, then $\triangle ABC$ has a right angle at C.

9. Sample Problems

   (a) Prove the Exterior Angle Theorem. Why is the Exterior Angle Theorem strictly a Euclidean theorem?

   (b) Show that a triangle's circumcenter is the center of its circumscribed circle.

   (c) Draw pictures showing that the circumcenter and orthocenter of a triangle could lie outside the triangle.

   (d) Write down all trigonometric ratios for a 30-60-90 triangle and a 45-45-90 triangle.

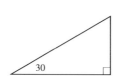

   (e) Write down all the trigonometric ratios for a right triangle with legs 8 and 15.

   (f) Can you define all the trigonometric ratios for 0 and 90 degree angles? If so, do it, and if not, why not?

   (g) Explain how the Triangle Inequality follows from the saying "the shortest distance between two points is a straight line."

   (h) Explain why you cannot have a triangle of side lengths 3, 4, and 8.

   (i) What happens if you apply the Law of Cosines to a triangle that has a right angle at C?

   (j) Find the remaining sides of $\triangle DEF$ if $d = 4$, $m\angle E = 40$, and $m\angle F = 60$. (This is called *solving* the triangle.)

(k) Prove the Pythagorean Theorem using similar triangles. [Hint: first, draw the altitude from the right angle. Then set up similarity ratios that lead to a^2 and b^2. Then add.]

10. Answers to Sample Problems

(a) Prove the Exterior Angle Theorem. Why is the Exterior Angle Theorem strictly a Euclidean theorem?

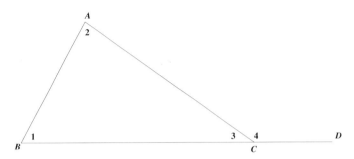

Given: $\triangle ABC$. Prove: $m\angle 4 = m\angle 1 + m\angle 2$.

Proof: Since $\angle 3$ and $\angle 4$ are supplementary, $m\angle 3 + m\angle 4 = 180$. So $m\angle 4 = 180 - m\angle 3$. In $\triangle ABC$, $m\angle 1 + m\angle 2 + m\angle 3 = 180$. Thus $m\angle 1 + m\angle 2 = 180 - m\angle 3$. By substitution, therefore, $m\angle 4 = m\angle 1 + m\angle 2$. □

The Exterior Angle Theorem is strictly Euclidean because it relies on the Euclidean fact that the angles of a triangle add up to 180 degrees.

(b) Show that a triangle's circumcenter is the center of its circumscribed circle.

We will first prove a lemma: If P is on the perpendicular bisector of $\overline{AB}$, then $\overline{PA} \cong \overline{PB}$.

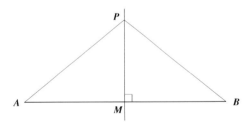

Proof: Draw the perpendicular bisector of $\overline{AB}$. By definition, it intersects $\overline{AB}$ at its midpoint, M, so that $\angle PMA$ and $\angle PMB$ are right angles. So $\angle PMA \cong \angle PMB$ and $\overline{AM} \cong \overline{BM}$. Clearly $\overline{PM} \cong \overline{PM}$. Thus, by SAS, $\triangle PMA \cong \triangle PMB$. Therefore $\overline{PA} \cong \overline{PB}$ by CPCTC. □

The perpendicular bisectors of the sides of $\triangle ABC$ are concurrent at the circumcenter. Hence, if P is the circumcenter, then $\overline{PA} \cong \overline{PB} \cong \overline{PC}$ by repeatedly invoking the lemma. Therefore, if we draw a circle with center P and radius PA, the circle will pass through all three vertices of the triangle, circumscribing it.

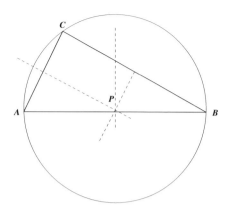

(c) Draw pictures showing that the circumcenter and orthocenter of a triangle could lie outside the triangle.

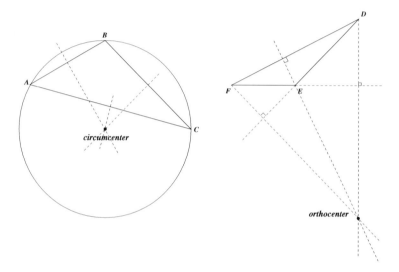

(d) Write down all trigonometric ratios for a 30-60-90 triangle and a 45-45-90 triangle.

Angle θ	$\sin\theta$	$\cos\theta$	$\tan\theta$	$\cot\theta$	$\sec\theta$	$\csc\theta$
30	$\frac{1}{2}$	$\frac{\sqrt{3}}{2}$	$\frac{1}{\sqrt{3}} = \frac{\sqrt{3}}{3}$	$\sqrt{3}$	$\frac{2}{\sqrt{3}} = \frac{2\sqrt{3}}{3}$	2
60	$\frac{\sqrt{3}}{2}$	$\frac{1}{2}$	$\sqrt{3}$	$\frac{1}{\sqrt{3}} = \frac{\sqrt{3}}{3}$	2	$\frac{2}{\sqrt{3}} = \frac{2\sqrt{3}}{3}$
45	$\frac{\sqrt{2}}{2}$	$\frac{\sqrt{2}}{2}$	1	1	$\sqrt{2}$	$\sqrt{2}$

(e) Write down all the trigonometric ratios for a right triangle with legs 8 and 15.

First, notice that the hypotenuse is $\sqrt{8^2 + 15^2} = \sqrt{289} = 17$.

Angle	$\sin\theta$	$\cos\theta$	$\tan\theta$	$\cot\theta$	$\sec\theta$	$\csc\theta$
opposite 8	$\frac{8}{17}$	$\frac{15}{17}$	$\frac{8}{15}$	$\frac{15}{8}$	$\frac{17}{15}$	$\frac{17}{8}$
opposite 15	$\frac{15}{17}$	$\frac{8}{17}$	$\frac{15}{8}$	$\frac{8}{15}$	$\frac{17}{8}$	$\frac{17}{15}$

(f) Can you define all the trigonometric ratios for 0 and 90 degree angles? If so, do it, and if not, why not?

Think of what happens as the angle A approaches 0 degrees. Then the opposite side shrinks to zero, and the adjacent side length approaches the length of the hypotenuse. So, $\sin(0) = 0$ and $\cos(0) = 1$. Thus, $\tan(0) = 0$ and $\sec(0) = 1$, but $\cot(0)$ and $\csc(0)$ are not defined because they have denominators equal to zero. Similarly, $\sin(90) = 1$ and $\cos(90) = 0$. So $\cot(90) = 0$ and $\csc(90) = 1$, while $\tan(90)$ and $\sec(90)$ are not defined.

(g) Explain how the Triangle Inequality follows from the saying "the shortest distance between two points is a straight line."

Consider two vertices of a triangle. There are two paths along the triangle leading from one vertex to the other. The first path is along the side joining the two vertices. The other path is along the other two sides, passing through the third vertex. According to the saying, the shortest path is the first one, the straight line joining the two vertices. Therefore, the sum of the other two side lengths must be greater than the length of the third side. This is exactly what the Triangle Inequality says.

(h) Explain why you cannot have a triangle of side lengths 3, 4, and 8.

Think of attaching the sides of length 3 and 4 to the opposite ends of the side of length 8. Then it's clear that the sides of length 3 and 4 cannot reach each other. Even pointing directly toward each other, they have a total length of 7, which is less than 8, the distance between their fixed endpoints.

(i) What happens if you apply the Law of Cosines to a triangle that has a right angle at C?

The Law of Cosines says that in $\triangle ABC$, $c^2 = a^2 + b^2 - 2ab(\cos C)$. So, if $\angle C$ is a right angle, then $\cos C = 0$. Therefore, $c^2 = a^2 + b^2$, which is really the Pythagorean Theorem. Therefore, the Law of Cosines is a generalization of the Pythagorean Theorem to any triangle.

(j) Find the remaining sides of $\triangle DEF$ if $d = 4$, $m\angle E = 40$, and $m\angle F = 60$. (This is called *solving* the triangle.)

Since the angle sum of a triangle is 180, $m\angle D = 80$. Using the Law of Sines and a calculator, we have

$$\frac{\sin 60}{f} = \frac{\sin 40}{e} = \frac{\sin 80}{4} \approx 0.2462.$$

Therefore, $e \approx 2.61$ and $f \approx 3.52$.

(k) Prove the Pythagorean Theorem using similar triangles. [Hint: first, draw the altitude from the right angle. Then set up similarity ratios that lead to a^2 and b^2. Then add.]

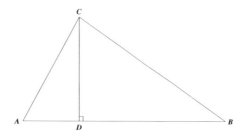

Let $a = BC$, $b = AC$, $c = AB$, $x = AD$, and $y = BD$. [Notice that $x + y = c$.] Recall that $\triangle ABC \sim \triangle CBD \sim \triangle ACD$. So, $\frac{c}{a} = \frac{a}{y}$ and $\frac{c}{b} = \frac{b}{x}$. After cross-multiplying, we get $a^2 = cy$ and $b^2 = cx$. Thus $a^2 + b^2 = cy + cx = c(y + x) = c^2$. $\square$

e. Apply and justify properties of polygons and circles from an advanced standpoint (e.g., derive the area formulas for regular polygons and circles from the area of a triangle)

1. What are some formulas for the area A of a triangle?

   There are many formulas, the most common of which is: $A = \frac{1}{2}bh$, where b is the length of the base and h the length of an altitude drawn to that base. There is a trigonometric formula for the area of $\triangle ABC$: $A = \frac{1}{2}ab \sin C$. There is also Heron's Formula, based only on the side lengths and the semiperimeter $s = \frac{1}{2}(a + b + c)$: $A = \sqrt{s(s - a)(s - b)(s - c)}$.

2. How do you use triangles to find the area of a regular polygon?

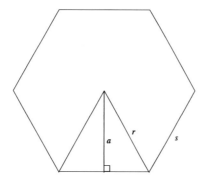

   In the diagram, we are looking at a hexagon, but you can imagine the polygon to have any number of sides. Also, r is called a *radius* and a an *apothem*. The side length s is just the perimeter of the polygon divided by n, the number of sides: $s = P/n$. Since the polygon is regular, drawing the radii will divide the polygon into n congruent triangles, each with base s and height a. So the total area of the polygon is: $A = n(\frac{1}{2}sa) = \frac{1}{2}aP$. Another way to see this formula is:

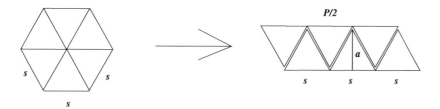

3. How do you use triangles to approximate the area of a circle?

   Think of a regular polygon having more and more sides. As the number of sides increases, the polygon looks more and more like a circle. So, if you think about what happens, you can determine that the apothem approaches the radius ($a \to r$) and the perimeter approaches the circumference ($P \to 2\pi r$) as the number of sections increases (as $n \to \infty$). Therefore,

   $$A = \frac{1}{2}aP \to \frac{1}{2}(r)(2\pi r) = \pi r^2.$$

4. Sample Problems

   (a) Find the area of a 3-4-5 triangle several different ways.

   (b) Find the area of an equilateral triangle of side length s. Compare it with the area of a square of side length s and the area of a regular hexagon of side length s.

   (c) Find the area of a regular octagon of side length s.

   (d) In a regular n-gon, a, r, P, and n are not independent quantities. Find the formula for the area in terms of n and a. [Hint: You will need trigonometry.]

5. Answers to Sample Problems

   (a) Find the area of a 3-4-5 triangle several different ways.

   Notice that there is a right angle between the sides of length 3 and 4. Thus, if 4 is the base, then 3 is the height. So the area is $\frac{1}{2}(4)(3) = 6$.

   Or, we can use the trigonometric formula, with any sides labeled a and b. If we use the typical labeling for a right triangle, then C is a right angle. So

   $$\frac{1}{2}ab\sin C = \frac{1}{2}(3)(4)(\sin 90) = 6.$$

   We could also use $a = 3$, $b = 5$, which means that C is opposite the side of length 4. Thus $\sin C = \frac{4}{5}$. So

   $$\frac{1}{2}ab\sin C = \frac{1}{2}(3)(5)\left(\frac{4}{5}\right) = 6.$$

   We can also use Heron's formula, where $s = \frac{1}{2}(3 + 4 + 5) = 6$.

   $$A = \sqrt{s(s-a)(s-b)(s-c)} = \sqrt{6(3)(2)(1)} = \sqrt{36} = 6.$$

   (b) Find the area of an equilateral triangle of side length s. Compare it with the area of a square of side length s and the area of a regular hexagon of side length s.

   Using the trigonometric formula for area, we get $\frac{1}{2}(s)(s)(\sin 60) = \frac{\sqrt{3}}{4}s^2$. The area of a square of side length s is s^2. A regular hexagon of side length s is composed of six equilateral triangles of side length s. So, the area of a regular hexagon of side length s is $6(\frac{\sqrt{3}}{4})s^2 = \frac{3\sqrt{3}}{2}s^2$.

   (c) Find the area of a regular octagon of side length s.

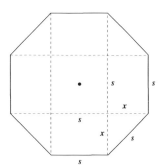

Notice that the regular octagon is made up of one square of side length s, four rectangles that are s by x, and four half-squares of side length x. Also, the Pythagorean Theorem implies that $2x^2 = s^2$, which means $x = \frac{s}{\sqrt{2}}$. So the total area is

$$s^2 + 4sx + 2x^2 = s^2 + \frac{4s^2}{\sqrt{2}} + 2\left(\frac{s^2}{2}\right) = (2 + 2\sqrt{2})s^2.$$

(d) In a regular n-gon, a, r, P, and n are not independent quantities. Find the formula for the area in terms of n and a. [Hint: You will need trigonometry.]

We know that $A = \frac{1}{2}aP = \frac{1}{2}a(ns)$, where s is the side length. Let θ be the angle formed at the center of the n-gon by a radius and an apothem. Then $\theta = \frac{360}{2n}$ and $\tan\theta = \frac{s}{2a}$. Hence, $s = 2a\tan\theta$. Therefore,

$$A = \frac{ans}{2} = \frac{an(2a\tan\theta)}{2} = a^2n\tan\left(\frac{360}{2n}\right).$$

f. Identify and justify the classical constructions (e.g., angle bisector, perpendicular bisector, replicating shapes, regular polygons with 3, 4, 5, 6, and 8 sides)

1. What makes a construction "classical?"

   The classical constructions are those that can be performed with a compass (for copying arcs of a given fixed length) and an unmarked straightedge (for drawing or extending lines if you are given two points). These were the geometry tools used by the ancient Greeks.

2. How do you copy an angle? Why does it work?

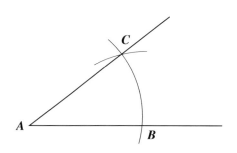
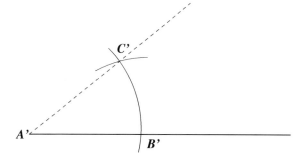

To copy the given $\angle A$ onto the given line at A', we first draw an arc through the sides of the angle. Label the points of intersection as B and C. Using the same compass setting, swing an arc centered at A'. Label its point of intersection with the line as B'. Now set the compass to the distance BC. Keeping the same compass setting, swing an arc centered at B' that intersects the first arc at a point C'. Then $\angle C'A'B' \cong \angle CAB$.

The reason that $\angle C'A'B' \cong \angle CAB$ is because $AB = AC = A'B' = A'C'$ and $BC = B'C'$. So by SSS, $\triangle C'A'B' \cong \triangle CAB$. Therefore, $\angle A \cong \angle A'$ by CPCTC.

3. How do you bisect an angle? Why does it work?

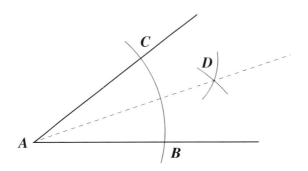

To bisect the given $\angle A$, we first draw an arc through the sides of the angle. Label the points of intersection as B and C. Using a new compass setting that is at least half the distance BC, swing two arcs, one centered at B and one centered at C, so that they intersect at a point D in the interior of angle A. Then $\overrightarrow{AD}$ bisects angle A.

The reason that $\overrightarrow{AD}$ bisects angle A is that $AB = AC$, $BD = CD$, and $AD = AD$. So, by SSS, $\triangle DAB \cong \triangle DAC$. Therefore, $\angle DAB \cong \angle DAC$ by CPCTC.

4. How do you perpendicularly bisect a line segment? Why does it work?

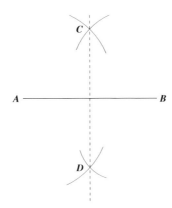

To perpendicularly bisect the given segment $\overline{AB}$, we first set the compass to a distance that is at least half of AB. Then swing arcs centered at A on both sides of $\overline{AB}$. Using the same compass setting, swing arcs centered at B on both sides of $\overline{AB}$ so that the new arcs intersect the old ones. Label the points of intersection C and D. Then $\overline{CD}$ perpendicularly bisects $\overline{AB}$.

The reason that $\overline{CD}$ perpendicularly bisects $\overline{AB}$ is that $AC = AD = BC = BD$, which makes $ADBC$ a rhombus. The diagonals of a rhombus perpendicularly bisect each other. (This can be proved using the methods of section **c** above.)

5. How do you divide a segment into n congruent pieces?

   We will show how to trisect a line segment, but the process can be repeated for any positive integer n. We will also use the construction for copying an angle.

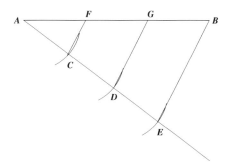

   To trisect the given segment $\overline{AB}$, we first draw a line segment from A in a different direction from B. Then we mark off three equal segments on this line: $AC = CD = DE$. Next, connect point E to point B. Then, copy $\angle AEB$ so that it has a vertex at D and then make another copy with its vertex at C. So $\angle ACF \cong \angle ADG \cong \angle AEB$. The points F and G trisect $\overline{AB}$.

   The reason this construction works is that $\triangle ACF \sim \triangle ADG \sim \triangle AEB$ by AA. Moreover, the triangles' side lengths are in the proportion $1 : 2 : 3$. Therefore, $AF = FG = GB$.

6. How do you construct a regular hexagon?

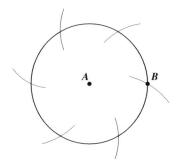

   To construct a regular hexagon, draw a circle centered at some point A. Select a point B on the circle. Using the same compass setting as you used to draw the circle, swing arcs around the circumference of circle A, starting at B. After six arcs, you should be back at B. The intersection points between the arcs and the circle are the vertices of a regular hexagon.

7. How do you double the number of sides in a given regular n-gon?

   If you are given a regular n-gon, you could construct the circumscribing circle. Then, perpendicularly bisect any side (say $\overline{AB}$) of the n-gon. Now find the intersection point C between the perpendicular bisector and the circumscribing circle. The length AC (or BC) is the side length for the $2n$-gon. Use this as a new compass setting and proceed around the rest of the circle to construct all the vertices of the regular $2n$-gon.

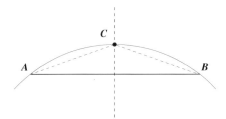

8. How do you construct a regular pentagon?

   This is a surprisingly tricky construction. To present it here would go beyond the scope of this text. Suffice it to say that you must first construct a 72 degree angle in order to construct the regular pentagon. One hint is that $\cos 72 = \frac{\sqrt{5}-1}{4}$, which is a constructible length.

9. What constructions are not classical? Why not?

   It is impossible to double the cube, square the circle, or trisect an arbitrary angle (though people tried for thousands of years). This means that a compass and straightedge cannot construct $\sqrt[3]{2}$ or $\sqrt{\pi}$, nor can they solve a general cubic equation. There is an algebraic proof of these facts that goes beyond many undergraduate mathematics curricula and certainly beyond this text, but suffice it to say that compasses and straightedges are good for finding distances, which means that rational numbers and square roots are OK, but it is not possible to construct irrational cube roots or $\sqrt{\pi}$.

   Also, there are an infinite number of regular polygons which cannot be constructed, again, for algebraic reasons beyond the scope of this text. A regular 7-gon is not constructible; neither are a 9-gon, 11-gon, 13-gon, nor a 19-gon. Gauss constructed a regular 17-gon in his teens, but he was pretty smart!

10. Sample Problems

    (a) Practice your basic constructions. Look in a textbook for more fancy constructions. How do the compass and straightedge provide evidence for geometric proofs?

    (b) Inscribe an equilateral triangle in a circle.

    (c) Inscribe a square in a circle.

    (d) Suppose one of your students claims that they have constructed a regular polygon with 14 sides. Explain how you know that they must be wrong.

11. Answers to Sample Problems

    (a) Practice your basic constructions. Look in a textbook for more fancy constructions. How do the compass and straightedge provide evidence for geometric proofs?

       The compass copies distances. This means that it can be used to show that line segments are congruent. The straightedge can be used to draw the line between two points or to extend lines. Mathematicians have shown that every construction that can be done with a compass and straightedge can actually be done with a compass alone!

(b) Inscribe an equilateral triangle in a circle.

Use the construction given above for a regular hexagon inscribed in a circle. Then connect every other vertex to form an equilateral triangle.

(c) Inscribe a square in a circle.

There are a number of ways to do this. A direct way is to draw a diameter of the circle, then perpendicularly bisect the diameter to find the perpendicular diameter. The four endpoints of these diameters are the vertices of a square. See the picture below.

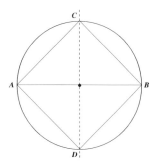

(d) Suppose one of your students claims that they have constructed a regular polygon with 14 sides. Explain how you know that they must be wrong.

If the student were correct, then by connecting every other vertex, the student would have constructed a regular 7-gon (heptagon), which is impossible to construct with a compass and straightedge. Therefore, the student must not be correct.

3.2 Coordinate Geometry

a. Use techniques in coordinate geometry to prove geometric theorems

1. What is coordinate geometry? How does it work?

   Coordinate geometry is the application of algebra to geometry. Often, we will place geometric objects on a Cartesian coordinate system and then use algebraic reasoning to discover, justify, show, or even prove a certain relationship.

   Example: Show that the diagonals of a rectangle are congruent. To prove this, we first need to place an arbitrary rectangle on a coordinate system. Since rotating and translating the rectangle will not affect the length of its diagonals, we can place the rectangle so that its vertices are at $(0,0)$, $(a,0)$, (a,b), and $(0,b)$. The specific values of a and b are unknown, and thus our proof methods will be sufficiently general.

   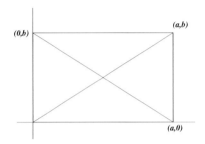

   Using the distance formula, the length of the diagonal from $(0,0)$ to (a,b) is found to equal $\sqrt{(a-0)^2 + (b-0)^2} = \sqrt{a^2 + b^2}$. The other diagonal has length $\sqrt{(a-0)^2 + (0-b)^2} = \sqrt{a^2 + b^2}$. Therefore, the diagonals of a rectangle are congruent.

   Advice: if your proof requires midpoints, then start with points like $(2a, 2b)$ instead of (a,b). You are still being completely arbitrary, but the math is easier.

2. Sample Problems

   (a) Write down and memorize the Distance Formula, the Midpoint Formula, the Slope Formula, the Slope-Intercept equation of a line, and the Point-Slope equation of a line.

   (b) Let $A = (2,3), B = (-2,5), C = (5,8)$, and $D = (1,10)$. Show that $ABDC$ is a parallelogram. Where is point E if $ABCE$ is a parallelogram?

   (c) Justify the Law of Cosines using the following picture.

   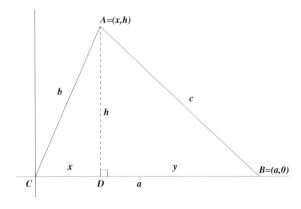

(d) Prove that the diagonals of a square are perpendicular to each other, bisect each other, and are the same length. How does the length of a diagonal compare with the length of a side of the square?

(e) Prove that the diagonals of a rectangle bisect each other. Is this true for any parallelogram? If so, prove it, and if not, give a counterexample.

(f) Show that if you join the four midpoints of the sides of a quadrilateral, then you form a parallelogram.

(g) Prove that the three medians of a triangle are concurrent.

3. Answers to Sample Problems

(a) Write down and memorize the Distance Formula, the Midpoint Formula, the Slope Formula, the Slope-Intercept equation of a line, and the Point-Slope equation of a line.

The distance between (x_1, y_1) and (x_2, y_2) is $\sqrt{(x_2 - x_1)^2 + (y_2 - y_1)^2}$.

The midpoint of the line segment between (x_1, y_1) and (x_2, y_2) is $\left(\dfrac{x_1 + x_2}{2}, \dfrac{y_1 + y_2}{2} \right)$.

The slope of the line passing through (x_1, y_1) and (x_2, y_2) is $\dfrac{y_2 - y_1}{x_2 - x_1}$.

If a line has slope m and y-intercept b, then its equation is $y = mx + b$.

If a line has slope m and passes through (h, k), then its equation is $y - k = m(x - h)$.

(b) Let $A = (2, 3), B = (-2, 5), C = (5, 8)$, and $D = (1, 10)$. Show that $ABDC$ is a parallelogram. Where is point E if $ABCE$ is a parallelogram?

(To see what's going on here, plot these points on a set of coordinate axes.) The slope of $\overline{AB}$ is $\frac{5-3}{-2-2} = -\frac{1}{2}$. The slope of $\overline{DC}$ is $\frac{10-8}{1-5} = -\frac{1}{2}$. So $\overline{AB} \parallel \overline{DC}$. The slope of $\overline{BD}$ is $\frac{10-5}{1-(-2)} = \frac{5}{3}$. The slope of $\overline{AC}$ is $\frac{8-3}{5-2} = \frac{5}{3}$. So $\overline{BD} \parallel \overline{AC}$. Therefore, $ABDC$ is a parallelogram.

Point E must be located at $(9, 6)$ so that $ABCE$ is a parallelogram.

(c) Justify the Law of Cosines using the following picture.

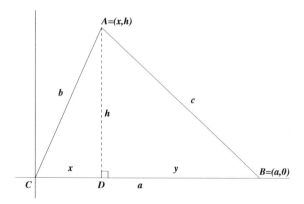

Notice that in right triangle ADC, $\cos C = \frac{x}{b}$. Thus $x = b \cos C$. Using the Distance Formula, we get $c = \sqrt{(x - a)^2 + (h - 0)^2}$. So,

$$\begin{aligned} c^2 &= (x - a)^2 + (h - 0)^2 = x^2 - 2ax + a^2 + h^2 \\ &= a^2 + (x^2 + h^2) - 2ax = a^2 + b^2 - 2ax, \end{aligned}$$

if we use the Pythagorean Theorem. Therefore, by substitution, $c^2 = a^2 + b^2 - 2ab \cos C$. $\square$

(d) Prove that the diagonals of a square are perpendicular to each other, bisect each other, and are the same length. How does the length of a diagonal compare with the length of a side of the square?

On a coordinate grid, we can put the vertices of the square at $(0,0), (2s,0), (2s,2s)$, and $(0,2s)$, where $2s$ is the side length of the square. The diagonal through $(0,0)$ and $(2s,2s)$ has slope $\frac{2s-0}{2s-0} = 1$. The other diagonal has slope $\frac{0-2s}{2s-0} = -1$. Since the slopes are negative reciprocals of each other, the diagonals are perpendicular. Using the distance formula, the diagonals must be congruent. (This was already proven above for any rectangle.) To see that the diagonals bisect each other, we need to show that their midpoints are the same point. The midpoint of the diagonal through the origin is $(\frac{0+2s}{2}, \frac{0+2s}{2}) = (s,s)$, and the midpoint for the other diagonal is $(\frac{0+2s}{2}, \frac{2s+0}{2}) = (s,s)$ also. Therefore, the diagonals of a square bisect each other.

(e) Prove that the diagonals of a rectangle bisect each other. Is this true for any parallelogram? If so, prove it, and if not, give a counterexample.

We will show that it is true for any parallelogram, which means that it would certainly be true for any rectangle. Place the vertices of the parallelogram at $(0,0), (2a,0), (2b,2c)$, and $(2a+2b, 2c)$.

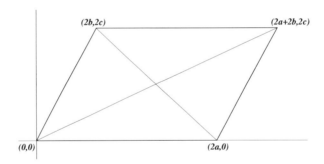

The midpoint of the diagonal that passes through the origin is $(\frac{0+2a+2b}{2}, \frac{0+2c}{2}) = (a+b, c)$. The midpoint of the other diagonal is $(\frac{2b+2a}{2}, \frac{2c+0}{2}) = (b+a, c)$. Since their midpoints coincide, the diagonals of a parallelogram bisect each other.

(f) Show that if you join the four midpoints of the sides of a quadrilateral, then you form a parallelogram.

In the following picture, we have drawn an arbitrary quadrilateral and labeled its vertices and the midpoints of its sides. We have also connected the midpoints.

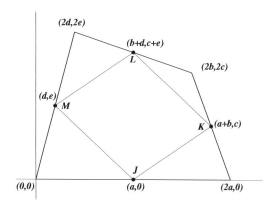

The slope of $\overline{JK}$ is $\dfrac{c-0}{a+b-a} = \dfrac{c}{b}$. The slope of $\overline{LM}$ is $\dfrac{c+e-e}{b+d-d} = \dfrac{c}{b}$.

The slope of $\overline{KL}$ is $\dfrac{c+e-c}{b+d-(a+b)} = \dfrac{e}{d-a}$. The slope of $\overline{MJ}$ is $\dfrac{e-0}{d-a} = \dfrac{e}{d-a}$.

Therefore $JKLM$ is a parallelogram.

(g) Prove that the three medians of a triangle are concurrent.

In the following picture, we have drawn an arbitrary triangle and labeled its vertices and the midpoints of its sides. We have also drawn in the medians. To prove that the medians are concurrent, we will find equations for all three lines, showing that they intersect. To make the calculations cleaner, we label the vertices with multiples of 6.

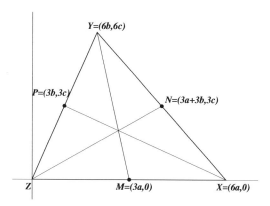

The slope of $\overline{ZN}$ is $\dfrac{3c}{3a+3b} = \dfrac{c}{a+b}$. So the equation of $\overline{ZN}$ is $y = \left(\dfrac{c}{a+b}\right)x$.

The slope of $\overline{YM}$ is $\dfrac{6c}{6b-3a} = \dfrac{2c}{2b-a}$. So the equation of $\overline{YM}$ in Point-Slope form is $y = \left(\dfrac{2c}{2b-a}\right)(x-3a)$.

These two lines intersect at a point. To find it, substitute $y = \left(\dfrac{c}{a+b}\right)x$ into the second equation, giving $\left(\dfrac{c}{a+b}\right)x = \left(\dfrac{2c}{2b-a}\right)(x-3a)$. Cross-multiplying gives:

$$\begin{aligned}
cx(2b-a) &= 2c(x-3a)(a+b) = (2cx-6ac)(a+b) \\
2bcx - acx &= 2acx - 6a^2c + 2bcx - 6abc \\
-3acx &= -6a^2c - 6abc \\
x &= 2a + 2b.
\end{aligned}$$

Plugging this into the equation for $\overline{ZN}$ gives $y = 2c$. So the first two medians intersect at the point $(2a + 2b, 2c)$. If this point lies on the third median, then we will have proven that the medians are concurrent.

The slope of $\overline{XP}$ is $\frac{3c-0}{3b-6a} = \frac{c}{b-2a}$. So the Point-Slope form of $\overline{XP}$ is $y = (\frac{c}{b-2a})(x - 6a)$. If we plug in $x = 2a + 2b$, then we get

$$y = \left(\frac{c}{b-2a}\right)(2a + 2b - 6a) = \left(\frac{c}{b-2a}\right)(2b - 4a) = 2c.$$

So the point $(2a + 2b, 2c)$ is also on $\overline{XP}$. Therefore, the three medians of a triangle are concurrent. $\square$

b. Model and solve mathematical and real-world problems by applying geometric concepts to two-dimensional figures

1. Sample Problems

   (a) A circle is inscribed in a square so that the diameter of the circle is equal to the side length of the square. Find:

      i. the ratio of the circumference of the circle to the perimeter of the square.

      ii. the ratio of the area of the circle to the area of the square.

   (b) Building off the previous problem, now place four circles inside the square according to the following diagram.

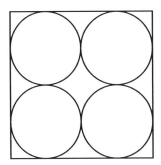

      i. Find the ratio of the total circumferences of all the circles to the perimeter of the square.

      ii. Find the ratio of the total area of the circles to the area of the square.

      iii. Compare these answers to the previous problem.

   (c) Suppose that you want to find the height of a tall building on a sunny day. You notice that a 1-meter stick casts a shadow of 14cm. Then you notice that the building casts a shadow of 2 meters. How tall is the building? (Hint: You can use similar triangles.)

   (d) Johnny's garden is an isosceles trapezoid with legs 10 feet and bases 20 feet and 8 feet. He would like to cover the garden with different plants, each of which requires 4 square feet of its own space to grow in. How many plants should Johnny get for his garden?

2. Answers to Sample Problems

(a) A circle is inscribed in a square so that the diameter of the circle is equal to the side length of the square. Find:

    i. the ratio of the circumference of the circle to the perimeter of the square. ANS: $\frac{\pi}{4}$. If s is the side length of the square, then the circumference is πs and the perimeter is $4s$.

    ii. the ratio of the area of the circle to the area of the square. ANS: $\frac{\pi}{4}$. The area of the circle would be $\frac{\pi}{4}s^2$, while the area of the square would be s^2.

(b) Building off the previous problem, now place four circles inside the square according to the following diagram.

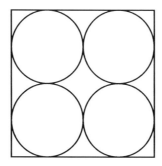

    i. Find the ratio of the total circumferences of all the circles to the perimeter of the square. ANS: $\frac{\pi}{2}$. Again, we let s be the side length of the square, which makes the radius of each little circle $\frac{s}{4}$. So the circumference of each is $2\pi(\frac{s}{4})$, which makes the total circumference of all four to be $2\pi s$. The perimeter of the square is still $4s$.

    ii. Find the ratio of the total area of the circles to the area of the square. ANS: $\frac{\pi}{4}$. The total area of the four little circles is still $\frac{\pi}{4}s^2$.

    iii. Compare these answers to the previous problem. We notice that while the circumference of the four little circles is twice the circumference of the one big circle, the area of the four little circles is equal to the area of the one big circle. So four little circles cover as much of the square as the one big circle did.

(c) Suppose that you want to find the height of a tall building on a sunny day. You notice that a 1-meter stick casts a shadow of 14cm. Then you notice that the building casts a shadow of 2 meters. How tall is the building? (Hint: You can use similar triangles.) Consider the figure below.

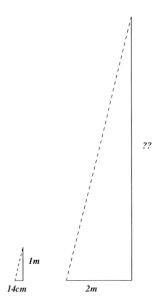

Setting up a proportion (and making sure to use the same units), we have $\dfrac{100}{14} = \dfrac{x}{200}$, or $x \approx 1429$ cm $= 14.29$ m.

(d) Johnny's garden is an isosceles trapezoid with legs 10 feet and bases 20 feet and 8 feet. He would like to cover the garden with different plants, each of which requires 4 square feet of its own space to grow in. How many plants should Johnny get for his garden? 28 plants.

The area of Johnny's garden can be found using the diagram below.

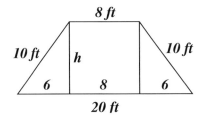

In particular, we can find the height h, since the trapezoid has two right triangles, one on each side. First, we can deduce that one leg of each right triangle is 6 feet. Thus, using the Pythagorean Theorem, we can deduce that the height h is 8 feet (6-8-10 triangle). Therefore the area is $\left(\dfrac{20+8}{2}\right)(8) = 112$ square feet. Since each plant requires 4 square feet, Johnny could plant $\dfrac{112}{4} = 28$ plants.

c. Translate between the geometric description and the equation for a conic section

1. What is a conic section?

   There are three types of conic sections: parabolas, ellipses, and hyperbolas. (A circle is a conic section, but a circle is a special case of an ellipse.) The term "conic section" refers to the fact that each of these shapes can be seen as the intersection between a cone and a plane.

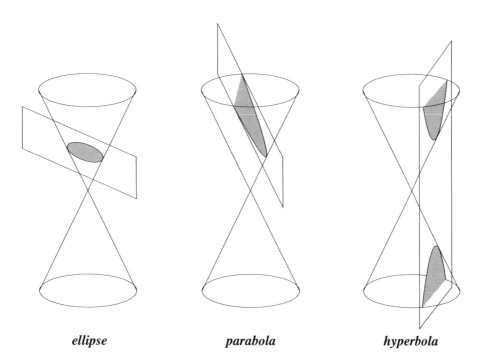

ellipse   *parabola*   *hyperbola*

2. What are the geometric descriptions of the conic sections?

    These definitions involve some special points called *foci* (singular: *focus*) and sometimes a special line called a *directrix*.

    The definition of an ellipse starts with two foci. A point P lies on an ellipse if the sum of the distances from P to the foci is a constant. If the foci are F_1 and F_2, then $PF_1 + PF_2$ has to be a constant.

    The definition of a hyperbola also starts with two foci. A point P lies on a hyperbola if the difference of the distances from P to the foci is a constant. If the foci are F_1 and F_2, then $|PF_1 - PF_2|$ has to be a constant.

    The definition of a parabola requires a focus and a directrix, with the focus not lying on the directrix. A point P lies on a parabola if the distance from P to the focus is equal to the shortest distance from P to the directrix.

3. What about a circle?

    A circle is a special case of an ellipse in that the two foci are coincident. So if $F = F_1 = F_2$, then $PF + PF$ (that is, $2PF$) is a constant. So PF is also a constant. In other words, a circle is the set of all points in the plane that are a given distance (called the radius – what we were calling PF) from a given point (called the center – what we were calling F).

4. How can we use the Pythagorean Theorem to define a Distance Formula?

    The Distance Formula is an important formula in coordinate geometry, but it is really just the Pythagorean Theorem! We will derive it generally now, but use a specific example below.

    Suppose we wish to find the distance between (s, t) and (h, k). We first draw a right triangle with hypotenuse going from (s, t) to (h, k). For the picture, $s > h$ and $t > k$, but for the formula, it doesn't really matter.

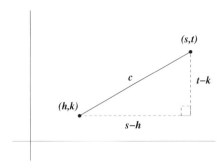

So, using the Pythagorean Theorem, the hypotenuse c satisfies: $c^2 = a^2 + b^2$.

$$c^2 = (s - h)^2 + (t - k)^2 \implies c = \sqrt{(s - h)^2 + (t - k)^2}.$$

This is the Distance Formula. You can see that it doesn't matter if $s > h$ or $t > k$; their corresponding differences are squared.

5. How can we use the Distance Formula to derive the equations of the conic sections?

   (a) The Circle.

      i. How can we use the definition to derive the equation of the circle?
         As an example, suppose that the center of the circle is at $(-1, 2)$ and the radius is 5. What is the equation of the circle? We need an equation that is satisfied by those points that are 5 units away from $(-1, 2)$ and only by those points. So, (x, y) is on the circle if and only if the distance between (x, y) and $(-1, 2)$ is 5. Using the Distance Formula:

         $$\sqrt{(x - (-1))^2 + (y - 2)^2} = 5 \implies (x + 1)^2 + (y - 2)^2 = 25.$$

         You can certainly square out the binomials if you wish, but as we will see, this format is much better for circles.

      ii. How can you read off the center and radius from the equation of a circle?
         If the equation of a circle is in its standard form: $(x - h)^2 + (y - k)^2 = r^2$, then this means the circle has radius r and is centered at the point (h, k). For example, if you are asked to describe the points that satisfy $x^2 + (y + 5)^2 = 4$, you could say with certainty that this equation describes a circle of radius 2, centered at the point $(0, -5)$.

     iii. Why do we have to complete the square?
         Given that the standard form of the equation of the circle is so helpful, we often want to put other equations into the standard form. This may require completing the square. For example, suppose you know that $x^2 + y^2 - 6x + 2y = 0$ describes a circle. What is the center of that circle? What is its radius? We have to complete the square to find out.

$$x^2 + y^2 - 6x + 2y = 0$$
$$x^2 - 6x + y^2 + 2y = 0$$
$$x^2 - 6x + \underline{9} + y^2 + 2y + \underline{1} = 0 + \underline{9} + \underline{1}$$
$$(x - 3)^2 + (y + 1)^2 = 10$$

(We underlined the numbers that had to be added to both sides of the equation to complete the square.) So, the circle has a radius of $\sqrt{10}$ and is centered at $(3, -1)$.

(b) The Parabola.

    i. What is the definition of a parabola?
A parabola is the set of all points that are the same distance from a given point (called the focus) as they are from a given line (called the directrix). The distance from a point on the parabola to the directrix is measured perpendicularly to the directrix. For simplicity, we will restrict ourselves only to horizontal or vertical directrices.

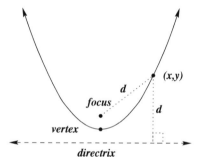

    ii. What is the Vertex Form of the equation of a parabola?
For up or down parabolas with a vertex at (h, k), the equation is of the form:

$$y - k = a(x - h)^2,$$

where the parabola opens upward if $a > 0$, downward if $a < 0$.
For right or left parabolas with a vertex at (h, k), the equation is of the form:

$$x - h = a(y - k)^2,$$

where the parabola opens to the right if $a > 0$, to the left if $a < 0$.

    iii. How can you find the distance from a point to a line?
We determined the Distance Formula above for the distance between two points. Now we need to determine a formula for the distance from a point to a horizontal or vertical line. These formulas can be seen in the following picture.

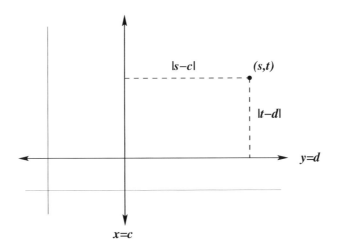

So the distance from (s,t) to the horizontal line $y = d$ is $|t - d|$. Similarly, the distance from (s,t) to the vertical line $x = c$ is $|s - c|$. We need the absolute value in case $s < c$ or $t < d$ (though these cases are not pictured).

iv. How can you derive the equation of a parabola from its definition?

We will show a specific example here, but the general formulas are not much harder to obtain. Suppose we have a parabola with a focus at $(1,4)$ and a directrix of $x = -3$. The parabola is the set of points (x, y) that are as far away from $(1,4)$ as they are from the line $x = -3$. So

$$\text{distance to focus} = \text{distance to directrix}$$
$$\sqrt{(x-1)^2 + (y-4)^2} = |x+3|.$$

Squaring both sides gives:

$$
\begin{aligned}
(x-1)^2 + (y-4)^2 &= (x+3)^2 \\
x^2 - 2x + 1 + (y-4)^2 &= x^2 + 6x + 9 \\
(y-4)^2 &= 8x + 8 \\
(y-4)^2 &= 8(x+1) \\
\frac{1}{8}(y-4)^2 &= x+1
\end{aligned}
$$

This is in Vertex Form, with the vertex at $(-1, 4)$ (halfway between the focus and directrix). Notice that this parabola opens to the right.

(c) The Ellipse.

i. What is the definition of an ellipse?

Recall that a point lies on an ellipse if the sum of the distances from the point to the two foci is constant. You can draw an ellipse by attaching a fixed length of string to two foci and then using a pencil to stretch the string taut. The figure you can draw is an ellipse.

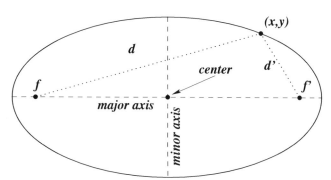

The foci are f and f'. The sum d + d' is constant.

ii. What is the standard form for the equation of an ellipse?

If an ellipse is centered at (h, k) and has an x-radius of a and a y-radius of b, then its equation is:

$$\frac{(x-h)^2}{a^2} + \frac{(y-k)^2}{b^2} = 1.$$

If $a > b$, as it is in the picture above, then the horizontal distance across the ellipse is called the major axis and the vertical distance is called the minor axis, and vice versa if $b > a$ (not pictured). (If $a = b$, then the ellipse is a circle!) In the picture above, the x-radius is half the length of the major axis and the y-radius is half the length of the minor axis.

iii. How do you derive the equation of an ellipse from its definition?

Again, we will show a specific example. A good Geometry or Algebra II textbook will have a general derivation. Suppose that the ellipse has foci at $(-4, 0)$ and $(0, 0)$ and that the sum of the distances to the two foci is $2\sqrt{13}$. So, distance from (x, y) to focus 1 plus distance from (x, y) to focus 2 equals $2\sqrt{13}$.

$$\sqrt{(x+4)^2 + y^2} + \sqrt{x^2 + y^2} = 2\sqrt{13}$$
$$\sqrt{(x+4)^2 + y^2} = 2\sqrt{13} - \sqrt{x^2 + y^2}.$$

Squaring both sides gives:

$$(x+4)^2 + y^2 = 52 - 4\sqrt{13(x^2 + y^2)} + x^2 + y^2$$
$$8x - 36 = -4\sqrt{13(x^2 + y^2)}$$
$$2x - 9 = -\sqrt{13x^2 + 13y^2}.$$

Again, squaring both sides, we get:

$$4x^2 - 36x + 81 = 13x^2 + 13y^2$$
$$81 = 9x^2 + 36x + 13y^2.$$

Completing the square, we add 36 to each side:

$$81 + 36 = 9(x^2 + 4x + 4) + 13y^2$$
$$117 = 9(x+2)^2 + 13y^2$$
$$1 = \frac{(x+2)^2}{13} + \frac{y^2}{9}.$$

This is the standard form for the equation of an ellipse. From it, you can see that its center is at $(-2, 0)$ (halfway between the foci) and that its x-radius is $\sqrt{13}$ and its y-radius is $\sqrt{9} = 3$.

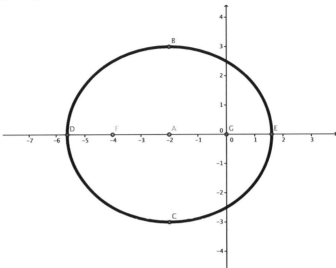

(d) The Hyperbola.

    i. What is the definition of a hyperbola?

    Given two points called foci, a point lies on a hyperbola if the difference of the distances from the point to the two foci is constant.

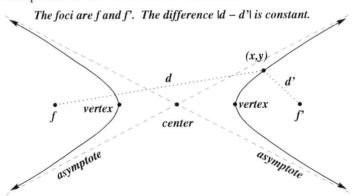

    ii. What are some features of a hyperbola?

    A hyperbola has two symmetric branches, and two asymptotes. Each end of each branch approaches one of the asymptotes, getting closer as you move farther from the center. We will assume our hyperbolas are in "standard form," meaning the branches either open up and down, or right and left. In either case, the asymptotes have slopes that are opposites of one another.

    iii. What is the standard form for the equation of a hyperbola?

    For an up-down hyperbola with a center at (h, k), and an x-radius of a, and a y-radius of b, the equation is

$$\frac{(y-k)^2}{b^2} - \frac{(x-h)^2}{a^2} = 1,$$

in which case the asymptotes have slopes $\pm\frac{b}{a}$ and intersect at the center. The vertices of this hyperbola are at $(h, k+b)$ and $(h, k-b)$. The term x-radius might be misleading here, since the hyperbola doesn't pass to the right or left of the center, but the value is helpful in determining that the slopes of the asymptotes are $\pm\frac{b}{a}$. For a left-right hyperbola with a center at (h, k), and an x-radius of a, and a y-radius of b, the equation is

$$\frac{(x-h)^2}{a^2} - \frac{(y-k)^2}{b^2} = 1,$$

in which case the asymptotes have slopes $\pm\frac{b}{a}$ and intersect at the center. The vertices of this hyperbola are at $(h+a, k)$ and $(h-a, k)$. The term y-radius might be misleading here, since the hyperbola does not pass above or below the center, but the value is helpful in determining that the slopes of the asymptotes are $\pm\frac{b}{a}$.

iv. How do you derive the equation of a hyperbola from its definition?

As with the ellipse, the derivation of the hyperbola equation is straightforward, but requires a lot of algebra. Again, we will show a specific example and refer the reader to a good Geometry or Algebra II textbook for a general derivation. Suppose that the hyperbola has foci at $(0, 5)$ and $(0, -1)$ and that the difference of the distances from any point on the hyperbola to the two foci is 4. So, distance from (x, y) to focus 1 minus the distance to focus 2 equals 4.

$$\begin{aligned}
\sqrt{x^2 + (y-5)^2} - \sqrt{x^2 + (y+1)^2} &= 4 \\
\sqrt{x^2 + (y-5)^2} &= 4 + \sqrt{x^2 + (y+1)^2}
\end{aligned}$$

Squaring both sides:

$$\begin{aligned}
x^2 + y^2 - 10y + 25 &= 16 + 8\sqrt{x^2 + (y+1)^2} + x^2 + y^2 + 2y + 1 \\
-8\sqrt{x^2 + (y+1)^2} &= 12y - 8 \\
-2\sqrt{x^2 + (y+1)^2} &= 3y - 2
\end{aligned}$$

Squaring again:

$$\begin{aligned}
4(x^2 + y^2 + 2y + 1) &= 9y^2 - 12y + 4 \\
4x^2 - 5y^2 + 20y &= 0
\end{aligned}$$

So now we complete the square (being very careful with signs):

$$\begin{aligned}
4x^2 - 5(y^2 - 4y + 4) &= 0 - 20 \\
4x^2 - 5(y-2)^2 &= -20 \\
\frac{4x^2}{-20} - \frac{5(y-2)^2}{-20} &= 1 \\
\frac{(y-2)^2}{4} - \frac{x^2}{5} &= 1.
\end{aligned}$$

This tells us the center of the hyperbola is at $(0, 2)$ (halfway between the foci), the vertices are at $(0, 4)$ and $(0, 0)$, and the asymptotes have slopes $\pm\frac{2}{\sqrt{5}}$ and pass through $(0, 2)$. See the picture below.

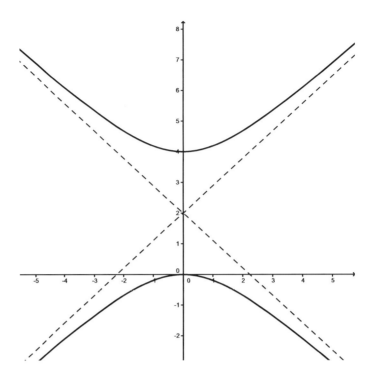

6. Sample Problems

    (a) Find equations for the following conic sections.

        i. the set of all points that are three units from the point $(-1, 4)$

        ii. the ellipse with foci at $(-1, 0)$ and $(1, 0)$ and passing through the point $(0, \sqrt{3})$

        iii. the hyperbola with foci at $(-3, 0)$ and $(3, 0)$ and passing through the point $(1, 0)$

        iv. the parabola with focus at $(-1, 0)$ and vertex at $(3, 0)$

    (b) Each if the following equations, if graphed, would correspond to a conic section. Identify which conic section corresponds to each.

        i. $x^2 + 5y^2 = 36$

        ii. $x^2 - 5y^2 = 36$

        iii. $x^2 - 5y = 36$

        iv. $x^2 + y^2 = 36$

7. Answers to Sample Problems

    (a) Find equations for the following conic sections.

        i. the set of all points that are three units from the point $(-1, 4)$

        This describes a circle. If (x, y) is on the circle, then the distance from (x, y) to $(-1, 4)$ is 3. So,

$$\sqrt{(x+1)^2 + (y-4)^2} = 3; \text{ or } (x+1)^2 + (y-4)^2 = 9.$$

        ii. the ellipse with foci at $(-1, 0)$ and $(1, 0)$ and passing through the point $(0, \sqrt{3})$

Since we know a point on the ellipse and the foci, we can figure out the constant associated with this ellipse, that is, the distance that is equal to the sum of the distances from the point to each focus. We'll find that first.

$$\sqrt{(0+1)^2 + (\sqrt{3}-0)^2} + \sqrt{(0-1)^2 + (\sqrt{3}-0)^2} = \sqrt{1+3} + \sqrt{1+3} = 4.$$

Now that we know this distance, we can set up the equation. If a point (x,y) is on this ellipse, then the distance from (x,y) to $(-1,0)$ plus the distance from (x,y) to $(1,0)$ must equal 4. Using the Distance Formula, we can write

$$\sqrt{(x+1)^2 + (y-0)^2} + \sqrt{(x-1)^2 + (y-0)^2} = 4.$$

We isolate one radical and square both sides of the equation, then simplify.

$$
\begin{aligned}
\sqrt{(x+1)^2 + y^2} &= 4 - \sqrt{(x-1)^2 + y^2} \\
(x+1)^2 + y^2 &= 16 - 8\sqrt{(x-1)^2 + y^2} + (x-1)^2 + y^2 \\
x^2 + 2x + 1 + y^2 &= 16 - 8\sqrt{(x-1)^2 + y^2} + x^2 - 2x + 1 + y^2 \\
4x - 16 &= 8\sqrt{(x-1)^2 + y^2} \\
x - 4 &= 2\sqrt{(x-1)^2 + y^2} \\
x^2 - 8x + 16 &= 4(x^2 - 2x + 1 + y^2) = 4x^2 - 8x + 4 + 4y^2 \\
12 &= 3x^2 + 4y^2
\end{aligned}
$$

In standard form, this is written: $\dfrac{x^2}{4} + \dfrac{y^2}{3} = 1.$

iii. the hyperbola with foci at $(-3,0)$ and $(3,0)$ and passing through the point $(1,0)$

As above, we can determine the constant difference between the distances from a point on the hyperbola to each focus. Since the distance from $(1,0)$ to $(-3,0)$ is 4 and the distance from $(1,0)$ to $(3,0)$ is 2, then the difference between these distances is 2. So, for a general point (x,y), we have

$$\left| \sqrt{(x+3)^2 + y^2} - \sqrt{(x-3)^2 + y^2} \right| = 2$$

To show how the absolute value affects the final answer, we'll use ± 2 for the right hand side and then we'll follow it through the calculations. We'll start by isolating a radical, like we did for the ellipse.

$$
\begin{aligned}
\sqrt{(x+3)^2 + y^2} &= \pm 2 + \sqrt{(x-3)^2 + y^2} \\
(x+3)^2 + y^2 &= 4 \pm 4\sqrt{(x-3)^2 + y^2} + (x-3)^2 + y^2 \\
x^2 + 6x + 9 + y^2 &= 4 \pm 4\sqrt{(x-3)^2 + y^2} + x^2 - 6x + 9 + y^2 \\
12x - 4 &= \pm 4\sqrt{(x-3)^2 + y^2} \\
3x - 1 &= \pm\sqrt{(x-3)^2 + y^2} \\
9x^2 - 6x + 1 &= x^2 - 6x + 9 + y^2 \\
8x^2 - y^2 &= 8
\end{aligned}
$$

In standard form, this is written: $x^2 - \dfrac{y^2}{8} = 1$. Notice that the $\pm$ sign did not affect the final equation.

iv. the parabola with focus at $(-1,0)$ and vertex at $(3,0)$

Since the focus and vertex lie on the x-axis, we know that the directrix must be perpendicular to the x-axis, and that the vertex must be equidistant between the focus and directrix. So the directrix is the line $x = 7$ so that the vertex is four units from the focus and four units from the directrix.

So now, a general point (x,y) on the parabola needs to be as far from $(-1,0)$ as it is from the line $x = 7$. Hence,

$$
\begin{aligned}
\sqrt{(x+1)^2 + y^2} &= |x - 7| \\
(x+1)^2 + y^2 &= (x-7)^2 \\
x^2 + 2x + 1 + y^2 &= x^2 - 14x + 49 \\
y^2 + 16x - 48 &= 0
\end{aligned}
$$

This is written in vertex form as $x - 3 = -\dfrac{y^2}{16}$.

(b) Each if the following equations, if graphed, would correspond to a conic section. Identify which conic section corresponds to each.

i. $x^2 + 5y^2 = 36$; ellipse. (The coefficients of x^2 and y^2 are not equal, but have the same sign.)

ii. $x^2 - 5y^2 = 36$; hyperbola. (The coefficients of x^2 and y^2 have different signs.)

iii. $x^2 - 5y = 36$; parabola. (Only one variable is squared.)

iv. $x^2 + y^2 = 36$; circle. (This is a special case of an ellipse where the coefficients of x^2 and y^2 are equal.)

d. Translate between rectangular and polar coordinates and apply polar coordinates and vectors in the plane

Section **1.1.f** (in the CSET Study Guide for Number and Quantity & Algebra) explains polar representations of complex numbers, and **5.1.e** (in the CSET Study Guide for Calculus) goes into more detail on the same topic. In general, though, you can use polar coordinates even if you are not working with complex numbers.

1. What are polar coordinates? What do they mean?

Polar coordinates describe points on the plane using two numbers: r (the distance to the origin), and θ, the angle from the positive x-axis to a ray pointing from the origin toward the desired point. The formulas for writing x and y as functions of r and θ are therefore $x = r\cos\theta$, $y = r\sin\theta$. See the picture below.

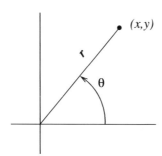

There's nothing unusual about polar coordinates; they are merely another way of describing points on the plane. Instead of using distances right or left, up or down from the origin, like (x, y), we use descriptors like distance from the origin and angle with the positive x-axis, (r, θ). If the Cartesian coordinates were used to describe a point in a town with a grid of streets, you might say that the point is the intersection of Third Street and Avenue D. If polar coordinates were used, you might say that the point was two miles from the center of town, on a bearing northeast from the center.

2. How do you translate between Cartesian and polar coordinates?

   We have already seen the formulas for x and y in terms of r and θ, namely $x = r\cos\theta$ and $y = r\sin\theta$. From these, one can deduce that $r = \sqrt{x^2 + y^2}$ and $\theta = \arctan\left(\dfrac{y}{x}\right)$. One also needs to choose the particular θ to be in the correct quadrant based on the individual signs of x and y. For example, the point $(-1, 1)$ would have $r = \sqrt{2}$ and $\theta = \dfrac{3\pi}{4}$ (in Quadrant II), whereas the point $(1, -1)$ would have the same r value, but would have $\theta = \dfrac{7\pi}{4}$ (in Quadrant IV). Notice that $\dfrac{y}{x} = -1$ in both cases.

3. How do you apply polar coordinates in the plane?

   The main application of polar coordinates in Geometry is through Transformational Geometry. In particular, one can use polar coordinates to describe the affects of a rotation of the plane on a specific point. See section **3.4.a** below for more details.

4. What is a vector?

   See sections **2.4.a** and **2.4.b** (in the CSET Study Guide for Number and Quantity & Algebra) for definitions and basic properties of vectors.

5. How do you apply vectors in the plane?

   The main way to apply vectors in Geometry is through Transformational Geometry. In particular, one often uses a vector to describe how a translation of the plane or of space affects a specific point. See section **3.4.a** below for more details.

3.3 Three-Dimensional Geometry

a. Demonstrate knowledge of the relationships between lines and planes in three dimensions (e.g., parallel, perpendicular, skew, coplanar lines)

1. What does it mean for a line to lie in a plane? ...to be perpendicular to a plane? ...to be parallel to a plane?

   A line lies in a plane if every point on the line is also a point in the plane. A line ℓ is perpendicular to a plane P if ℓ intersects P at one point A and if ℓ is perpendicular to any line through point A that lies in plane P. [Aside: in advanced math, planes are described by their perpendicular lines, often called "normal vectors."] A line is parallel to a plane if the line and the plane do not intersect.

2. What does it mean for two planes to be parallel? ...perpendicular?

   Two planes are parallel if they do not intersect. Also, two planes are parallel if they are both perpendicular to the same line. Two planes are perpendicular if they intersect at a right angle.

   More precisely, suppose plane P is perpendicular to line ℓ and plane Q is perpendicular to line m. Then plane P is parallel to plane Q if lines ℓ and m are parallel, and P is perpendicular to Q if ℓ is perpendicular to m.

3. What does it mean to say that two lines are "coplanar"?

   Two lines are coplanar if there is a plane that contains both lines.

4. Are all non-intersecting pairs of lines "parallel?"

   No, just because two lines in space do not intersect does not mean they are "parallel." In space, we have the possibility of "skew" lines. The difference is this: two lines are parallel if they do not intersect and there exists a plane containing both of them, whereas two lines are skew if they do not intersect and there is no plane that contains them both. As an example, if you think of a road that goes across a highway on an overpass, that road and the highway are skew.

5. Sample Problems

   (a) Explain why skew lines cannot intersect.

   (b) In what ways can two or three lines intersect on a plane?

   (c) In what ways can two or three lines intersect in space?

   (d) In what ways can two or three planes intersect in space?

   (e) In what ways can a line and a plane intersect in space?

   (f) How many points determine a line? ...a plane? ...space?

6. Answers to Sample Problems

   (a) Explain why skew lines cannot intersect.
      Skew lines cannot intersect because they lie on parallel planes, which by definition do not intersect.

(b) In what ways can two or three lines intersect on a plane?

On a plane, two lines could be parallel, or they could intersect in one point. Three lines could all be parallel, or two could be parallel and one a transversal, or any two of them could intersect in distinct points, or the three lines might be concurrent at a single point.

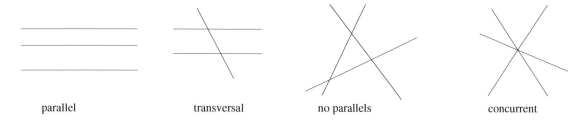

parallel   transversal   no parallels   concurrent

(c) In what ways can two or three lines intersect in space?

In space, two lines could be parallel or skew, in which case they do not intersect. If they are neither parallel nor skew, then the two lines intersect in one point. Three lines could exhibit the same behavior as in the previous problem, or if two of the lines are skew, then the third line could intersect one of them, both of them, or neither of them.

(d) In what ways can two or three planes intersect in space?

In space, two planes could be parallel, or else they could intersect in a line. Three planes could all be parallel, or two could be parallel and one could intersect each of the others in a line, or all three planes could intersect in a single point (like two walls and the floor intersect at the corner of a room), or the three planes could intersect in a line, or the three planes could intersect two at a time, with the three resulting lines of intersection being parallel.

(e) In what ways can a line and a plane intersect in space?

Either the line lies on the plane, is parallel to the plane, or else it intersects that plane in a single point.

(f) How many points determine a line? ...a plane? ...space?

Two points determine a line. Three non-collinear points determine a plane. Four non-coplanar points determine space.

b. Apply and justify properties of three-dimensional objects (e.g., the volume and surface area formulas for prisms, pyramids, cones, cylinders, spheres)

1. What are the volume and surface area of a cube?

If a cube has side length s, then its volume is s^3 and its surface area is $6s^2$ because it has six squares for its sides.

2. What are the other solids and what are their volume and surface area formulas?

The other solids (roughly in order of increasing complexity) are:

- rectangular prism - congruent rectangle bases lying in parallel planes (one directly aligned with the other) with corresponding vertices joined, making four rectangular lateral faces

- prism - congruent polygon bases lying on parallel planes with corresponding vertices joined, making parallelogram lateral faces (PRISMS CAN BE SLANTED!)

- pyramid - polygon base with each vertex joined to a point (called "the" vertex) on a different plane, making triangular lateral faces (PYRAMIDS CAN BE SLANTED!)

- cylinder - congruent circular bases lying on parallel planes, joined by one lateral face (CYLINDERS CAN BE SLANTED!)

- cone - a circular base joined to a vertex on a different plane, making one curved lateral face (CONES CAN BE SLANTED!)

- sphere - the set of all points in space which lie a certain distance (called the radius) from a given point (called the center)

Solid	Volume	Surface Area, if not slanted
prism	Bh, where B is area of base	$2B + Ph$, where P is perimeter of base
pyramid	$\frac{1}{3}Bh$	B plus areas of triangle sides
cylinder	$\pi r^2 h$	$2\pi r^2 + 2\pi rh$
cone	$\frac{1}{3}\pi r^2 h$	$\pi r^2 + \pi r\ell$, where ℓ is slant height
sphere	$\frac{4}{3}\pi r^3$	$4\pi r^2$

3. How are these volume formulas obtained?

You can obtain all of the volume formulas using calculus. However, you can also find convincing geometric justifications as well. Euclid finds the volumes of the Platonic solids in Book XIII of the *Elements*.

The volumes of a prism and a cylinder are of the form Bh, where B is the area of the base. This is plausible because each slice perpendicular to the height has exactly the same area.

To find the volume of a pyramid, you can subdivide a cube into 3 congruent pyramids of the same base area and height as the original cube, which explains why $\frac{1}{3}$ shows up in the volume of a pyramid.

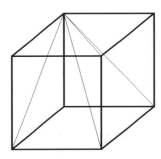

The relationship of a cone to a cylinder is analogous to the relationship of a pyramid to a prism of the same base and height. So, the volume of a cone is one-third that of the cylinder of the same base and height.

Archimedes found the volume of a sphere by showing that the ratio of the volume of a sphere to the volume of its circumscribing cylinder is 2:3. He was so proud of this result that he reportedly wanted it put on his tombstone.

Here's how it works. Archimedes noticed that if you take a double cone, a sphere, and a cylinder, all of the same radius r and height $2r$, and if you take circular slices through all three of them at the same height, then the area of the cylinder slice is the sum of the areas of the double cone slice and the sphere slice.

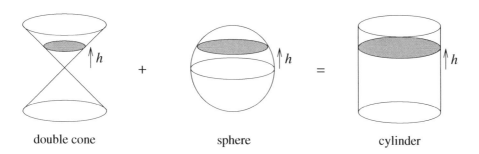

double cone   sphere   cylinder

To see this, assume that the double cone, sphere, and cylinder are centered at a height of zero. Hence for the cone, if the slice is at height h, then the radius of the slice is h. For the sphere, however, the radius of the slice is $\sqrt{r^2 - h^2}$, since the side view of the sphere is a circle. So the sum of the areas of these slices is

$$\pi h^2 + \pi(\sqrt{r^2 - h^2})^2 = \pi h^2 + \pi(r^2 - h^2) = \pi r^2,$$

which is precisely the area of the cylinder slice at height h.

So, by Cavalieri's Principle[1], the volume of the cylinder is the sum of the volumes of the sphere and the volume of the cone. In other words:

$$(\pi r^2)(2r) = V_{sph} + 2\left(\frac{1}{3}\pi r^2 r\right).$$

From this, one obtains $V_{sph} = 2\pi r^3 - \frac{2}{3}\pi r^3 = \frac{4}{3}\pi r^3$.

4. How are these surface area formulas obtained?

The surface areas of a prism or a pyramid are found by adding up the areas of their polygonal faces. If the pyramid is not slanted, then its slant height ℓ (the height of each triangular face) is constant. In this case, its surface area would be $B + \frac{1}{2}P\ell$, where B is the area of the base and P is the perimeter of the base.

For a cylinder, the surface has three faces, two circular bases plus one lateral side. If you think of a soup can label, this lateral side can be "unrolled" into a rectangle whose dimensions are the circumference of the base ($2\pi r$) and the height h. So the surface area of a cylinder is $2\pi r^2 + 2\pi r h$. For a cone, if we use an analogous argument as in the pyramid case, we find that its surface area is $\pi r^2 + \frac{1}{2}P\ell = \pi r^2 + \pi r\ell$, because the perimeter P equals $2\pi r$, the circumference of the base.

For a sphere, calculus can be used to find its surface area somewhat directly, although Archimedes certainly knew the formula. One can project the sphere onto the lateral side

---

[1]Cavalieri's Principle says that if you take two solids and if parallel planes through those solids always intersect both solids so that the areas of intersection are equal, then the volumes of the solids must be equal.

of its circumscribing cylinder (like projecting the surface of Earth onto a rectangular map) in such a way that areas are preserved. The lateral side of the cylinder of radius r and height $2r$ has area $(2\pi r)(2r) = 4\pi r^2$. Hence, $4\pi r^2$ is the surface area of a sphere of radius r.

5. Sample Problems

    (a) Find the volume of the Great Pyramid of Cheops, with square base of side length 754ft, and a height of 482ft.

    (b) Find the surface area of the four sides of the Great Pyramid of Cheops (not the base).

    (c) Find the volume of an equilateral triangular prism with base side length 4cm and height 5cm.

    (d) Find the volume of a pyramid with an equilateral triangle base of side length 4cm and height 5cm.

    (e) Find the volume of a cylindrical soda can of height 12cm and base diameter 6.5cm. Assuming 1 cubic cm holds 1mL of liquid, and 1mL equals 0.0338 fluid oz, how many ounces would this can hold?

    (f) Find the volume and surface area of a cone of radius 5 and height 5.

    (g) Several of the formulas involve the height. The volume formulas still work if the solid is slanted, provided the height is measured perpendicularly to the base. Justify this using Cavalieri's Principle.

    (h) Which volume formulas take the form: volume equals area of base times height? ... volume equals one-third area of base times height?

    (i) Suppose that a can of tennis balls is a cylinder that is just large enough to hold three spherical tennis balls. Find the ratio of the total volume of the tennis balls to the total volume of the can if a tennis ball has radius 3cm.

    (j) In the previous problem, what is the surface area of the three tennis balls? What is the lateral surface area of the can (not including the bases)? What is the ratio of the two?

    (k) Do your answers to the previous two questions really depend on the radius of the tennis balls? [What would Archimedes say?]

6. Answers to Sample Problems

    (a) Find the volume of the Great Pyramid of Cheops, with square base of side length 754ft, and a height of 482ft.

    The volume of a pyramid is $\frac{1}{3}Bh$, where B is the area of the base. So,

$$V = \frac{1}{3}(754)^2(482) \approx 91{,}340{,}000 \text{ cubic feet.}$$

    (b) Find the surface area of the four sides of the Great Pyramid of Cheops (not the base).

    We know that the sides are triangles, but we don't know the height of each triangle. (The slant height of the pyramid is the height of each triangular side.) A cut-away side view shows how we can use the Pythagorean Theorem to determine the slant height.

So $\ell^2 = (482)^2 + (377)^2$, or $\ell \approx 612$ feet. Therefore, the total surface area of the sides of the Great Pyramid is

$$4\left[\frac{1}{2}(754)(612)\right] \approx 923{,}000 \text{ square feet.}$$

(c) Find the volume of an equilateral triangular prism with base side length 4cm and height 5cm.

The volume of a prism is Bh, where B is the area of the base. Using trigonometry (or the 30-60-90 right triangle ratios), we find $B = \frac{\sqrt{3}}{4}s^2$, where s is the side length of the triangle. So, the volume is

$$\frac{\sqrt{3}}{4}(4^2)(5) = 20\sqrt{3} \approx 34.6 \text{ cm}^3.$$

(d) Find the volume of a pyramid with an equilateral triangle base of side length 4cm and height 5cm.

The volume of a pyramid is one-third of its corresponding prism. So the answer to this problem is one-third of the answer to the previous problem: $V = \frac{20\sqrt{3}}{3} \approx 11.5 \text{ cm}^3$.

(e) Find the volume of a cylindrical soda can of height 12cm and base diameter 6.5cm. Assuming 1 cubic cm holds 1mL of liquid, and 1mL equals 0.0338 fluid oz, how many ounces would this can hold?

The radius of the can is 3.25 cm. So the volume is $\pi r^2 h = \pi(3.25)^2(12) \approx 398 \text{ cm}^3$. The can holds $398(0.0338) \approx 13.5$ fluid ounces.

(f) Find the volume and surface area of a cone of radius 5 and height 5.

The volume is $\frac{1}{3}\pi r^2 h = \frac{1}{3}\pi(25)(5) \approx 131$ cubic units. The surface area is πr^2 (for the base) plus $\pi r \ell$, where ℓ is the slant height. Since the radius is equal to the height, this cone has a 45 degree slant angle. So, $\ell = 5\sqrt{2}$. Therefore, the surface area is

$$\pi(25) + \pi(5)(5\sqrt{2}) = \pi(25 + 25\sqrt{2}) \approx 190 \text{ square units.}$$

(g) Several of the formulas involve the height. The volume formulas still work if the solid is slanted, provided the height is measured perpendicularly to the base. Justify this using Cavalieri's Principle.

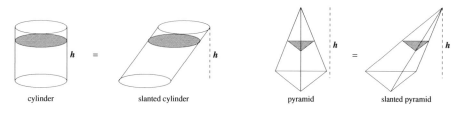

Since the area of each slice is the same in the solid as it is in the slanted version of the solid, Cavalieri's Principle says that the volumes of the two solids have to be equal to each other.

(h) Which volume formulas take the form: volume equals area of base times height? ...volume equals one-third area of base times height?

The volumes of prisms and cylinders are of the form $V = Bh$, where B is the area of the base. The volumes of pyramids and cones are of the form $V = \frac{1}{3}Bh$.

(i) Suppose that a can of tennis balls is a cylinder that is just large enough to hold three spherical tennis balls. Find the ratio of the total volume of the tennis balls to the total volume of the can if a tennis ball has radius 3cm.

Notice that the height of the can is 18cm.

$$V_{sphs} = 3\left(\frac{4}{3}\pi \cdot 3^3\right) = 108\pi \text{ cm}^3$$

$$V_{cyl} = \pi(3^2)(18) = 162\pi \text{ cm}^3$$

The ratio is therefore $108\pi : 162\pi = 2 : 3$.

(j) In the previous problem, what is the surface area of the three tennis balls? What is the lateral surface area of the can (not including the bases)? What is the ratio of the two?

$$SA_{sphs} = 3(4\pi \cdot 3^2) = 108\pi \text{ cm}^2$$

$$SA_{cyl} = 2\pi(3)(18) = 108\pi \text{ cm}^2$$

The ratio is therefore $1 : 1$.

(k) Do your answers to the previous two questions really depend on the radius of the tennis balls? [What would Archimedes say?]

Archimedes knew that these ratios did not depend on the radius of the spheres. To be more general, let's assume a radius r.

$$V_{sphs} = 3\left(\frac{4}{3}\pi r^3\right) = 4\pi r^3$$

$$V_{cyl} = \pi r^2(6r) = 6\pi r^3$$

$$SA_{sphs} = 3(4\pi r^2) = 12\pi r^2$$

$$SA_{cyl} = 2\pi r(6r) = 12\pi r^2$$

Therefore, in general, the ratio $V_{sphs} : V_{cyl} = 2 : 3$ and the ratio $SA_{sphs} : SA_{cyl} = 1 : 1$.

c. Model and solve mathematical and real-world problems by applying geometric concepts to three-dimensional figures

We have just done several problems involving three-dimensional objects. Here are a few more.

1. Sample Problems

(a) A cardboard box measures 12 inches by 20 inches by 8 inches. Is it possible to place a 24-inch rigid stick in the box? (Hint: find the length of the diagonal of the box.)

(b) A right circular cone has radius 10cm and height 13cm. What is the volume of the cone? What is the volume of the smallest cylindrical box into which the cone will fit?

(c) Separate the cube below into three pyramids.

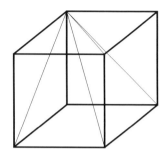

Suppose you now want to paint all the sides of the three pyramids. If the cube side length is 6 feet, and if one pint of paint will cover 40 square feet, how many pints of paint do you need?

(d) Using the same ratio (1 pint of paint covers 40 square feet), determine how much paint is needed to cover the side and the top of a cylindrical water tank of height 16 feet and radius 5 feet. (The bottom is sitting on the ground and will not need to be painted.)

2. Answers to Sample Problems

(a) A cardboard box measures 12 inches by 20 inches by 8 inches. Is it possible to place a 24-inch rigid stick in the box? (Hint: find the length of the diagonal of the box.) Yes. Consider the picture.

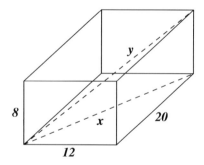

Here, we can determine x because it is the hypotenuse of a right triangle on the base of the box with legs 12 and 20. So $x^2 = 144 + 400 = 544$. Thus $x = \sqrt{544}$. But then y is the hypotenuse of a right triangle with legs x and 8. So,

$$y^2 = x^2 + 64 \implies y^2 = 544 + 64 = 608 \implies y = \sqrt{608} \approx 24.66 \text{ inches} > 24 \text{ inches.}$$

(b) A right circular cone has radius 10cm and height 13cm. What is the volume of the cone? What is the volume of the smallest cylindrical box into which the cone will fit?

The volume of the cone is $\frac{1}{3}\pi r^2 h = \frac{1}{3}\pi(10)^2(13) = \frac{1300\pi}{3} \approx 1361.36$ cubic centimeters. The smallest cylindrical box that could contain the cone has the same dimensions as the cone, and is therefore three times bigger. (Compare volume formulas to see this.) So the cylinder would have a volume of $1300\pi \approx 4084.07$ cubic centimeters.

(c) Separate a cube into three pyramids, as shown below.

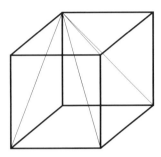

Suppose you now want to paint all the sides of the three pyramids. If the cube side length is 6 feet, and if one pint of paint will cover 40 square feet, how many pints of paint do you need? 9.22 pints.

We have to do a little investigating here. Each of the three pyramids is congruent to the others, and each has one square base (6' by 6'), two sides that are right triangles with legs 6' and 6', and two sides are right triangles with legs 6' and $6\sqrt{2}$ feet (i.e., the length of the diagonal of one of the square sides of the cube). So the total surface area of one pyramid is

$$1(6)(6) + 2\left(\frac{1}{2}\right)(6)(6) + 2\left(\frac{1}{2}\right)(6)(6\sqrt{2}) = 72 + 36\sqrt{2} = 36(2 + \sqrt{2}).$$

Thus the total surface area of all three pyramids is $108(2 + \sqrt{2}) \approx 368.74$ square feet. We divide this by 40 to obtain about 9.22 pints of paint, or one gallon plus 1.22 pints.

(d) Using the same ratio (1 pint of paint covers 40 square feet), determine how much paint is needed to cover the side and the top of a cylindrical water tank of height 16 feet and radius 5 feet. (The bottom is sitting on the ground and will not need to be painted.)

Here, the sides to be painted are one circle (the top) and one side, which we can "unroll" into a rectangle of the same height as the cylinder, but with a length equal to the cylinder's circumference. So, the area is

$$\pi(5)^2 + 2\pi(5)(16) = 185\pi \approx 581.19 \text{ square feet},$$

which would require $\dfrac{185\pi}{40} \approx 14.53$ pints of paint, or one gallon plus 6.53 pints.

3.4 Transformational Geometry

a. Demonstrate knowledge of isometries in two- and three-dimensional space (e.g., rotation, translation, reflection), including their basic properties in relation to congruence

1. What is an isometry?

   An isometry is a function that maps points on the plane (or in space) to other points on the plane (or in space) in such a way that all distances are preserved. So, if we call our isometry F, then the distance between points A and B is equal to the distance between $F(A)$ and $F(B)$. A common notation is to use primes for the transformed points. So, under an isometry, $A'B' = AB$. The most common isometries are rotations, reflections in a line (or in a plane), and translations.

2. How are the ideas of isometry and congruence related?

   Many people have a common-sense notion of what it means for two figures to be congruent: the figures need to be "the same." But a precise definition can be tricky. Transformational geometry uses a definition of congruence based in transformations, namely, that two figures are congruent if one can be transformed to the other via a sequence of isometries. (The Common Core State Standards have adopted this approach.)

3. How do you use the definition of congruence in terms of isometries to decide if two figures are congruent?

   The short answer to this question is that you have to determine whether there is a series of isometries that would cause one figure ultimately to coincide with the other one. Since we are only allowed to use rigid motions, we know that if the two figures aren't the same size, then there is no way for them to be congruent.

4. What are the basic properties of isometries?

   Because isometries preserve lengths, they also preserve any geometric property that follows from lengths, such as congruence of triangles, and thus of angles, polygons, and solids, too. Areas and volumes are also preserved by isometries.

5. How do you determine the image of a figure transformed by a rotation?

   See table below for the image of the point (a, b) under a counter-clockwise (ccw) rotation centered at the origin.

If the ccw rotation around the origin measures:	then the image of (a, b) is:
90 degrees	$(-b, a)$
180 degrees	$(-a, -b)$
270 degrees	$(b, -a)$

   To draw a rotated figure, then, rotate the important points first. For example, suppose you are rotating a triangle around the origin ccw 90 degrees and its vertices are at $(0, 5)$, $(-1, -2)$, and $(4, 3)$. Then the transformed triangle will have vertices at $(-5, 0)$, $(2, -1)$, and $(-3, 4)$. Connect the vertices to draw the rotated triangle.

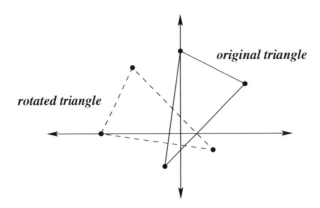

One can use polar coordinates to help with this process, but without going into too much detail on the geometry of complex multiplication, we can probably only do examples involving "nice" polar coordinate points. If rotating a point with polar coordinates r and θ around the origin ccw by an angle α, the resulting point will have polar coordinates r and $\theta + \alpha$. See Sample Problems below for an example.

6. How do you determine the image of a figure transformed by a reflection?

   Say you wanted to draw a triangle ($\triangle ABC$) and its image under reflection across one of its sides ($\overline{AB}$). Draw the same triangle on two different transparencies. Then flip one sheet over and lay it back down so that the two A vertices are on top of each other and the two B vertices are on top of each other. Then you are looking at the reflection of $\triangle ABC$ in side $\overline{AB}$.

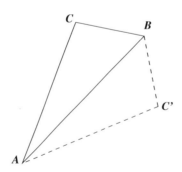

Reflections using graph paper (and coordinates) are a little trickier, unless the line of reflection is one of the following: $y = x$, $y = -x$, the x-axis, or the y-axis. See the following table for the image of (a, b) under reflections in these four lines.

If the line of reflection is:	then the image of (a, b) is:
$y = x$	(b, a)
$y = -x$	$(-b, -a)$
$y = 0$ (x-axis)	$(a, -b)$
$x = 0$ (y-axis)	$(-a, b)$

As before, simply draw the images of important points first and then determine the figure. For example, suppose you are reflecting the earlier triangle across the y-axis. (Recall that its vertices were at $(0,5)$, $(-1,-2)$, and $(4,3)$.) Then the reflected triangle will have vertices at $(0,5)$, $(1,-2)$, and $(-4,3)$. Now simply connect the vertices to draw the reflected triangle. Notice that the first vertex didn't change. That's because it is on the y-axis, and therefore its reflection is also on the y-axis.

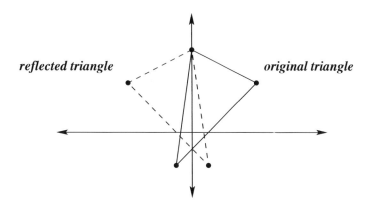

7. How do you determine the image of a figure transformed by a translation?

With graph paper and coordinates, translations are pretty straightforward, assuming we know the coordinates to which the origin moves under the translation (i.e., assuming we know the vector of translation). If the origin moves to the point (h,k), then the image of any point (a,b) under this translation will be $(a+h, b+k)$.

As above, simply draw the images of important points first and then determine the figure. For example, suppose you are translating the earlier triangle. (Recall that its vertices were at $(0,5)$, $(-1,-2)$, and $(4,3)$.) If the origin moves to the point $(3,-1)$ under this translation, then the translated triangle will have vertices at $(3,4)$, $(2,-3)$, and $(7,2)$. Now simply connect the vertices to draw the translated triangle. Notice that there are no fixed points under a translation.

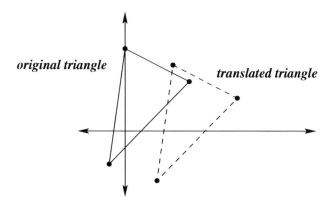

8. How can you show that two triangles are congruent if their corresponding pairs of sides and corresponding pairs of angles are congruent?

We assume that the corresponding pairs of sides and corresponding pairs of angles are congruent. Then we must show how to transform one of the triangles so that it coincides with the other. To make it easier, let's say that $\triangle ABC$ and $\triangle A'B'C'$ meet the hypotheses, and that each vertex corresponds with its primed counterpart: A with A', etc. We need to explain the steps to take $\triangle ABC$ to $\triangle A'B'C'$.

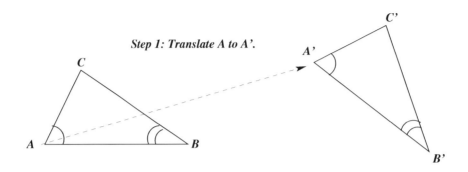

Step one: translate the original figure so that A moves to A'.

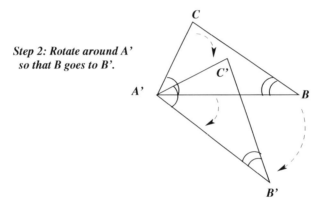

Step two: rotate around point A' until side $\overline{AB}$ lines up with its image. Since $AB = A'B'$, we know that B will land on B'.

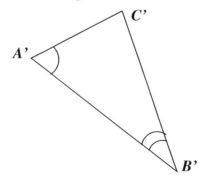

Thus after two isometry transformations – a translation followed by a rotation – these two triangles coincide. Point C has wound up on top of C' and we already knew that all the corresponding angles were congruent. Therefore, these two triangles are congruent.

9. How can you show that the corresponding pairs of sides and corresponding pairs of angles of two triangles are congruent if the triangles are congruent?

    This is the converse of the previous statement. Here, we assume that two triangles are congruent. That means, by definition, that there is a sequence of rigid motions that takes one triangle to the other. Suppose we perform those rigid motions. What does the final picture look like?

    It looks like one triangle because the one triangle will be lying exactly on top of the other one. They coincide. Therefore, each side (respectively, each angle) of the first triangle corresponds to a side (respectively, an angle) of the second triangle. Corresponding pairs of sides and corresponding pairs of angles are congruent.

    Notice that the previous two statements combine to demonstrate the statement: Two triangles are congruent if and only if corresponding pairs of sides and corresponding pairs of angles are congruent.

10. Sample Problems

    (a) What information is necessary to describe a rotation? ...a translation? ...a reflection?

    (b) List the image of the point $(1, \sqrt{3})$ under the following transformations.

        i. a rotation of 90 degrees around the origin. ...by 30 degrees around the origin.

        ii. a translation by the vector $(1, -1)$. ...by the vector $(-1, 0)$.

        iii. a reflection in the x-axis. ...in the line $y = x$.

    (c) Prove that if T is an isometry, then $\triangle ABC \cong \triangle T(A)T(B)T(C)$.

    (d) Draw and label an equilateral triangle. List all the different isometries that don't really change the equilateral triangle. (Such an isometry is called a *symmetry*.) Repeat for a square, a rectangle, and a parallelogram.

    (e) Justify the Isosceles Triangle Theorem using transformational geometry.

    (f) If you draw a diagonal of a parallelogram, you obtain two congruent triangles. What isometry maps one of these triangles to the other?

    (g) Is the composition of two isometries another isometry? Explain.

11. Answers to Sample Problems

    (a) What information is necessary to describe a rotation? ...a translation? ...a reflection?

        To describe a rotation, you need to state the center of rotation and the angle of rotation. (Or, in three dimensions, you need to state an axis of rotation and an angle of rotation.) To describe a translation, you need to give a vector of translation; that is, you need to state a direction in which to translate and how far to move in that direction. To describe a reflection, you need to state a line of reflection. (Or, in three dimensions, you need to state a plane of reflection.)

    (b) List the image of the point $(1, \sqrt{3})$ under the following transformations.

i. a rotation of 90 degrees around the origin. $(-\sqrt{3}, 1)$. ... by 30 degrees around the origin. $(0, 2)$.

To answer the first question, one can use the table above. For the second question, one can use polar coordinates. The starting point, $(1, \sqrt{3})$ has $r = 2$ and $\theta = \dfrac{\pi}{3}$. So its image under rotation by $\dfrac{\pi}{6}$ is a point where $r = 2$ still, but θ is now $\dfrac{\pi}{3} + \dfrac{\pi}{6} = \dfrac{\pi}{2}$. Converting back to Cartesian coordinates, we get $(0, 2)$.

ii. a translation by the vector $(1, -1)$. $(2, \sqrt{3} - 1)$. ... by the vector $(-1, 0)$. $(0, \sqrt{3})$.

For these, we simply add the translation vector to each point, coordinate by coordinate.

iii. a reflection in the x-axis. $(1, -\sqrt{3})$. ... in the line $y = x$. $(\sqrt{3}, 1)$.

For these, one can use the table above.

(c) Prove that if T is an isometry, then $\triangle ABC \cong \triangle T(A)T(B)T(C)$.

Proof: Since T is an isometry, by the definition of congruence,

$$\triangle ABC \cong \triangle T(A)T(B)T(C). \quad \square$$

(d) Draw and label an equilateral triangle. List all the different isometries that don't really change the equilateral triangle. (Such an isometry is called a *symmetry*.) Repeat for a square, a rectangle, and a parallelogram.

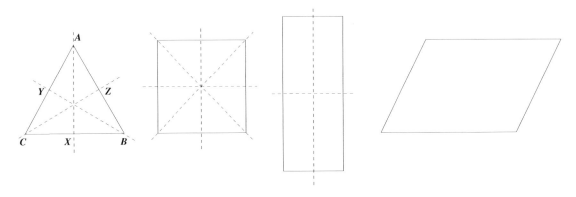

In the triangle above, there are six symmetries: three reflections in the dashed lines $\overline{AX}$, $\overline{BY}$, and $\overline{CZ}$; and rotations by 120 degrees, 240 degrees, and 0 degrees. Even though rotation by zero degrees doesn't really do anything, it is an important symmetry of the triangle, in roughly the same way that zero is an important concept in addition.

In the square, there are eight symmetries: four reflections in the dashed lines, and four rotations, by 90, 180, 270, and 0 degrees.

In the rectangle, there are four symmetries: two reflections in the dashed lines, and rotations by 180 and 0 degrees.

In the parallelogram, there are only two symmetries: rotations by 180 and 0 degrees.

(e) Justify the Isosceles Triangle Theorem using transformational geometry.

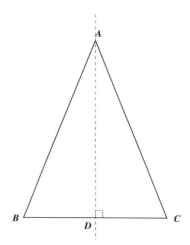

Proof: The hypothesis is that $\overline{AB} \cong \overline{AC}$. Let $\overline{AD}$ be the perpendicular bisector of $\overline{BC}$. Let R represent reflection in $\overline{AD}$. Then it is clear that $R(B) = C$, $R(C) = B$, and $R(A) = A$. Since R is an isometry, $\angle ABC \cong \angle R(A)R(B)R(C) = \angle ACB$. □

(f) If you draw a diagonal of a parallelogram, you obtain two congruent triangles. What isometry maps one of these triangles to the other? a 180 degree rotation around the center of the parallelogram.

(g) Is the composition of two isometries another isometry? Explain.

Yes, the composition of two isometries is another isometry. If F and G both preserve distances, then doing F followed by G would still preserve distances. Consider $G(F(A))G(F(B))$. Since G preserves distances, $G(F(A))G(F(B)) = F(A)F(B)$. Since F preserves distances, $F(A)F(B) = AB$. So, $G(F(A))G(F(B)) = AB$. Therefore, G composed with F (denoted $G \circ F$) is an isometry.

b. Demonstrate knowledge of dilations (e.g., similarity transformations or change in scale factor), including their basic properties in relation to similarity, volume, and area

1. What is a dilation?

A dilation (or change of scale) is a transformation of the plane with the property that the ratio of the distance between the image of a point and a fixed point (called the "center" of the dilation) to the distance between the original point and the center is equal to a constant (called the "scale factor" of the dilation.) Moreover, the original point, its image, and the center of the dilation are collinear, with the point and its image on one side of the center. (For our purposes, the center cannot be between the point and its image.) The center of the dilation is fixed; the dilation does not move it.

In other words, consider the dilation with a scale factor k, centered at P. Let A' denote the image of A under the dilation and B' the image of B. Then $\frac{A'P}{AP} = \frac{B'P}{BP} = k$, or $A'P = k(AP)$ and $B'P = k(BP)$. In the picture below, $k = 3$. That's because $A'P$ is three times as long as AP. Similarly, $B'P = 3(BP)$. Notice that because $k > 1$, the points move away from P after the dilation.

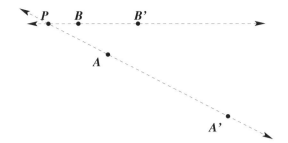

By the way, I use the term "dilation" if $k > 1$ because then points seem to be moving away from the center. If $k < 1$, I would call it a "contraction" because points are moving toward the center, with distances getting smaller, but "dilation" has become rather common for both types, and so I will follow that usage from here on.

2. What is a similarity transformation?

   A dilation is an example of a similarity transformation. More generally, a similarity transformation is a transformation that may be composed of dilations and isometries, done one after the other.

3. How do you verify properties of similarity transformations experimentally?

   Probably the most precise way is to play around with geometry software. It can conduct these dilations for you and you can use the software to measure various distances and to construct ratios. However, you can also just get out pencil and paper and a ruler to experiment with dilations. We will draw pictures for each of the properties above, which provide some evidence as to why they are true.

4. What are some basic properties of similarity transformations?

   (a) A dilation takes a line not passing through the center of the dilation to a parallel line, and leaves a line passing through the center unchanged.

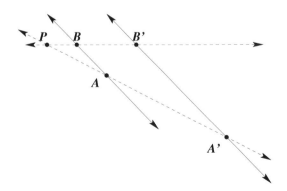

   Notice that $\overleftrightarrow{A'B'}$ appears to be parallel to $\overleftrightarrow{AB}$. Moreover, lines through P are not changed: $\overleftrightarrow{A'P}$ is the same line as $\overleftrightarrow{AP}$; $\overleftrightarrow{B'P}$ is the same line as $\overleftrightarrow{BP}$.

   (b) The dilation of a line segment is longer or shorter in the ratio given by the scale factor.

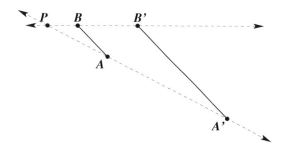

We know from how the dilation is defined that $\frac{A'P}{AP} = \frac{B'P}{BP} = k$. (In this picture, $k = 3$.) But if you draw precisely and measure closely, you will find that $\frac{A'B'}{AB}$ also equals 3. In general, any line segment $\overline{ST}$ will transform under a dilation with scale factor k to $\overline{S'T'}$ with $S'T' = k(ST)$.

(c) A dilation preserves angles.

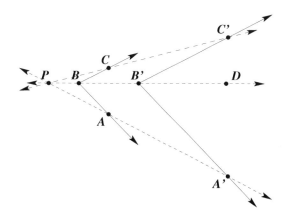

Here, $\angle ABC$ is congruent to $\angle A'B'C'$. Unlike the previous two properties, we can actually prove this one using parallel lines and transversals, and assuming that the first property above is true.

To see this, notice that $\angle ABB' \cong \angle A'B'D$ because they are corresponding angles when parallel lines $\overleftrightarrow{AB}$ and $\overleftrightarrow{A'B'}$ are cut by transversal $\overleftrightarrow{PD}$. Similarly, $\angle CBB' \cong \angle C'B'D$. So, by what is sometimes called the Angle Addition Property, we can deduce that $\angle ABC$ (made up of $\angle ABB'$ and $\angle CBB'$) must be congruent to $\angle A'B'C'$ (made up of $\angle A'B'D$ and $\angle C'B'D$, which are congruent, respectively, to $\angle ABB'$ and $\angle CBB'$).

5. Why do we need to verify properties of similarity transformations experimentally? Why can't we just prove them?

Remember that there are undefined terms in geometry, like point and line. The reason for that is that you have to start somewhere without a definition so that subsequent terms can be defined in terms of those words.

A similar situation occurs in a logical system, like geometry. You can't just prove everything. A proof relies on other facts and other statements. Some of those statements must just be assumed to be true so that there is a starting point. Such statements are called "axioms" or "postulates."

Often the topic of similarity in geometry is introduced using a postulate that two triangles are similar if two pairs of their corresponding angles are congruent. All the subsequent properties of similarity, including the properties of similarity transformations that we just examined and verified experimentally, can then be proved as logical consequences of this postulate.

Transformational geometry often defines similarity based on similarity transformations. (The Common Core State Standards follow this approach.) Then two triangles (or other figures) are defined to be similar if one is the image of the other under a similarity transformation. This is our starting point. Then, we will deduce the other properties of similarity from this starting point. These properties that we just verified, then, are like the postulates of our system. One advantage of using transformational geometry as the basis of your logical system is that you can verify its postulates experimentally. By measuring and drawing pictures, you can convince yourself that the postulates really should be true.

6. Which properties of dilations are also true of similarity transformations in general?

   Recall that a similarity transformation is composed of dilations and isometries. This means that the first property is not necessarily true of a general similarity transformation. If you rotate or reflect a line, its image does not have to be parallel to the original line.

   However, an isometry does not change lengths of segments. So, composing dilations and isometries still means that each line segment's length will be changed by the same scale factor.

   Finally, angles are still preserved. Since every dilation and isometry preserves angles, any combination of them must also preserve angles.

7. How are areas and volumes affected by a similarity transformation?

   If you have a similarity transformation with scale factor k, then any area will be transformed to an area that measures k^2 times the original area. Moreover, any volume will be transformed to a volume that measures k^3 times the original volume.

8. Sample Problems

   (a) Sketch square $ABCD$ and its image under a dilation of scale factor two ...

      i. centered at the center of the square.
      ii. centered at point A.
      iii. centered at the midpoint of $\overline{CD}$.

   (b) Consider $\triangle ABC$ with $a = 3$, $b = 4$, and $c = 5$. Draw altitude $\overline{CD}$. Find the scale factor of the contraction that maps ...

      i. $\triangle ABC$ to $\triangle CBD$.
      ii. $\triangle ABC$ to $\triangle ACD$.

   (c) Is the composition of two similarity transformations another similarity transformation? Explain. If so, what is its scale factor?

   (d) Is the composition of a similarity transformation and an isometry another similarity transformation? Explain. If so, what is its scale factor?

(e) Join the midpoints of the sides of a square to obtain a smaller square. What is the exact similarity transformation that maps the first square to the second square? Is there more than one right answer?

(f) What scale factor is needed for a similarity transformation to transform a square into a square with twice the area?

(g) What scale factor is needed for a similarity transformation to transform a cube into a cube with twice the volume?

9. Answer to Sample Problems

(a) Sketch square $ABCD$ and its image under a dilation of scale factor two ...

    i. centered at the center of the square.

    ii. centered at point A.

    iii. centered at the midpoint of $\overline{CD}$.

In each picture, $A'B'C'D'$ is the image of $ABCD$ after the transformation.

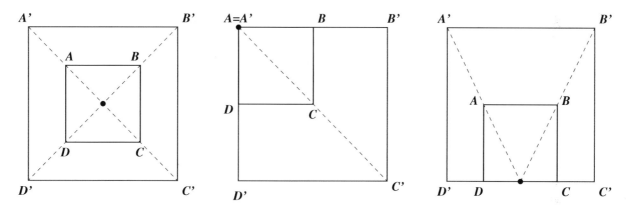

(b) Consider $\triangle ABC$ with $a = 3$, $b = 4$, and $c = 5$. Draw altitude $\overline{CD}$. Find the scale factor of the contraction that maps ...

    i. $\triangle ABC$ to $\triangle CBD$. $\frac{3}{5}$

    ii. $\triangle ABC$ to $\triangle ACD$. $\frac{4}{5}$

(c) Is the composition of two similarity transformations another similarity transformation? Explain. If so, what is its scale factor?

The composition of two similarity transformations is a similarity transformation and the scale factor of the composition is the product of the scale factors of the individual similarity transformations. If S_1 is a similarity transformation with scale factor k_1 and S_2 is a similarity transformation with scale factor k_2, then $S_1 \circ S_2$ is a similarity transformation with scale factor $k_1 k_2$.

(d) Is the composition of a similarity transformation and an isometry another similarity transformation? Explain. If so, what is its scale factor?

The composition of a similarity transformation and an isometry is another similarity transformation. Moreover, the composition has a scale factor equal to the scale factor of the first similarity transformation. If S is a similarity transformation with scale factor k and T is an isometry, then $S \circ T$ is a similarity transformation with scale factor k.

(e) Join the midpoints of the sides of a square to obtain a smaller square. What is the exact similarity transformation that maps the first square to the second square? Is there more than one right answer?

There are several right answers. This transformation is composed of a dilation and a rotation. The dilation is centered at the center of the square and has a scale factor of $\frac{1}{\sqrt{2}} = \frac{\sqrt{2}}{2}$. This is followed by a rotation of 45 degrees around the center of the square.

(f) What scale factor is needed for a similarity transformation to transform a square into a square with twice the area? $\sqrt{2}$

(g) What scale factor is needed for a similarity transformation to transform a cube into a cube with twice the volume? $\sqrt[3]{2}$

4.1 Probability

a. Prove and apply basic principles of permutations and combinations

1. What are permutations and combinations?

   A permutation is a partial sequence of elements from a set. The order of that sequence is important. For instance, a permutation problem might involve determining the number of ways that you can rank the students in your class. If you have ten students, then there would be 10! or 3,628,800 ways to rank your students. If you want to know how many ways you can choose the first place student, the second place student, and the third place student, there are $10 \times 9 \times 8 = 720$ ways to do so. In general, the number of ways to rank k objects from a set of n objects is often denoted $_nP_k$ and is equal to $\dfrac{n!}{(n-k)!}$. So $_{10}P_3 = 720$.

   A combination is a selection of a certain number of elements from a set. The order in which the selection is chosen is not important. The number of ways to choose k objects from a set of n objects is often denoted $_nC_k$ (read "n choose k") or $\begin{pmatrix} n \\ k \end{pmatrix}$ and is equal to $\dfrac{n!}{k!(n-k)!}$. So if you were to choose a committee of three students from a group of ten, there would be $_{10}C_3$ (or 120) ways to do that.

2. What are the basic rules of counting?

   There are a few basic rules of counting:

   - If there are n total outcomes, and if k of those outcomes meet condition A, then the number of outcomes than do *not* meet condition A is $n - k$.

   - If two choices are to be made in succession, and there are m ways to make the first choice and n ways to make the second choice, then the total number of ways to make both choices is mn.

   - The total number of events that meet condition A or condition B is the total number that meet A plus the total number that meet B minus the number that meet both A and B (due to overcounting).

   As an example of this last rule, suppose you want to count the number of students in your class who are 14 years old or female. (Let's say you have six boys who are 13 and nine boys who are 14, as well as seven girls who are 13 and eight girls who are 14.) Then you could add the total number of students who are 14 years old (17) to the total number of female students (15). This would give you 32. But then you would have to subtract 8, the number of female students who are 14 years old because you would have counted them twice. So the answer is that there are 24 students who are 14 years old or female (i.e., the nine boys who are 14, plus the 15 girls, makes 24).

3. What are the basic principles of permutations and combinations? How are they related?

   Permutations often use multiplication. To count the number of ways to pick first, second, and third place from 10 students, we start by seeing that there are 10 ways to choose the first place student. After that, there are 9 contestants from which to choose the second place student. Then, there are only 8 left from which to choose the third place student. So, there are $(10)(9)(8) = 720 = {}_{10}P_3$ ways to choose the top three places, which we calculated above.

Combinations are similar, except that order doesn't matter. So, if we were to count the number of ways to pick a committee of 3 students from a class of 10, we are not interested in ranking them. We could still count them using the rankings above, but then we are overcounting because sometimes different rankings will be made up of the same three people. In fact, there are $3! = 6$ ways to rank three people, and so we have overcounted the number of combinations by a factor of 6. Therefore, there are only $\frac{720}{6} = 120 = {}_{10}C_3$ possible committees of three students from a class of ten.

4. Sample Problems

   (a) How many ways are there to select a three-course meal from 6 appetizers, 3 entrées, and 5 desserts?

   (b) How many California license plates are there (assuming fixed placement, i.e. one number is followed by three letters and then three more numbers)?

   (c) How many ways are there to pick a committee of 4 students from a class of 33?

   (d) How many ways are there to pick a committee of 4 students consisting of 2 girls and 2 boys from a class of 12 girls and 21 boys?

   (e) Explain why ${}_9C_5 = \dfrac{{}_9P_5}{5!}$

   (f) Suppose that you want a password that is 8 characters long, and that you are allowed to choose from a total of 100 characters. Repeated characters are allowed.

      i. How many possible passwords are there?

      ii. Now suppose that a hacker can check 1 million passwords a second. How long would it take the hacker to go through all the passwords?

      iii. How often should you change your password, or should you not really worry?

5. Answers to Sample Problems

   (a) How many ways are there to select a three-course meal from 6 appetizers, 3 entrées, and 5 desserts? $(6)(3)(5) = 90$

   (b) How many California license plates are there (assuming fixed placement, i.e. one number is followed by three letters and then three more numbers)? $(10^4)(26^3) = 175{,}760{,}000$

   (c) How many ways are there to pick a committee of 4 students from a class of 33? ${}_{33}C_4 = 40{,}920$

   (d) How many ways are there to pick a committee of 4 students consisting of 2 girls and 2 boys from a class of 12 girls and 21 boys? $({}_{12}C_2)({}_{21}C_2) = 13{,}860$

   (e) Explain why ${}_9C_5 = \dfrac{{}_9P_5}{5!}$

      The number ${}_9P_5$ counts how many ways there are to rank 5 people from a group of 9. However, if we are interested in combinations, then we do not care about the actual ranking. For example, the ranking A, B, C, D, E is different from the ranking A, B, C, E, D, but as far as combinations are concerned, these two sets of five elements are the same. So to calculate $_9C_5$, we need to divide $_9P_5$ by the total number of ways in which 5 people can be ranked, which is 5!.

(f) Suppose that you want a password that is 8 characters long, and that you are allowed to choose from a total of 100 characters. Repeated characters are allowed.

   i. How many possible passwords are there? $100^8 = 10^{16}$

   ii. Now suppose that a hacker can check 1 million passwords a second. How long would it take the hacker to go through all the passwords? 10^{10} seconds, which is over 317 years

   iii. How often should you change your password, or should you not really worry? If you change your password each year, then the hacker has only a 0.3% chance of finding your password each year.

b. Illustrate finite probability using a variety of examples and models (e.g., the fundamental counting principles, sample space)

1. What is finite probability? What is sample space?

Finite probability measures the probability of certain outcomes when there are only a finite number of outcomes possible. The set of all possible outcomes is called the *sample space*. In finite probability, if all possible outcomes are equally likely, then the probability of an event A is the ratio of the number of outcomes in which A occurs to the total number of outcomes. For example, if you roll a die, what is the likelihood of rolling a multiple of 3? Since there are two multiples of 3 out of a sample space of six possible rolls $\{1,2,3,4,5,6\}$, the probability of rolling a multiple of 3 is $\frac{2}{6} = \frac{1}{3}$. Notice that A can be thought of as a subset of the sample space; here, $A = \{3,6\}$. In general, an *event* is a subset of the sample space.

2. What are the basic principles of probability?

There are a few basic principles of probability. In the following, A and B are events in the sample space, S.

- The total probability of all possible outcomes must be 1.

- If A is an event, then $P(A)$, the probability of A occurring is $\dfrac{|A|}{|S|}$. (Here, $|X|$ indicates the number of elements of the set X.)

- If the probability of event A is $P(A)$, then the probability that A does *not* happen ($\overline{A}$, called the *complement* of A) is: $P(\overline{A}) = 1 - P(A)$.

- If two events (A and B) are *independent* of each other, then the probability of both occurring (A AND B) is: $P(A \cap B) = P(A)P(B)$. This is called the *Multiplication Rule*.

- If A and B are two events, then the probability of either one of them happening (A OR B) is: $P(A \cup B) = P(A) + P(B) - P(A \cap B)$, where, as in the counting case, we subtract the probability of both A and B happening due to having counted it twice.

- In the special case when two events (A and B) are *mutually exclusive*, then the probability that either one of them occurs (A OR B) is: $P(A \cup B) = P(A) + P(B)$. This is called the *Addition Rule*.

3. What are some common examples and models for finite probability?

The simplest example is flipping a coin, which is a good model for an event (heads or tails) to occur with probability $p = \frac{1}{2}$. Another simple example involves rolling a die, in which the numbers 1 through 6 come up, each with probability $p = \frac{1}{6}$. Rolling two independent dice and calculating their sum is slightly more complicated, because then different sums have different probabilities, based on the number of ways they can occur. (See the Sample Problems.) Finally, a standard deck of 52 playing cards can be described via a finite probability model. In a standard deck, there are four suits, each with 13 cards. In fact, in poker, the ranking of poker hands is determined by their relative probabilities.

4. What is the difference between selecting with replacement or without replacement?

When you are asked to select two cards from a standard deck, there is a big difference between drawing with replacement or drawing without replacement. If you are drawing with replacement, then you draw one card, record it, and then put it back in the deck before drawing a second card. If we assume that each draw is a random event and that the draws are independent, then there is a small chance you might draw the same card again.

On the other hand, if you are drawing two cards without replacement, then there is no chance you would draw the same card twice. Instead, you would draw one card, record it, and then you would draw another card from the remaining cards in the deck. This will change the probabilities.

As a quick example, suppose you draw two cards. What is the probability that both are hearts if you draw with replacement? ...without replacement? With replacement, the probability is $\frac{13}{52} = \frac{1}{4}$ of drawing a heart. If we replace the first card, then the probability is still $\frac{1}{4}$ of drawing a heart for the second card. Assuming these two draws are independent, then the probability of drawing two hearts is $\frac{1}{4} \cdot \frac{1}{4} = \frac{1}{16} = 0.0625$. On the other hand, if drawing without replacement, the probability of drawing a heart on the first draw is still $\frac{1}{4}$. But if you have drawn a heart, then the remainder of the deck will have 12 hearts and 51 cards left. So the probability of drawing a second heart after drawing one already is $\frac{12}{51} = \frac{4}{17}$. Multiplying these gives

$$\frac{1}{4} \cdot \frac{4}{17} = \frac{1}{17} \approx 0.0588,$$

which is slightly smaller than the result obtained with replacement.

5. Sample Problems

   (a) Suppose you flip three fair coins: a penny, a quarter, and a nickel. What is the probability that all three come up heads? ...that two come up heads? Explain (in terms of the symmetry of heads and tails) why your two answers should add up to 50%.

   (b) How many possible outcomes are there for rolling two dice?

   (c) Complete the table for rolling two dice:

sum	2	3	4	5	6	7	8	9	10	11	12
prob											

(d) If you choose 5 cards at random from a deck of cards, without replacement, what is the probability that all five cards will be hearts? ... will be from the same suit?

(e) Repeat the previous problem, but with replacing each card after it is drawn.

(f) Draw four cards at random, without replacement. What is the probability that all four cards are from different suits?

6. Answers to Sample Problems

(a) Suppose you flip three fair coins: a penny, a quarter, and a nickel. What is the probability that all three come up heads? ... that two come up heads? Explain (in terms of the symmetry of heads and tails) why your two answers should add up to 50%.

Since the three coin flips are independent events, the probability of getting three heads is $\left(\frac{1}{2}\right)\left(\frac{1}{2}\right)\left(\frac{1}{2}\right) = \frac{1}{8}$. Another way to see this is that of the eight possible outcomes, only HHH has all three coins coming up heads.

There are three ways for two coins to come up heads: HHT, HTH, THH. So the probability of this event is $\frac{3}{8}$.

The other two possible numbers of heads are zero and one. But obtaining one head is the same event as obtaining two tails. So, by symmetry, the probability of getting one head is the same as the probability of getting two heads. Similarly, the probability of getting no heads (and three tails) is the same as the probability of getting three heads. Since the total probability has to be 1, the sum of our two answers has to be 50% or $\frac{1}{2}$.

(b) How many possible outcomes are there for rolling two dice? There are 36 different outcomes, which are equally likely. If you are measuring the sum of the two dice, then there are eleven different sums, but they are not equally likely.

(c) Complete the table for rolling two dice:

sum	2	3	4	5	6	7	8	9	10	11	12
prob	$\frac{1}{36}$	$\frac{2}{36}$	$\frac{3}{36}$	$\frac{4}{36}$	$\frac{5}{36}$	$\frac{6}{36}$	$\frac{5}{36}$	$\frac{4}{36}$	$\frac{3}{36}$	$\frac{2}{36}$	$\frac{1}{36}$

(d) If you choose 5 cards at random from a deck of cards, without replacement, what is the probability that all five cards will be hearts? ... will be from the same suit?

The probability that the first card is a heart is $\frac{13}{52}$. Assuming that the first card was a heart, there are now only 12 hearts left in the deck of 51 cards. So, the probability that the second card is a heart is $\frac{12}{51}$. Continuing in this way,

$$\left(\frac{13}{52}\right)\left(\frac{12}{51}\right)\left(\frac{11}{50}\right)\left(\frac{10}{49}\right)\left(\frac{9}{48}\right) = \frac{33}{66,640} \approx 0.000495$$

is the probability that all five cards will be hearts.

The probability that all five cards will be from the same suit is four times this quantity, because there are four suits, or $\frac{33}{16,660} \approx 0.00198$.

(e) Repeat the previous problem, but with replacing each card after it is drawn.

This means that for each card, the probability of drawing a heart is $\frac{1}{4}$. So, the probability that all five cards will be hearts is $\left(\frac{1}{4}\right)^5 = \frac{1}{1024} \approx 0.000977$. The probability that all five cards will be from the same suit is thus $\frac{4}{1024} = \frac{1}{256} \approx 0.0039$.

(f) Draw four cards at random, without replacement. What is the probability that all four cards are from different suits?

The first card could be anything. So the probability of selecting an OK card is 1. However, once the first card is drawn, you can no longer draw a card from that suit. So there are 39 "good" cards left out of the 51 remaining cards. The probability that the second card is OK is thus $\frac{39}{51} = \frac{13}{17}$. The probability that the third card is OK is thus $\frac{26}{50} = \frac{13}{25}$. And finally, the probability that the fourth card is OK is $\frac{13}{49}$. Hence, the probability that all four cards are from different suits is

$$\left(\frac{13}{17}\right)\left(\frac{13}{25}\right)\left(\frac{13}{49}\right) = \frac{2197}{20{,}825} \approx 0.1055,$$

or almost 11%.

c. Use and explain the concepts of conditional probability and independence

1. What is conditional probability?

Conditional probability deals with probabilities of events happening under certain conditions, i.e., when certain information is known. The notation $P(A|B)$ means the probability of event A happening when event B has already happened. The basic formula is:

$$P(A|B) = \frac{P(A \cap B)}{P(B)}.$$

2. How is conditional probability used?

One common example where conditional probability is important lies in medical testing. For instance, suppose that there is an HIV test that is 95% accurate, meaning that in 95% of tests, the test results match the actual HIV status of the subject. Now suppose that you take an HIV test and the result comes back positive. What is the likelihood that you have HIV?

It might surprise you to know that the answer is less than 95%, and that in fact, the answer depends on the actual percentage of the population that has HIV. In order to make the numbers easier, let's assume that the probability that a randomly chosen individual in the population has HIV is 1%. We will now calculate the probability of a false positive test result. Let's assume that 1 million people take the HIV test.

(a) How many of those people actually have HIV? How many people do not have HIV?

ANS: Since we are assuming that 1% of the population has HIV, 10,000 have HIV, which means that 990,000 do not have HIV.

(b) Of those that have HIV, how many tested positive? (That is, how many true positives were there?)

ANS: Of those that have HIV, 95% of them got a test score which matched their status. So, there were 9,500 true positive test results.

(c) Of those that do not have HIV, how many tested positive? (That is, how many false positives were there?)

ANS: Again, 95% obtained a test result that matched their status. So, 5% got a false reading, for a total of $(0.05)(990,000) = 49{,}500$ false positive test results.

(d) Looking at the previous two answers, how many total positive test results were there?

ANS: There were $9{,}500 + 49{,}500 = 59{,}000$ total positive test results.

(e) What is the probability that a given positive test result is false?

ANS: The probability that a given positive test result is false is therefore $\dfrac{49{,}500}{59{,}000} \approx 0.839$, or almost 84%.

In the language of conditional probability, we would say that the probability that a person is HIV negative, given a positive test result, is 0.839 or 83.9% . This may seem counterintuitive, but there are far more false positive test results in this artificial example than there are true positive test results.

3. How does independence relate to conditional probability?

Recall that we defined two events A and B as independent if $P(A \cap B) = P(A)P(B)$. This means that we can simplify the formula for $P(A|B)$ to get just $P(A)$. This makes sense, because it's like saying that the conditional probability of A happening given that B happens is just the same as the probability of A happening on its own. This seems to capture the idea of A being independent from B.

4. Sample Problems

(a) In the previous example, we said that the HIV test was 95% accurate. State what this means in terms of conditional probability.

(b) In the HIV example, find $P(T+)$, the probability of a positive test result.

(c) In the HIV example, are the probability of getting a positive test result and the probability of being HIV positive independent events?

(d) If two dice are rolled, find the probability that their sum is 8, given that each die has an even number showing.

(e) Flip two coins. What is the probability that both are heads, given that at least one of them is heads?

5. Answers to Sample Problems

(a) In the previous example, we said that the HIV test was 95% accurate. State what this means in terms of conditional probability.

This means that the probability of getting a positive test result, given that the person is HIV+, is 95%. It also means that the probability of getting a negative test result, given that the person is HIV-, is 95%. (In practice, these two probabilities might not be the same for a given test. Ask your health care provider for more information if you are curious to know more about the accuracy of medical tests. I am NOT a medical professional!)

(b) In the HIV example, find $P(T+)$, the probability of a positive test result.

Method #1: There were a total of 59,000 positive test results out of 1,000,000 tests. So, the probability of getting a positive test result is 0.059. This means that 5.9% of the people taking the test got a positive test result.

Method #2: We will use the basic formula twice. Notice that

$$P(T+\,|+) = \frac{P(T+\cap+)}{P(+)}, \text{ and } P(+|T+) = \frac{P(+\cap T+)}{P(T+)}.$$

From these two equations, it follows that $P(T+\,|+)P(+) = P(+|T+)P(T+)$, because both sides are equal to $P(T+\cap+)$. We know that $P(T+\,|+) = 0.95$ and $P(+) = 0.01$, and we found in the example above that $P(+|T+)$, the probability of being HIV+ given a positive test result, is $\frac{9{,}500}{59{,}000} \approx 0.161$. Putting all this together, we get

$$P(T+) = \frac{P(T+\,|+)P(+)}{P(+|T+)} = \frac{(0.95)(0.01)}{0.161} = 0.059.$$

(c) In the HIV example, are the probability of getting a positive test result and the probability of being HIV positive independent events?

No. We can see this by comparing $P(+)$ with $P(+|T+)$. If these events are independent, then these probabilities should be the same. We are given $P(+) = 0.01$. However, we found out that $P(+|T+) = 0.161$ above. It also doesn't make sense that these events would be independent. One would expect a relationship between HIV status and the outcome of the HIV test.

(d) If two dice are rolled, find the probability that their sum is 8, given that each die has an even number showing.

Method #1: If we know that there are two even numbers showing, then the only possibilities for each die are 2, 4, 6. The following table lists the sums in each case.

	2	4	6
2	4	6	8
4	6	8	10
6	8	10	12

So the only possible sums are 4, 6, 8, 10, and 12. Their conditional probabilities can be calculated directly by counting up the number of times each sum occurs, and then dividing by the total number of outcomes in this reduced sample space.

sum	4	6	8	10	12
prob	$\frac{1}{9}$	$\frac{2}{9}$	$\frac{3}{9}$	$\frac{2}{9}$	$\frac{1}{9}$

So, the probability of getting an 8, given that there are two even numbers showing, is $\frac{1}{3}$.

Method #2: Let A be the event that the dice add up to 8. Let B be the event that each die has an even number showing. Then $P(A \cap B) = \frac{3}{36} = \frac{1}{12}$ and $P(B) = \frac{1}{4}$. Therefore,

$$P(A|B) = \frac{1/12}{1/4} = \frac{1}{3}.$$

(e) Flip two coins. What is the probability that both are heads, given that at least one of them is heads?

Method #1: Since we know that at least one of the two coins was heads, the only possibilities are: HH, HT, and TH, each of which is equally likely. So, the probability that both are heads is $\frac{1}{3}$.

Method #2: Let A be the event of getting two heads and let B be the event of getting at least one head. Then $P(A \cap B) = \frac{1}{4}$ and $P(B) = \frac{3}{4}$. Therefore,

$$P(A|B) = \frac{1/4}{3/4} = \frac{1}{3}.$$

d. Compute and interpret the probability of an outcome, including the probabilities of compound events in a uniform probability model

e. Use normal, binomial, and exponential distributions to solve and interpret probability problems

1. What are some ways to interpret the probability of an outcome?

   As we have seen already, probabilities can be interpreted as a ratio. The first part of the ratio is the number of events in which a desired outcome occurs, while the second part of the ratio is the total number of events. For example, the probability of rolling a 7 on two dice is $\frac{1}{6}$ because, in six of the 36 possible rolls, the two dice add up to 7.

   Probability can also be interpreted as the likelihood of a given event occurring on a given trial. For example, if you toss a coin, you would expect a heads in about half of all independent trials.

2. What is a compound event?

   Let's use the definition that a compound event is made up of two or more events, with conjunctions "and" or "or." For example, we could calculate the probability that when rolling two dice, we obtain a sum that is even AND each of the two dice is odd. In addition, we could calculate the probability of rolling an even number OR a 3 when rolling one die. We will find these probabilities below.

3. What are some ways to compute the probability of a compound event in a uniform probability model?

   Before we describe some methods, let's revisit independent events and mutually exclusive events.

   Recall that if two events A and B are independent, then the probability of both events occurring is the product of their individual probabilities: $P(A \cap B) = P(A)P(B)$. If the events are not independent, then one method could be to list all the possible outcomes in the compound sample space, and count how many times both A and B occur. In our first example above, the events A (rolling a sum that is even) and B (rolling two odd numbers) are not independent. (See Sample Problems.) Notice that $B \subseteq A$; in other words, if we roll two odd numbers, then we certainly have rolled an even sum. So $P(A \cap B) = P(B)$ in this case.

   The probability of rolling an odd number on one die is $\frac{1}{2}$. Hence the probability of rolling an odd number on two (independent) dice is $\frac{1}{4}$. Therefore, there is a 25% chance that when rolling two dice, you will get an even number and the numbers on the two dice will be odd.

Recall that if two events are mutually exclusive, then the probability of either one happening is the sum of their individual probabilities: $P(A \cup B) = P(A) + P(B)$. If the events are not mutually exclusive, then $P(A \cup B) = P(A) + P(B) - P(A \cap B)$. In our second example above, the events are mutually exclusive. If you roll a 3, then your roll cannot also be an even number. The probability of rolling an even number is $\frac{1}{2}$. The probability of rolling a 3 is $\frac{1}{6}$. So the probability of rolling an even number or a 3 is $\frac{1}{2} + \frac{1}{6} = \frac{2}{3}$.

More examples can be found in the sample problems.

4. What is the normal distribution? When and how is it used?

The normal distribution (or bell curve) is very important in statistics, as we will see later. For the purposes of probability, the normal curve is centered at the mean value of your variable and the standard deviation is the horizontal distance from the center to the steepest point on the curve (inflection point). See section **4.2.b** for more information about standard deviation.

Probabilities are equal to areas under the bell curve and are interpreted using the 68-95-99.7 rule: approximately 68% of the area under the curve lies within one standard deviation of the mean, 95% within two standard deviations, and 99.7% within three standard deviations. For an example, suppose that heights of adult men in the US are distributed normally with mean 178cm and standard deviation 7cm. This means that about 68% of adult men in the US have heights between 171cm and 185cm (178 ± 7), 95% are between 164cm and 192cm tall (178 ± 14) and only 0.3% are shorter than 157cm or taller than 199cm (178 ± 21).

5. What is the binomial distribution? When and how is it used?

The binomial distribution is used when you have several independent trials, each with the same probability of "success," such as flipping a coin several times, or rolling a die several times and looking for a specific value. Here, we use the binomial distribution to find $B(n, k, p)$, the probability of having k successes in n trials, if each trial's probability of success is p. The formula is:

$$B(n, k, p) = {}_nC_k \, p^k (1 - p)^{n-k}.$$

As an example, the probability of getting three heads when you flip a coin ten times is $B(10, 3, 0.5) = {}_{10}C_3(0.5)^3(0.5)^7 = \frac{120}{1024} \approx 0.117$, or almost 12%. The probability of getting 6 heads when you flip a coin 20 times is $B(20, 6, 0.5) \approx 0.037$, which is less than 4%.

As another example, the probability of rolling exactly two 6s when rolling 3 dice is $B(3, 2, \frac{1}{6}) = {}_3C_2(\frac{1}{6})^2(\frac{5}{6}) = \frac{15}{216} = \frac{5}{72} \approx 0.0694$.

6. What is the exponential distribution? When and how is it used?

Suppose there is an event that happens randomly but at a constant average rate. Then the time between events is a random variable that is exponentially distributed. For example, if you are studying a radioactive element, and you are measuring the time between two decay events, you would find that the time between events follows the exponential distribution.

The time you have to wait until your next phone call might also be exponentially distributed (assuming that phone calls occur randomly, but with a constant average rate). The probability distribution is exponential. The probability of waiting longer than x is e^{-rx}, where r is the average rate of the process. The expected wait time is $\frac{1}{r}$. See section **f** for more on expected values.

As an example, if you work at a job where you answer phones, and if calls come in randomly but are exponentially distributed at an average rate of 20 calls per hour, then the call rate is $r = \frac{1}{3}$ of a call per minute. So your average wait time between calls would be 3 minutes. Also, the probability of waiting longer than five minutes for your next call would be $e^{-5/3} \approx 0.1889$, or almost 19%.

7. Sample Problems

   (a) When the weather report says a 20% chance of rain tomorrow, what does that mean?

   (b) When rolling two dice, why are the events "rolling an even sum" and "rolling two odd numbers" NOT independent?

   (c) Find probabilities for the following events. Assume a standard 52-card deck with four suits of 13 cards each.

      i. choosing a card that is red and a face card (Jack, Queen, or King)

      ii. choosing one card from each of two identical decks, and obtaining a sum that is even and each card is a 2, a 3, or a 4

      iii. choosing a card that is red or a face card

      iv. choosing a card that is either a spade or a red face card

   (d) What does it mean to say that the probability of a positive test result, given that the subject has HIV, is 95%?

   (e) Find the probability of getting less than two heads on six coin tosses.

   (f) We saw earlier that the probability of getting three heads on ten coin tosses was almost 12%, while the probability of getting six heads on twenty coin tosses was less than 4%. Why aren't these two binomial probabilities equal? After all, both represent a 30% heads rate on the coin.

   (g) Find the probability of getting exactly 30 heads on 100 coin tosses.

   (h) Find the probability of rolling exactly four 6s when rolling six dice.

   (i) Scores on a common IQ test are normally distributed with mean 100 and about 68% of people scoring between 85 and 115. What is the standard deviation of the scores on this test?

   (j) Suppose that the heights of US women (age 18-24) are distributed normally with mean 65.5in and standard deviation 2.5in. Find the percentage of US women (age 18-24) who are between 65.5in and 70.5in.

   (k) Suppose that the bus service in your town is so bad that the busses come at random and their arrivals at your bus stop are exponentially distributed, with an average rate of four busses every hour. You arrive at the bus stop at 7am.

    i. How long would you expect to wait for a bus?

    ii. What is the probability that you will have to wait 45 minutes before a bus comes?

8. Answers to Sample Problems

(a) When the weather report says a 20% chance of rain tomorrow, what does that mean?

This means that historically, similar climate conditions have led to rainfall in about 20% of previous cases.

(b) When rolling two dice, why are the events "rolling an even sum" and "rolling two odd numbers" NOT independent?

These events are not independent because the probability of rolling an even sum is $\frac{1}{2}$, while the probability of rolling an even sum, given that the two dice are odd, is 1. Since these two probabilities are different, these two events are NOT independent.

(c) Find probabilities for the following events. Assume a standard 52-card deck with four suits of 13 cards each.

    i. choosing a card that is red and a face card (Jack, Queen, or King). $\frac{3}{26}$. There are six red face cards in the deck. Thus the probability of choosing one is $\frac{6}{52} = \frac{3}{26}$. Or, put another way, the probability of choosing a red card is $\frac{1}{2}$, and the probability of choosing a face card is $\frac{3}{13}$. Since these are independent events, the probability of both happening is the product: $\frac{3}{26}$.

    ii. choosing one card from each of two identical decks, and obtaining a sum that is even and each card is a 2, a 3, or a 4. $\frac{5}{169}$. Notice that the suits don't really matter here. So let's reduce the problem to two 13-card decks, and ask the same question. This will not change the probability of our compound event. Choosing one card from each deck gives 169 possibilities for the two cards: $(A, A), (A, 2), (A, 3), \ldots, (A, K), (2, A), (2, 2), \ldots, (K, K)$. Of these 169 possible choices, only 5 meet the two criteria: $(2, 2), (2, 4), (3, 3), (4, 2), (4, 4)$. So the probability is $\frac{5}{169}$.

    iii. choosing a card that is red or a face card. $\frac{8}{13}$. These events are not mutually exclusive (There are red face cards.), and so we use the formula: $P(A \cup B) = P(A) + P(B) - P(A \cap B)$. We found the probability of choosing a red face card above: $\frac{3}{26}$. We know the probability of choosing a red card is $\frac{1}{2}$, and the probability of choosing a face card is $\frac{3}{13}$, and so we find that the probability of choosing a card that is red or a face card is

$$\frac{1}{2} + \frac{3}{13} - \frac{3}{26} = \frac{13 + 6 - 3}{26} = \frac{16}{26} = \frac{8}{13}.$$

iv. choosing a card that is either a spade or a red face card. $\dfrac{19}{52}$. These events are mutually exclusive. (There are no red spades.) The probability of choosing a spade is $\dfrac{1}{4}$ and the probability of choosing a red face card is $\dfrac{3}{26}$. So the probability of selecting a spade or a red face card is

$$\frac{1}{4} + \frac{3}{26} = \frac{13+6}{52} = \frac{19}{52}.$$

(d) What does it mean to say that the probability of a positive test result, given that the subject has HIV, is 95%?

This means that if a person has HIV and takes this test repeatedly, they will receive a positive test result in about 95% of trials. It also means that if 100 independent people had HIV and they each took this HIV test, the expected number of positive test results would be 95. (See expected values in the next section.)

(e) Find the probability of getting less than two heads on six coin tosses.

We can find this probability by adding the probability of getting zero heads to the probability of getting one head.

$$B(6, 0, 0.5) + B(6, 1, 0.5) = (0.5)^6 + 6(0.5)^6 = 0.109375,$$

or about 11%.

(f) We saw earlier that the probability of getting three heads on ten coin tosses was almost 12%, while the probability of getting six heads on twenty coin tosses was less than 4%. Why aren't these two binomial probabilities equal? After all, both represent a 30% heads rate on the coin.

These two numbers are not equal because of the way probability works in a large number of trials. In only ten trials, getting three heads is not too unlikely. If only two more coin tosses had gone the other way, then you would have had exactly 50% heads. But with twenty coin tosses, getting six heads means that you are four coin tosses away from 50%, which is less likely to happen. Notice in the next question how small the probability is of getting 30 heads out of 100 coin tosses. As the number of trials increases, we expect the number of heads to get closer and closer to 50%.

(g) Find the probability of getting exactly 30 heads on 100 coin tosses.

$$B(100, 30, 0.5) = {}_{100}C_{30}(0.5)^{100} \approx 0.00002317.$$

(h) Find the probability of rolling exactly four 6s when rolling six dice.

$$B\left(6, 4, \frac{1}{6}\right) = {}_6C_4 \left(\frac{1}{6}\right)^4 \left(\frac{5}{6}\right)^2 \approx 0.0080.$$

(i) Scores on a common IQ test are normally distributed with mean 100 and about 68% of people scoring between 85 and 115. What is the standard deviation of the scores on this test? 15

(j) Suppose that the heights of US women (age 18-24) are distributed normally with mean 65.5in and standard deviation 2.5in. Find the percentage of US women (age 18-24) who are between 65.5in and 70.5in.

Since the standard deviation is 2.5in, about 95% of women are between 60.5in and 70.5in tall. Assuming from the symmetry of the normal distribution that half of these are above the mean and half are below, 47.5% of women are between 65.5in and 70.5in tall.

(k) Suppose that the bus service in your town is so bad that the busses come at random and their arrivals at your bus stop are exponentially distributed, with an average rate of four busses every hour. You arrive at the bus stop at 7am.

  i. How long would you expect to wait for a bus? 15 minutes

  ii. What is the probability that you will have to wait 45 minutes before a bus comes? About 5%. Since $r = \frac{1}{15}$, we have $e^{-45/15} = e^{-3} \approx 0.0498$, or about 5%.

f. Calculate expected values and use them to solve problems and evaluate outcomes of decisions

1. What does "expected value" mean? How do you interpret expected value?

   The expected value of a random variable is like the average of all possible values of that variable, weighted by the probability of each value's occurrence. For example, if we roll a fair die (with probability $\frac{1}{6}$ of attaining each roll from 1 to 6), then the expected value is the average of the numbers 1 through 6, which is 3.5.

   As for interpretation, you can think of the expected value as the long-term mean (or average) for the values of the random variable. Notice in our example of a die that the expected value is 3.5. This is not one of the possible rolls of a die. You could roll a 3 or a 4, but not a 3.5. However, in the long run, if you kept rolling the die and kept averaging the numbers you obtained, your average would approach 3.5. The more rolls, the closer to 3.5 your average would eventually become.

2. How do you calculate expected value?

   For finite probability, we calculate expected value by calculating the weighted average of all outcomes. So, if there are n outcomes in our sample space, and the probability of outcome x_i is p_i, then the expected value (denoted $\bar{x}$) is

   $$\bar{x} = \sum_{i=1}^{n} p_i x_i.$$

   (For continuous random variables, the definition requires calculus and integration: $\bar{x} = \int x p(x) \, dx$, where the integral ranges over all possible values of the variable x, and $p(x)$ represents the probability distribution function. See section **4.2.a** and **4.2.b** for more information about continuous random variables.)

   As an example, we double-check the calculation for rolling one die:

   $$\bar{x} = (1)\left(\frac{1}{6}\right) + (2)\left(\frac{1}{6}\right) + (3)\left(\frac{1}{6}\right) + (4)\left(\frac{1}{6}\right) + (5)\left(\frac{1}{6}\right) + (6)\left(\frac{1}{6}\right) = \frac{21}{6} = \frac{7}{2} = 3.5.$$

As a non-uniform example, suppose we have an unfair die that rolls 1 through 5 each with probability $\frac{1}{10}$, and rolls a six with probability $\frac{1}{2}$. (Notice the total probability of all outcomes has to be 1.) What is the expected value for this die?

$$\bar{x} = (1)\left(\frac{1}{10}\right) + (2)\left(\frac{1}{10}\right) + (3)\left(\frac{1}{10}\right) + (4)\left(\frac{1}{10}\right) + (5)\left(\frac{1}{10}\right) + (6)\left(\frac{1}{2}\right) = \frac{45}{10} = \frac{9}{2} = 4.5.$$

If we were to roll this die many times, we would expect a higher average than if we were to roll a fair die the same number of times. The expected value quantifies that by pointing out than *on average*, each roll of the unfair die is one more than each roll of the fair die.

3. How can expected value help you evaluate outcomes of decisions?

   We will talk about two applications of expected value: casinos and lotteries. In a casino, the player has an expected value (of winnings) that is slightly lower than the cost to play the game. This means, in the long run, the casino will make money regardless of who is playing the game. For example, let's consider a roulette wheel that has the numbers 1 through 36 (half of which are red and half of which are black) and two green spaces: 0, and 00. The payout for betting on red or black is 100%. If you bet $10 on red and the wheel comes up red, you win $20 ($10 in addition to your initial $10 bet). But if the wheel doesn't come up red, then you win $0. What is the expected value of a $10 bet on red?

   $$(20)\left(\frac{18}{38}\right) + (0)\left(\frac{20}{38}\right) \approx 9.47.$$

   This means that on average, the casino will win about 53 cents on each $10 bet on red. With many people betting and many roulette wheels operating, the casino will make money.

   A lottery example is similar. Suppose you are trying to win a lottery where you have to pick six numbers from 1 to 50. What is the probability that you will pick the winning numbers at random? Well, there are $_{50}C_6$, or 15,890,700 possibilities. So the probability of winning is $\frac{1}{15,890,700}$.

   How does expected value play a role? Well, if you know what the jackpot prize value is, you can calculate your expected value of buying a ticket. Then you can see if it's worth your while to purchase a ticket. Let's say each ticket costs $2 and the jackpot is $28.5 million. Should you buy a ticket?

   Calculating the expected value in this case, we would get $\frac{28,000,000}{15,890,700} \approx 1.76$. So, your two dollar tickets would win $1.76 on average. So probably you wouldn't buy a ticket. Or maybe you're feeling lucky ....

4. Sample Problems

   (a) In addition to the regular six-sided die, some games (like Dungeons and Dragons) use other regular polyhedra as dice, having four, eight, twelve, and twenty sides, each numbered consecutively, starting with 1. Calculate the expected value for each of these dice. What is the expected value for rolling an n-sided die?

(b) Suppose you roll three six-sided dice at once. What is the expected number of 6s you roll? (Hint: start by calculating the probability of rolling zero, one, two, or three sixes.)

(c) Suppose that you have an unfair die that rolls 1 and 2 each with probability $\frac{1}{4}$. Then it rolls 3, 4, 5, and 6 each with probability $\frac{1}{8}$. Find the expected value of this die.

(d) Consider a game where you pay \$1 to roll three six-sided dice. You win \$10 if all three dice show a 6. Otherwise, you win \$2 for each 6 showing. Would you win money in the long run if you played this game?

(e) (This classic problem, called the St. Petersburg Paradox, has an interesting expected value.) Consider a game where you win \$2 if you toss a coin and it comes up heads. If not, you toss a coin a second time and you win \$4 if it comes up heads. If not, you toss the coin again and win \$8 if it comes up heads. If not, you toss the coin again and win \$16 if it comes up heads. The game continues until the first heads is obtained. So, if you obtain your first heads on the k-th toss, then you get paid 2^k dollars. Suppose the casino is charging \$20 to play the game. Would you win money in the long run if you played this game?

5. Answers to Sample Problems

(a) In addition to the regular six-sided die, some games (like Dungeons and Dragons) use other regular polyhedra as dice, having four, eight, twelve, and twenty sides, each numbered consecutively, starting with 1. Calculate the expected value for each of these dice. What is the expected value for rolling an n-sided die?

The four-sided die has an expected roll of 2.5; the eight-sided die, 4.5; the twelve-sided die, 6.5; the twenty-sided die, 10.5. In general, an n-sided die would have an expected roll of $\frac{n+1}{2}$.

(b) Suppose you roll three six-sided dice at once. What is the expected number of 6s you roll? (Hint: start by calculating the probability of rolling zero, one, two, or three sixes.) $\frac{1}{2}$.

Using the binomial formula, we can calculate the probability of zero, one, two, and three 6s. The probability of zero 6s is $B(3, 0, \frac{1}{6}) = {}_3C_0(\frac{1}{6})^0(\frac{5}{6})^3 = (\frac{5}{6})^3 \approx 0.5787$. Similarly, the probability of one 6 is $B(3, 1, \frac{1}{6}) \approx 0.3472$. The probability of two 6s is $B(3, 2, \frac{1}{6}) \approx 0.0694$. And lastly, the probability of three 6s is $B(3, 3, \frac{1}{6}) = (\frac{1}{6})^3 = 0.0046$. The expected number of sixes is thus approximately

$$(0)(0.5787) + (1)(0.3472) + (2)(0.0694) + (3)(0.0046) = 0.4998.$$

Now, if we had kept the exact values, rather than rounded off at each stage, we would have gotten exactly 0.5, or $\frac{1}{2}$. In other words, if you roll six dice, you would expect about one 6. So if you roll three dice, you would expect $\frac{1}{2}$ of a 6 *on average.*

(c) Suppose that you have an unfair die that rolls 1 and 2 each with probability $\frac{1}{4}$. Then it rolls 3, 4, 5, and 6 each with probability $\frac{1}{8}$. Find the expected value of this die. 3.

$$(1)\left(\frac{1}{4}\right) + (2)\left(\frac{1}{4}\right) + (3)\left(\frac{1}{8}\right) + (4)\left(\frac{1}{8}\right) + (5)\left(\frac{1}{8}\right) + (6)\left(\frac{1}{8}\right) = \frac{3}{4} + \frac{18}{8} = \frac{12}{4} = 3.$$

(d) Consider a game where you pay \$1 to roll three six-sided dice. You win \$10 if all three dice show a 6. Otherwise, you win \$2 for each 6 showing. Would you win money in the long run if you played this game? Yes. Using the approximate probabilities above, we can estimate our expected winnings:

$$(10)(0.0046) + (4)(0.0694) + (2)(0.3472) = 1.018.$$

So, yes, you would win money in the long run because you would expect to win about 1.8 cents on average each time you play it. The expected winnings are greater than the cost of the game.

(e) (This classic problem, called the St. Petersburg Paradox, has an interesting expected value.) Consider a game where you win \$2 if you toss a coin and it comes up heads. If not, you toss a coin a second time and you win \$4 if it comes up heads. If not, you toss the coin again and win \$8 if it comes up heads. If not, you toss the coin again and win \$16 if it comes up heads. The game continues until the first heads is obtained. So, if you obtain your first heads on the k-th toss, then you get paid 2^k dollars. Suppose the casino is charging \$20 to play the game. Would you win money in the long run if you played this game? Yes.

Let's look at the expected value of winning. You win \$2 if you get a heads on the first toss, \$4 if you get a tails first, then a heads, \$8 if you get two tails followed by a heads, etc. So your expected winnings are:

$$(2)\left(\frac{1}{2}\right) + (4)\left(\frac{1}{4}\right) + (8)\left(\frac{1}{8}\right) + \ldots = 1 + 1 + 1 + \ldots,$$

which is infinite! So yes, you should play this game at any price! (Curiously, this problem has been studied since about 1700. Some interesting resolutions of this paradox can be found online.) Practically, of course, the casino could only pay out a certain finite limit, and so there would be some gamblers that the casino couldn't afford to pay.

Curiously, if you calculate the probability that you get a heads on one of the first four rolls, you would get $\frac{15}{16}$. So that means that you would win less than \$20 in most of your games. So if you play this game, be prepared to lose a lot of money before you see a big win.

4.2 Statistics

a. Compute and interpret the mean and median of both discrete and continuous distributions

1. What is a discrete distribution? What is a continuous distribution?

   A discrete distribution describes a variable that can only take on discrete values, that is, values which are separated by some finite distance, such as natural numbers. In a continuous distribution, the variable can take on any real number value over some interval.

2. What notation will we be using?

   In the following discrete distributions, we will assume that our data set is finite: $\{x_1, x_2, \ldots, x_n\}$. In the continuous distributions, we will assume that our data set is infinite: x is a real number. In each case, we will assume that our random variable x has a probability density function given by $p(x)$.

   For $p(x)$ to be a discrete probability density function, we must have $p(x_i) \geq 0$ (meaning the probability of the variable taking the value x_i is non-negative) and $\sum_{i=1}^{n} p(x_i) = 1$ (meaning the probability that the variable takes a value in the set $\{x_1, x_2, \ldots, x_n\}$ is 100%).

   For $p(x)$ to be a continuous probability density function, we must have $p(x) \geq 0$ for all values of x (meaning that probability of the variable taking the value x is non-negative) and $\int_{-\infty}^{\infty} p(x)\,dx = 1$ (meaning that the probability that the variable takes a value between negative and positive infinity is 100%).

3. What is the mean of a discrete distribution? What is the mean of a continuous distribution?

   The mean of discrete data is usually denoted μ and is equal to $\sum_{i=1}^{n} p(x_i)x_i$. If the data are uniformly distributed, then $\mu = \frac{1}{n} \sum_{i=1}^{n} x_i = \frac{x_1 + x_2 + \ldots + x_n}{n}$.

   The mean of a continuous distribution is the "center of mass" or "balancing point" of the distribution. In calculus, the mean is $\mu = \int_{-\infty}^{\infty} xp(x)\,dx$.

   Another name for the mean is the "average" or "expected" value.

4. What is the median of a discrete distribution? What is the median of a continuous distribution?

   The median of a uniform discrete distribution is the middle value, when all the values are listed in order, except that the median is not counted in either half of the data. So, half (or almost half) of the data points lie below the median and half above. For example, in $\{1, 2, 4, 7, 9\}$, the median is 4. In $\{1, 2, 4, 7, 9, 11\}$, the median is 5.5, the average of 4 and 7.

In a continuous distribution, the median is the x-value which separates the area under the distribution in half. In calculus terms, M is the median if and only if $\int_{-\infty}^{M} p(x)\,dx = \frac{1}{2}$.

5. Sample Problems

   (a) Suppose that your driver's license number is 5686788. Find the mean and median of the digits in your driver's license.

   (b) Assume that you have five data points: 1, 4, 5, 7, and x, where we do not know x, but we do know that $3 \le x \le 13$.

      i. What are the possible values of the mean of this data?

      ii. What are the possible values of the median of this data?

   (c) List data in which the mean is equal to the median.

   (d) List data in which the mean is greater than the median.

   (e) In real estate, why are median home prices listed, rather than mean home prices?

6. Answers to Sample Problems

   (a) Suppose that your driver's license number is 5686788. Find the mean and median of the digits in your driver's license.
   The mean is $\frac{1}{7}(5 + 6 + 8 + 6 + 7 + 8 + 8) = \frac{48}{7} \approx 6.86$. The median is 7.

   (b) Assume that you have five data points: 1, 4, 5, 7, and x, where we do not know x, but we do know that $3 \le x \le 13$.

      i. What are the possible values of the mean of this data? The mean is $\frac{17+x}{5}$, which will lie between 4 and 6.

      ii. What are the possible values of the median of this data? The median is either 4 (if $x \le 4$), 5 if ($x \ge 5$), or x (if $4 < x < 5$).

   (c) List data in which the mean is equal to the median. Answers may vary. The data set $\{1, 2, 3\}$ has mean 2 and median 2.

   (d) List data in which the mean is greater than the median. Answers may vary. The data set $\{1, 2, 6\}$ has mean 3 and median 2.

   (e) In real estate, why are median home prices listed, rather than mean home prices? The reason that median home prices are listed is that the median is a better measure of the typical home price in this case. Home prices are rarely normally distributed. Instead, there are often several homes near the lower end of the market, and a few very expensive homes (ranches, farms, large estates, etc.). These few expensive homes could noticeably raise the mean home price, but they would have little effect on the median home price.

b. Compute and interpret quartiles, range, interquartile range, and standard deviation of both discrete and continuous distributions

1. What are the quartiles of a discrete distribution? ...of a continuous distribution?

   In both discrete and continuous distributions, the first quartile is the median of the set of data points that are less than the original median. The third quartile is the median of the set of data points that are bigger than the original median. [The original median is also called the second quartile.] This means that one-fourth of the data lies below the first quartile, one-fourth between the first quartile and the original median, one-fourth between the original median and the third quartile, and one-fourth above the third quartile.

2. What is the range of a discrete distribution? ...of a continuous distribution?

   The range of a discrete distribution is the maximum value of the data minus the minimum value. In a continuous distribution, the range is the difference between the maximum and minimum x-values for which $p(x) > 0$. The range of a distribution can be infinite, but the range of a finite discrete distribution is finite.

3. What is the interquartile range of a discrete distribution? ...of a continuous distribution?

   In each case, the interquartile range (IQR) of a distribution is the range between the first and third quartiles. You could loosely call it the range in which the "middle half" of the data occurs, since one-fourth of the data would be less than the first quartile, and one-fourth would be greater than the third quartile. The IQR is often used in a common definition of "outliers," namely, an *outlier* is a data point that lies either more than 1.5(IQR) above the third quartile or less than 1.5(IQR) below the first quartile.

4. What is the standard deviation of a discrete distribution? ...of a continuous distribution?

   Before defining standard deviation, we define variance, which is a measure of how spread out your data are. The variance of a set of discrete data with mean μ is $\sum_{i=1}^{n} p(x_i)(x_i - \mu)^2$. If the data are uniformly distributed, then the variance is $\frac{1}{n} \sum_{i=1}^{n} (x_i - \mu)^2$.

   The variance of a continuous variable with mean μ is $\int_{-\infty}^{\infty} (x - \mu)^2 p(x) \, dx$.

   The standard deviation is the square root of the variance. It is another commonly used measure for the spread of your data. Recall from section **4.1.e** that if data is normally distributed, then about 68% of the population lies within one standard deviation from the mean, 95% within two standard deviations, and 99.7% within three standard deviations.

5. Sample Problems

   (a) Why would someone want to take the square root of the variance?

   (b) Consider the data sets $\{1, 2, 3, 4, 3, 2, 1\}$ and $\{10, 20, 30, 40, 30, 20, 10\}$. Which data set has a larger standard deviation? Why?

   (c) If your data is $\{1, 3, 4, 4, 6, 9, 12, 13, 13, 14, 15, 15\}$, then list the mean, median, quartiles, range, and IQR.

(d) If you add 100 to each element in the set above, then find the new mean, median, quartiles, range, and IQR. Would the standard deviation of your new set be different from its value in the old set? Why or why not?

(e) Calculate the mean and standard deviation of the probability distribution of a six-sided die.

6. Answers to Sample Problems

(a) Why would someone want to take the square root of the variance? One reason could be so that the standard deviation has the same units as the quantity being measured. If we are measuring height in centimeters, the variance would be in square centimeters. By taking the square root, the standard deviation has units of centimeters, like the height.

(b) Consider the data sets $\{1, 2, 3, 4, 3, 2, 1\}$ and $\{10, 20, 30, 40, 30, 20, 10\}$. Which data set has a larger standard deviation? Why?

From the formula for variance, it follows that the variance of the second set is 100 times larger than the variance of the first set because the data points are ten times larger. So, the standard deviation of the second set will be ten times larger than the standard deviation of the first set.

(c) If your data is $\{1, 3, 4, 4, 6, 9, 12, 13, 13, 14, 15, 15\}$, then list the mean, median, quartiles, range, and IQR.

The mean is $\frac{109}{12} \approx 9.08$. The median is 10.5. The first quartile is 4 and the third quartile is 13.5. The range is $15 - 1 = 14$. The IQR is $13.5 - 4 = 9.5$.

(d) If you add 100 to each element in the set above, then find the new mean, median, quartiles, range, and IQR. Would the standard deviation of your new set be different from its value in the old set? Why or why not?

The new mean, median, and quartiles would be increased by 100. The new range would be the same as the old range, and the new IQR would also be the same as the old one. The standard deviation would not be changed, since it measures how spread out the data are. Adding 100 to each data point does not spread them out at all. Looking at the formula for variance, you can see that if you add 100 to each x_i and to μ, then each difference $(x_i - \mu)$ is unchanged.

(e) Calculate the mean and standard deviation of the probability distribution of a six-sided die.

The mean is $\frac{1}{6}(1) + \frac{1}{6}(2) + \ldots + \frac{1}{6}(6) = \frac{21}{6} = 3.5$, which we found earlier as the expected value. The variance is thus

$$\frac{1}{6}\sum_{i=1}^{6}(i - 3.5)^2 = \frac{17.5}{6} = \frac{35}{12} \approx 2.92,$$

which means that the standard deviation is $\sqrt{\dfrac{35}{12}} \approx 1.71$.

c. Select and evaluate sampling methods appropriate to a task (e.g., random, systematic, cluster, convenience sampling) and display the results

1. What is a sample? What is a population?

   A sample is a subset of the population. Often you want to examine a sample because it is simpler than taking a census, which involves examining the entire population. This is really the fundamental question of inferential statistics: how do you extrapolate information from a sample to deduce information about a population?

   Let's talk about notation briefly. Most books use Greek letters (like μ and σ) to refer to *parameters*, i.e. pieces of information about the population as a whole. In contrast, they use Roman letters (like $\bar{x}$ or s_x) to refer to *statistics*, i.e. pieces of information that come from a sample of the population. The heart of inferential statistics lies in using statistics (from a sample) to infer information about parameters (of the population). For this reason, how you choose your sample is very important.

2. What are some different sampling methods?

   One familiar method is the Voluntary Response Sample, in which individuals are asked to respond if they wish. This is a form of convenience sampling, in which the people conducting the survey are surveying those individuals for whom it is convenient to do so. Such a sampling method is almost guaranteed to be biased.

   A Simple Random Sample (SRS) of n individuals from a population is defined to be a sample chosen in such a way that every subset of n individuals is equally likely to be chosen as the sample.

   A Stratified Random Sample is one in which the population is broken into groups (or strata), and then an SRS is chosen from each stratum and combined into the overall sample.

   An example of systematic sampling is perhaps to select every 25th item on a list and then put those items into your sample. That is, you are taking a systematic (not entirely random) approach to constructing the sample.

   Cluster sampling occurs when individuals are divided into clusters (often geographically), and then certain clusters are chosen at random to belong to the sample, (or individuals are chosen at random from the randomly-chosen clusters).

3. Which methods are appropriate for which situations?

   A lot of statistical sampling is driven by cost or time constraints. With sufficient resources, we would just survey the entire population for data. A stratified random sample or a cluster sample might be more appropriate than a simple random sample if you would like your sample to contain members of different groups. The stratification takes advantage of the assumption that individuals within a group are similar to each other, thereby eliminating the need to have a large sample from within each group.

   Convenience sampling is certainly convenient, but it rarely gives usable conclusions. Worse still is to ask people to participate in a certain survey, because it almost guarantees that the only responses to your survey will be from individuals with strong opinions.

4. How are data displayed?

   To display one-variable quantitative data, we use dot plots, histograms, stem and leaf plots, and box plots. To display one-variable categorical data, we use percentage counts, bar graphs, and pie charts. To display two-variable quantitative data, we often plot points on coordinate axes. The independent variable (if there is one) goes on the x-axis.

See section **g** below for more information on displaying one-variable data.

5. Sample Problems

   (a) Suppose that Congress decided to abolish the Census. Of the following, which sampling method would give Congress the best information about the US population?

      i. They should systematically contact every 500th Social Security Number holder and ask that person survey questions.

      ii. They should set up a phone line and a website for people to enter their census data because it will be most convenient.

      iii. They should combine some stratification with cluster sampling to try to obtain individuals from all sorts of different living situations.

      iv. They should take a simple random sample of the entire US population in order to be completely random.

   (b) Suppose that Johnny wants to determine which battery lasts longer: Battery A or Battery B. So Johnny goes down to the store and buys one package of Battery A and one of Battery B.

      i. What sampling method did Johnny use?

      ii. How could Johnny improve the validity of his results? (What would be a better way to sample?)

   (c) Big Giant News Corporation conducts an online poll after a recent political debate. They find that 65% favored candidate P, while 33% favored candidate Q, and 2% were undecided. Are these results reliable? Why or why not?

6. Answers to Sample Problems

   (a) Suppose that Congress decided to abolish the Census. Of the following, which sampling method would give Congress the best information about the US population?

      i. They should systematically contact every 500th Social Security Number holder and ask that person survey questions.

      ii. They should set up a phone line and a website for people to enter their census data because it will be most convenient.

      iii. They should combine some stratification with cluster sampling to try to obtain individuals from all sorts of different living situations.

      iv. They should take a simple random sample of the entire US population in order to be completely random.

ANS: iii. It is important to have data about people from all different walks of life in order to build a reliable data set. The systematic approach relies too heavily on Social Security Number, which may not be randomly assigned. Also, not everyone has a Social Security Number. Phone lines and web surveys are bad because not all people have a phone line or access to the web, and even those with access may not respond. An SRS might underrepresent certain groups, sort of like the way in which choosing a random sample of congress members might leave out the smaller states entirely.

(b) Suppose that Johnny wants to determine which battery lasts longer: Battery A or Battery B. So Johnny goes down to the store and buys one package of Battery A and one of Battery B.

    i. What sampling method did Johnny use? Johnny used a form of convenience sampling. He purchased batteries from a single nearby store.

    ii. How could Johnny improve the validity of his results? (What would be a better way to sample?) Johnny could at least sample different packages of batteries from different stores. Ideally, he could pick up a random selection of batteries from the factory. But he shouldn't tell them when he's coming. A dishonest battery manufacturer might give Johnny only their best batteries to be tested.

(c) Big Giant News Corporation conducts an online poll after a recent political debate. They find that 65% favored candidate P, while 33% favored candidate Q, and 2% were undecided. Are these results reliable? Why or why not?

Online polls (voluntary sampling polls) are rarely, if ever, reliable. People are far more likely to respond if they have a strong opinion on the subject and a strong desire to make their opinion known. Plus, they would have to have a computer with internet access. A more random sampling method would be better.

d. Apply the method of least squares to linear regression

1. What is linear regression?

Regression is done on scatterplots when you have an independent (explanatory) variable and a dependent (response) variable. Then you can find the equation of the regression line (or line of best fit) and use it to make predictions.

2. What is the method of least squares? How do you apply least squares to regression?

To find the line of best fit, we use the method of least squares, which minimizes the sum of the squares of the vertical distances of the data points to the line. For a discrete data set, $\{(x_1, y_1), (x_2, y_2), \ldots, (x_n, y_n)\}$, suppose the line of best fit is $y = mx + b$. Then the values of m and b are chosen to minimize

$$\sum_{i=1}^{n} (y_i - (mx_i + b))^2.$$

After some calculus, it follows that

$$m = \frac{\sum_{i=1}^{n}(x_i - \overline{x})(y_i - \overline{y})}{\sum_{i=1}^{n}(x_i - \overline{x})^2} \quad \text{and} \quad b = \overline{y} - m\overline{x}.$$

One consequence of these formulas is that the point $(\overline{x}, \overline{y})$ always lies on the regression line.

3. Sample Problems

   (a) Find the formula for the regression line through the following data:
       $\{(1,1),(2,2),(3,4),(4,5),(5,8)\}$.

   (b) Suppose that a class measured each student's armspan and height. Then they calculated the following least-squares regression line predicting armspan (y, in cm), given an individual's height (x, also in cm): $y = -42.7 + 1.3x$.

       i. Johnny is 180cm tall. What would you predict his armspan to be?

       ii. Suppose that the mean armspan of students in the class was 170.3cm. What, if anything, can be said about the mean height of students in the class?

4. Answers to Sample Problems

   (a) Find the formula for the regression line through the following data:
       $\{(1,1),(2,2),(3,4),(4,5),(5,8)\}$.

       First, we calculate $\bar{x} = 3$ and $\bar{y} = 4$. So, $(3,4)$ is on the regression line. Next, we have

       $$m = \frac{\sum_{i=1}^{5}(x_i - 3)(y_i - 4)}{\sum_{i=1}^{5}(x_i - 3)^2} = \frac{6 + 2 + 0 + 1 + 8}{4 + 1 + 0 + 1 + 4} = \frac{17}{10} = 1.7.$$

       Thus the y-intercept is $\bar{y} - m\bar{x} = 4 - (1.7)(3) = -1.1$. So the regression line is $y = 1.7x - 1.1$.

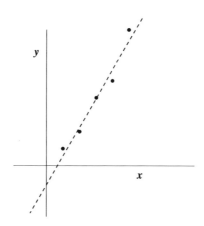

   (b) Suppose that a class measured each student's armspan and height. Then they calculated the following least-squares regression line predicting armspan (y, in cm), given an individual's height (x, also in cm): $y = -42.7 + 1.3x$.

       i. Johnny is 180cm tall. What would you predict his armspan to be? Using the formula, his armspan is predicted to be $-42.7 + 1.3(180) = 191.3$cm.

ii. Suppose that the mean armspan of students in the class was 170.3cm. What, if anything, can be said about the mean height of students in the class? We know that $(\overline{x}, \overline{y})$ is always on the regression line. So, if $\overline{y} = 170.3$, then

$$170.3 = -42.7 + 1.3\overline{x} \Rightarrow \overline{x} = \frac{170.3 + 42.7}{1.3} \approx 163.8\text{cm}.$$

So the average height of students in the class was 163.8cm.

e. Apply the chi-square test

1. What is the chi-square test?

The chi-square (χ^2 or X^2) test is a test of statistical inference, which means that you are evaluating how unlikely a certain data set would be under certain assumptions. See section **h** below for more examples of hypothesis testing. The chi-square test applies to two-way tables in which two categorical variables are being compared. The null hypothesis is that the two variables are not related. In that case, you would expect your population to be distributed a certain way throughout the table. The chi-square test statistic measures the difference between what you observed and what you would expect to observe if the variables were not related.

2. How do you apply the chi-square test?

To calculate X^2, you need to calculate the expected count within each cell of the table. If you are given a table of values, you can calculate the expected count in a cell via the formula

$$\text{expected count} = \frac{(\text{row total})(\text{column total})}{(\text{table total})}.$$

Then, summing over all the cells in the table, you calculate:

$$X^2 = \sum_{\text{all cells}} \frac{(\text{observed count} - \text{expected count})^2}{\text{expected count}}.$$

You also need to find the number of degrees of freedom,

$$df = (\#\text{ rows} - 1)(\#\text{ columns} - 1).$$

3. How do you interpret the chi-square test?

Once you have your test statistic, X^2 and your degrees of freedom, df, you can look up your p-value in a table (or on your calculator). This p-value is the probability of getting data as extreme as yours if the null hypothesis is true, that is, if there is no relationship between the two variables. So, a high p-value means that data as extreme as yours are very likely if the null hypothesis were true, and therefore there is no reason to disbelieve the null hypothesis. A low p-value means that data as extreme as yours would be rare if the null hypothesis were true, and so the null hypothesis might be invalid. A low p-value would lead you to suspect that the two variables are, in fact, related. For more examples of p-values, see section **h** below.

4. What is an example of the chi-square test?

The following table represents the grades received by 50 students in a calculus course. Is there good evidence for a relationship between the sex of the student and the grade she or he received in the course?

Observed Counts	A	B	C	D	F	Total
Female	9	9	4	0	0	22
Male	2	11	10	4	1	28
Total	11	20	14	4	1	50

We begin by filling in the expected count for each cell, based on the null hypothesis that there is no relationship between the sex of the student and the grade she or he received in the course. For instance, the expected number of female students getting an A would be $\frac{(22)(11)}{(50)} = 4.84$.

Expected Counts	A	B	C	D	F	Total
Female	4.84	8.8	6.16	1.76	0.44	22
Male	6.16	11.2	7.84	2.24	0.56	28
Total	11	20	14	4	1	50

Notice that $df = (5-1)(2-1) = 4$. Using a calculator to find X^2, we get $X^2 = 11.674$, with $p = 0.020$. This means that if there were no relationship between the sex of the student and the grade she or he received, then the likelihood of obtaining data at least as extreme as this is about 2%, which is not very likely. Therefore, we have good evidence that there really is some relationship between the sex of the student and the grade she or he received in the calculus course.

It is important to note that statistically, we have only shown that there is probably a relationship. We have not shown that the relationship is one of *causation*. Thus, one should *not* conclude from this data that women are better at calculus than men. Perhaps the female students worked harder and completed more of the homework, or perhaps the instructor graded the men more harshly. In any case, there is good evidence for a relationship, but much more research is needed to determine what that relationship may entail.

5. What is another example of the chi-square test?

[This example and many others listed below come from a standard textbook, Moore and McCabe[2], (p. 644).] Suppose that a company had a large work force and unfortunately had to fire some employees. Someone suspects that the company was more likely to fire older employees rather than younger ones. Are their suspicions valid? The following table has the data separated by age group and termination status.

---

[2]Moore and McCabe, *Introduction to the Practice of Statistics*. Fourth ed. W.H. Freeman and Company: New York, 2003.

Observed Counts	Under 40	Over 40	Total
Fired	16	78	94
Not Fired	585	765	1350
Total	601	843	1444

The first thing we need to do is calculate the expected counts in each cell. As before, this is done by looking at the totals in each row and column and figuring out how the numbers would be evenly distributed, given these totals. So, in the first cell (upper left), we would expect $(94)(601)/(1444)$ or 39.12. Continuing in this way, we obtain:

Expected Counts	Under 40	Over 40	Total
Fired	39.12	54.88	94
Not Fired	561.88	788.12	1350
Total	601	843	1444

Now we calculate X^2, the chi-square test statistic, and the degrees of freedom, $df = (2 - 1)(2 - 1) = 1$. You should get $X^2 = 25.04$. Then you go to the table (or use your calculator) to find that p is *very* small ($p < 0.0005$). So, if there were no relationship between the age of the employee and their termination status, then data at least as extreme as ours would happen with a likelihood of less than 0.05%. This is excellent evidence that in fact, the age of the employee *is* related to their termination status.

6. Sample Problems

   (a) In the calculus class data given above, suppose that students need a C or better to take the next class. Then we could make the following table.

Observed Counts	Passing	Not Passing	Total
Female	22	0	22
Male	23	5	28
Total	45	5	50

   Does this table present good evidence that there is a relationship between the sex of the student and whether or not the student passed the course? Calculate the chi-square test statistic and corresponding p-value to support your answer.

   (b) Suppose that someone comes to you and claims that their teacher is not grading the male students fairly. They ran a chi-square test on the relevant data and came up with $X^2 = 1.31$, with $p = 0.8597$. Do you believe their claim? Why or why not? Interpret their p-value.

   (c) (from Moore & McCabe, *ibid.*, p. 647) A survey was sent to three groups: those who received a preliminary letter about the survey, those who received a preliminary phone call about the survey, and those who received no contact prior to the survey. The numbers in the table refer to how many people returned the survey within two weeks.

Observed Counts	Letter	Phone	None	Total
Within 2 weeks	171	146	118	435
Not within 2 weeks	220	68	455	743
Total	391	214	573	1178

Fill in the Expected Counts table below. Then calculate the chi-square test statistic and its corresponding p-value. Interpret your results.

Expected Counts	Letter	Phone	None	Total
Within 2 weeks				435
Not within 2 weeks				743
Total	391	214	573	1178

7. Answers to Sample Problems

(a) In the calculus class data given above, suppose that students need a C or better to take the next class. Then we could make the following table.

Observed Counts	Passing	Not Passing	Total
Female	22	0	22
Male	23	5	28
Total	45	5	50

Does this table present good evidence that there is a relationship between the sex of the student and whether or not the student passed the course? Calculate the chi-square test statistic and corresponding p-value to support your answer.

First, we will find the expected counts in each cell.

Expected Counts	Passing	Not Passing	Total
Female	19.8	2.2	22
Male	25.2	2.8	28
Total	45	5	50

So, the chi-square test statistic is

$$\frac{(22 - 19.8)^2}{19.8} + \frac{(0 - 2.2)^2}{2.2} + \frac{(23 - 25.2)^2}{25.2} + \frac{(5 - 2.8)^2}{2.8} = 4.365.$$

We also have $df = 1$. Thus, the p-value, according to the calculator, is 0.0367. This means that if there were no relationship between the sex of the student and whether or not they passed the class, then data at least as extreme as ours would happen with a likelihood of about 3.7%, which is not very likely. So there is good evidence of a relationship between the sex of the student and whether or not they passed the class.

(b) Suppose that someone comes to you and claims that their teacher is not grading the male students fairly. They ran a chi-square test on the relevant data and came up with $X^2 = 1.31$, with $p = 0.8597$. Do you believe their claim? Why or why not? Interpret their p-value.

They have not presented good evidence to support their claim. Their p-value means that if there were no relationship between the sex of the student and their grade, then the likelihood of obtaining data at least as extreme as theirs is about 86%, which is highly likely. This data does *not* support the claim of unfair treatment.

(c) A survey was sent to three groups: those who received a preliminary letter about the survey, those who received a preliminary phone call about the survey, and those who received no contact prior to the survey. The numbers in the table refer to how many people returned the survey within two weeks.

Observed Counts	Letter	Phone	None	Total
Within 2 weeks	171	146	118	435
Not within 2 weeks	220	68	455	743
Total	391	214	573	1178

Fill in the Expected Counts table below. Then calculate the chi-square test statistic and its corresponding p-value. Interpret your results.

Expected Counts	Letter	Phone	None	Total
Within 2 weeks	144.38	79.02	211.59	435
Not within 2 weeks	246.62	134.98	361.41	743
Total	391	214	573	1178

Running the chi-square test on the calculator (with $df = 2$) gives: $X^2 = 163.412$ and $p = 3.28 \times 10^{-36}$, which is *incredibly* small. Therefore, we have extremely good evidence of a relationship between how the person was contacted beforehand and whether or not the survey was returned within two weeks.

f. Interpret scatter plots for bivariate data to investigate patterns of association between two quantities (e.g., correlation), including the use of linear models

1. What is correlation?

   The correlation of two variables is a number that measures the direction and strength of the linear relationship between them. If there are n data points: (x_1, y_1), (x_2, y_2), $\ldots$, (x_n, y_n), then the formula for the correlation r is

   $$r = \frac{1}{n-1} \sum_{i=1}^{n} \left(\frac{x_i - \overline{x}}{s_x} \right) \left(\frac{y_i - \overline{y}}{s_y} \right),$$

   where $\overline{x}$ [respectively, $\overline{y}$] is the mean of the x [resp., y] data, and s_x [resp., s_y] is the standard deviation of the x [resp., y] data.

   One result of this formula is that $-1 \leq r \leq 1$. The sign of r is determined by the slope of the linear relationship. The closer r is to zero, the less correlated the data are. Thus, a scatterplot that lacks a linear relationship has a correlation close to zero, whereas a scatterplot that looks close to a downward-sloping line has a correlation close to -1.

2. How are correlation and regression related?

   Recall that the correlation coefficient r is between -1 and 1. So, $0 \leq r^2 \leq 1$. In terms of regression, r^2 measures the fraction of the variation in the y-values that is explained by the least-squares regression line. For instance, if there is a perfect linear fit, then $r^2 = 1$, and so 100% of the variation in y-values is explained by this linear relationship. On the other extreme, if r^2 is very close to zero, then there is almost no discernible linear relationship between the two variables. So, the regression line would explain very little of the variation in y-values.

   There is a relationship between the slope of the line of best fit, the standard deviations of the x and y data, and r. In particular, the slope of the line of best fit is $\dfrac{r s_y}{s_x}$. Since the standard deviations are positive, this can explain why the sign of r matches the sign of the slope. To be more precise, r is the slope of the best fitting line, if the data have been normalized. In other words, if we replace each data point (x, y) with $\left(\dfrac{x - \bar{x}}{s_x}, \dfrac{y - \bar{y}}{s_y} \right)$, then the line of best fit of these points would have slope r, and would pass through the origin.

3. Sample Problems

   (a) Rank these pictures in increasing order of their corresponding correlation coefficients.

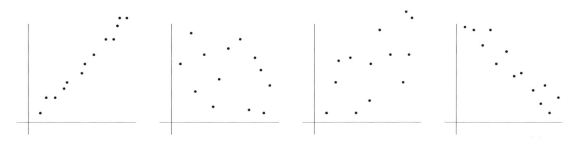

   (b) Janey found that for a certain regression line, $r = -0.9$. She concluded that her regression line explained 90% of the variation in her data. Calculate r^2. Then interpret r and r^2 for Janey.

4. Answers to Sample Problems

   (a) Rank these pictures in increasing order of their corresponding correlation coefficients.

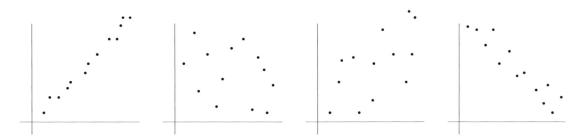

   The correlation coefficients in order are very negative, somewhat negative, somewhat positive, and very positive. See below.

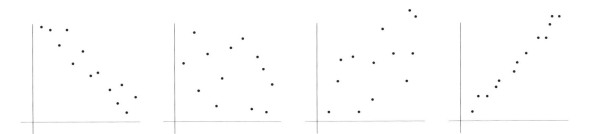

(b) Janey found that for a certain regression line, $r = -0.9$. She concluded that her regression line explained 90% of the variation in her data. Calculate r^2. Then interpret r and r^2 for Janey.

Janey confused r and r^2. In her case, $r^2 = 0.81$, which means that 81% of the variation in the data is explained by the linear relationship between her variables. Her value of r describes the direction of the relationship, which in this case would be a negative correlation (sloping downward). As the explanatory variable gets bigger, the response variable gets smaller.

g. Interpret data on a single count or measurement variable presented in a variety of formats (e.g., dot plots, histograms, box plots)

1. How are data displayed?

   To display one-variable quantitative data, we use dot plots, histograms, stem and leaf plots, and box plots. To display one-variable categorical data, we use percentage counts, bar graphs, and pie charts.

2. What are all these different ways of displaying data? What does each one show?

   This will probably be clearer if we use a set of quantitative data and display it in these various ways. Suppose that you give an exam in your math class and you get the following grades: 77, 46, 44, 59, 75, 86, 94, 52, 82, 86, 81, 35, 66, 75, 77, 87, 48, 74, 66, 77, 92, 49, 77, 52, 61, 82, and 78. We will display these data in multiple ways. (A big shout out to Geogebra, the free software that makes a lot of these displays possible. Box plots were done online at http://www.alcula.com/calculators/statistics/box-plot/.)

   - *Dot plot.* A dot plot represents each data point with a single dot. Dots are placed above a number line at their corresponding value. If there are multiple data points with the same value, then the dots are placed above one another. Our data generates the following dot plot. Notice that four students earned a 77.

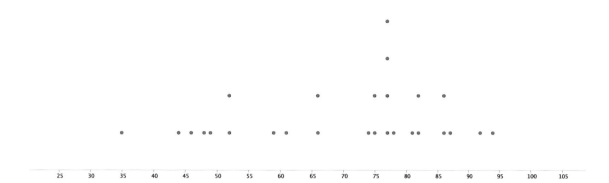

- *Histogram.* A histogram represents quantitative data by putting the data into subintervals. Each subinterval of data should have the same length and each data point should be put into a subinterval. In the following histogram, the range has been divided into ten subintervals. Since the range is 59 (low: 35, high: 94), each box represents a subinterval of 5.9 points. Notice that eight students were in the range from about 77 to about 83.

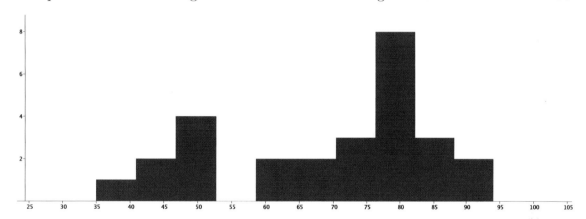

- *Stem and Leaf Plot.* Like a histogram, a stem and leaf plot also looks at the data in groupings, usually groups of ten. In our case, the "stem" will be the tens digit, and the "leaves" will be the ones digits corresponding to each data point. So the first row below represents the scores of 92 and 94. Notice that eight students scored in the 70s, and that four earned a 77.

9	2 4
8	1 2 2 6 6 7
7	4 5 5 7 7 7 7 8
6	1 6 6
5	2 2 9
4	4 6 8 9
3	5

- *Box Plot.* A box plot is a way of summarizing the data into a single visual. One draws a rectangle from the first to the third quartiles, with a transverse line drawn at the median. Then one adds other lines (sometimes called "whiskers") to reach the maximum and minimum values of the data, provided that they are not outliers. The box plot can give you a sense of center (median), as well as IQR (length of rectangle) and overall range (distance between extremes).

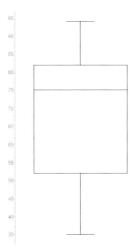

Now we'll display some categorical data using different methods. Suppose we have the following answers on a survey question about favorite color: blue, blue, green, purple, blue, red, purple, green, green, yellow, orange, green, purple, orange, blue.

- *Percentage Count.* This just lists the percentage of responses that fall into each category. We can list those percentages in a table. Notice that because of rounding, it might not look like the percentages all add up to 100%.

Blue	Green	Purple	Orange	Red	Yellow
26.67%	26.67%	20%	13.33%	6.67%	6.67%

- *Bar Graph.* A bar graph looks like a histogram, but it is used for categorical data. To drive this point home, often the bars for different discrete options do not touch each other, whereas they do for histograms. Note that the category counts are listed.

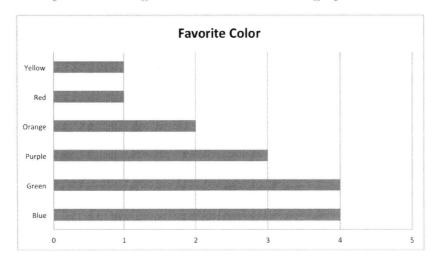

- *Pie Chart.* A pie chart maps the categorical variable onto a full circle, and then devotes sectors to each selection in the category. The size of each sector is proportional to the specific count of its corresponding selection. This gives a visual picture of relative sizes of the different groups.

Favorite Color

3. Sample Problems

(a) The following data represent the birthweights (in oz) of 15 babies in North Carolina: 158, 146, 128, 150, 119, 132, 132, 110, 127, 96, 111, 106, 112, 108, 107. (The data come from 1995 birth registry data at the North Carolina State Center for Health and Environmental Statistics. Thank you, Hope College Math Department! Retrieved online at http://www.math.hope.edu/swanson/statlabs/data.html.) Graph this data using

   i. a dot plot.
   ii. a stem and leaf plot.

(b) The following data represent the diastolic blood pressure numbers for seven young men (age 19 through 31). (Data from Golino, Hudson (2013): Men's dataset from the "Predicting increased blood pressure using Machine Learning" paper. figshare. http://dx.doi.org/10.6084/m9.figshare.845665.) 120, 100, 107, 120, 127, 170, 130. Graph this data using

   i. a histogram with 7 subdivisions.
   ii. a box plot.

(c) The following data represent the rolls of a six-sided die: 4, 3, 4, 2, 6, 2, 6, 5, 1, 5. Are these data quantitative or categorical? Explain. How would you display the results visually?

(d) Suppose that, of 100 randomly selected workplace accidents, 21 occurred on a Monday, 16 on a Tuesday, 13 on a Wednesday, 17 on a Thursday, and 33 on a Friday. How would you display these results visually?

4. Answers to Sample Problems

(a) The following data represent the birthweights (in oz) of 15 babies in North Carolina: 158, 146, 128, 150, 119, 132, 132, 110, 127, 96, 111, 106, 112, 108, 107. Graph this data using

    i. a dot plot.

    ii. a stem and leaf plot.

9	6
10	6 7 8
11	0 1 2 9
12	7 8
13	2 2
14	6
15	0 8

(b) The following data represent the diastolic blood pressure numbers for seven young men (age 19 through 31): 120, 100, 107, 120, 127, 170, 130. Graph this data using

    i. a histogram with 7 subdivisions.

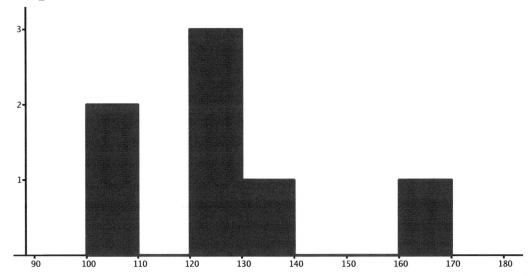

    ii. a box plot. (Notice that the outlier is not connected to the interquartile box.)

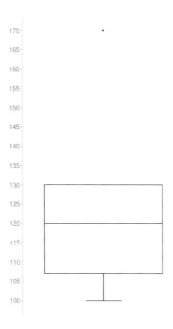

(c) The following data represent the rolls of a six-sided die: 4, 3, 4, 2, 6, 2, 6, 5, 1, 5. Are these data quantitative or categorical? Explain. How would you display the results visually?

I would say that this variable is categorical, since there are only six possible outcomes. If the six sides of the die were labeled with colors, like a Rubik's Cube, then the results would be more clearly categorical. But we have "assigned" the numbers 1 through 6 to the selections in the category. This allows us to come up with quantitative results. Nevertheless it's probably best if we display the results of our rolls using the categorical approaches. We will give a percentage table and a bar graph.

1	2	3	4	5	6
10%	20%	10%	20%	20%	20%

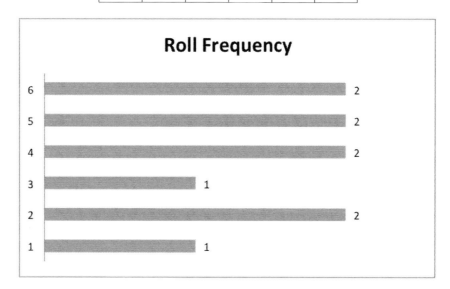

(d) Suppose that, of 100 randomly selected workplace accidents, 21 occurred on a Monday,

16 on a Tuesday, 13 on a Wednesday, 17 on a Thursday, and 33 on a Friday. How would you display these results visually?

These data may appear quantitative, but they are really categorical. One could use a bar graph or a pie chart to show the data. The pie chart makes it easy to see that more than 50% of workplace accidents happened on a Monday or a Friday.

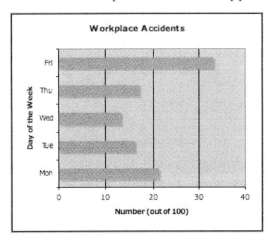
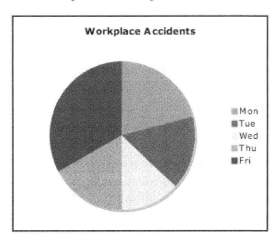

h. Demonstrate knowledge of P-values and hypothesis testing

In this section, we will use p-value instead of P-value.

1. What is a p-value? How do you interpret a p-value?

   A p-value is a probability, and hence is a number between 0 and 1. In practice, p-values are often reported with the results of an experiment. They are the quantitative measure by which experimenters determine if their experiments have had the desired effect or not. More precisely, a p-value is the likelihood of obtaining experimental results at least as extreme as the ones obtained assuming that the treatment really had no effect on the outcome. (Such an assumption is called the null hypothesis.)

   So, the smaller the p-value, the less likely that the treatment had no effect, i.e., the less likely that the results obtained were just due to random variation in the population. Small p-values provide evidence that a treatment is effective. On the other hand, the larger the p-value, the weaker the evidence that the treatment really had an effect. Larger p-values mean that it is more likely to obtain results at least as extreme as the ones obtained, if the null hypothesis is true.

2. What is a null hypothesis?

   A null hypothesis is the assumption that a treatment has no effect, or that there is no difference between two products, etc. When talking about drug trials, for example, one assumes that the null hypothesis (that the drug has no effect) is true. This assumption is required in order to calculate the proper p-value.

3. What is an alternative hypothesis?

   Contrary to the null hypothesis, there is the notion of an alternative hypothesis, which can be one- or two-sided. This is probably best explained via some examples below. We will deal mostly with two-sided alternative hypotheses in this book.

4. What is hypothesis testing?

Hypothesis testing is a key application of statistics to experiments. We have already described one type of hypothesis testing in section **e** above on the chi-square test.

Again, using the language of drug trials, when one is testing whether a drug is effective or not, one runs an experiment, which involves a treatment group and a control group. Then the outcomes of the treatment group and the control group are compared, under the assumption that the drug treatment will have no effect on the outcomes. A one-sided alternative hypothesis in this case would be that the treatment group will have a *better* outcome than the control group. A two-sided alternative hypothesis would just be that the treatment group will have a *different* outcome than the control group. One then calculates a p-value based on the outcomes observed and the particular alternative hypothesis being tested. As stated above, this p-value tells you the likelihood of obtaining (at random) outcomes that are at least as extreme as the ones obtained in the experiment, if the drug really had no effect. A smaller p-value is better evidence that perhaps the drug has an effect. A larger p-value means there is less evidence to reject the null hypothesis.

5. What are some examples of hypothesis testing?

Suppose that we want to determine which soft drink tastes better: A or B. The null hypothesis is that there is no difference between the two, and so we would expect about 50% of people to prefer A over B and 50% to prefer B over A. (We will ignore the possibility of a tie in this example.) An experimenter runs the experiment with the two-sided alternative hypothesis that A and B do not taste the same. The experimenter comes to you and says that more people preferred A to B, and that the p-value was 0.28. What can you conclude?

You would likely decide that the results were inconclusive. This p-value indicates that even if there is no difference between the two soft drinks, the random variation of the population would provide results at least as extreme as what the experimenter obtained in 28% of the experiments. That doesn't seem like a strong case that A tastes better than B.

If the p-value had been less than 0.05, a commonly used cutoff point for statistical significance, then yes, that would mean that if there were no real difference between the two, then results as extreme as that would only happen at random in less than 5% of the samples. This seems like a much stronger case that A tastes better than B.

Of course, there are many more variables to consider in an experiment like this: how are people selected to participate? Is it double-blind, meaning is it also true that the experimenter doesn't know which soft drink is which? If the experimenter were to know, then she or he might subtly influence the people tasting the soft drink samples. Experiments are tricky!

6. Sample Problems

   (a) State the null hypothesis in each case. Then state a one-sided and a two-sided alternative hypothesis in each case.

      i. The Census Bureau says that households spend on average 31% of their income on housing. You want to sample households in your area to see if that figure is correct for your town.

ii. You want to sample your high school's students' scores on the SAT test to see if the students in your class did better than the students in other classes.

(b) Suppose that someone studies the relationship between exercise and performance on a math test. Their null hypothesis was that exercising before a math test had no effect on math test performance, and their alternate hypothesis was that exercise did have an effect (maybe good or bad) on math test performance. The result was that students who exercised did better, and the p-value listed was 0.43. Interpret this result, including what it means for students who are about to take a math test.

(c) Suppose that a college samples a few of its graduates as to their salaries after graduation. They report that on average, male graduates earn significantly more than female graduates (with p-value 0.018) and that white graduates earn more than Latino graduates but that the difference was not significant (with p-value 0.649). State the null hypothesis in each case and interpret the two p-values.

7. Answers to Sample Problems

(a) State the null hypothesis in each case. Then state a one-sided and a two-sided alternative hypothesis in each case.

i. The Census Bureau says that US households spend on average 31% of their income on housing. You want to sample households in your area to see if that figure is correct for your town. The null hypothesis is that there is no difference between the average spending on housing in your town and the average spending on housing in the US. A one-sided alternative hypothesis could be that the average spending on housing in your town is more than the average spending on housing in the US. A two-sided alternative hypothesis would be that the average spending on housing in your town is not the same as the average spending on housing in the US.

ii. You want to sample your high school's students' scores on the SAT test to see if the students in your class did better than the students in other classes. The null hypothesis is that there is no difference between the students in your class and the students in other classes in terms of their SAT performance. A one-sided alternative hypothesis could be that the students in your class perform better on the SATs than students in other classes. A two-sided alternative hypothesis would be that the students in your class perform differently on the SATs than students in other classes.

(b) Suppose that someone studies the relationship between exercise and performance on a math test. Their null hypothesis was that exercising before a math test had no effect on math test performance, and their alternate hypothesis was that exercise did have an effect (maybe good or bad) on math test performance. The result was that students who exercised did better, and the p-value listed was 0.43. Interpret this result, including what it means for students who are about to take a math test.

This means that in the sample they studied, the students who exercised did better than those who did not. However, the p-value indicates that, if there really were no difference in math test performance between the two groups, there was a likelihood of 43% that a random sample would have obtained a difference in test scores at least as extreme as the one the researchers obtained. So this is not very convincing evidence that exercising before a test can improve your math score.

(c) Suppose that a college samples a few of its graduates as to their salaries after graduation. They report that on average, male graduates earn significantly more than female graduates (with p-value 0.018) and that white graduates earn more than Latino graduates but that the difference was not significant (with p-value 0.649). State the null hypothesis in each case and interpret the two p-values.

In the first comparison, the null hypothesis is that there is no difference in average income between male graduates and female graduates. The small p-value of 0.018 indicates that if the null hypothesis were true, then only 1.8% of random samples would have given an average income difference that was at least as extreme as the one obtained in the sample taken by the college. This is pretty convincing evidence that there really is a difference in the average income between male graduates and female graduates.

In the second comparison, the null hypothesis is that there is no difference in average income between white graduates and Latino graduates. The college's sample did show a difference in income, with white graduates earning more. However, the p-value of 0.649 indicates that an income difference at least as extreme as the one the college obtained would have shown up in 64.9% of random samples if the null hypothesis were true. This is not convincing evidence of a true difference in average income between white graduates and Latino graduates, which is why the result is described as "not significant."

i. Demonstrate knowledge of confidence intervals

1. What is a confidence interval? How do you interpret a confidence interval?

A confidence interval is a range of values that is likely to contain the parameter you are seeking. For example, suppose you are trying to estimate the average height of adult men in your town. You probably don't want to measure every man's height and then find the average. Instead, you take a sample of adult men in your town and measure their heights. From this, given a few other assumptions, you can determine a confidence interval for the average height of all men in your town. This would be a range of values, together with an idea of how confident you are that your interval has captured the true average height.

For the purposes of this book, we will focus primarily on confidence intervals at a 95% confidence level. This means that there is 95% chance that your confidence interval will contain the true value of the parameter you are seeking. Put another way, in about 95% of samples, the confidence interval constructed from that sample will contain the true value of the parameter.

2. How do you calculate a confidence interval for a population mean?

Suppose you are trying to determine the value of μ, the mean value of some characteristic (like height, weight, etc.) for your population. We will assume that you know the standard deviation of this statistic, σ. Since sampling the entire population is usually not feasible, suppose that you select a simple random sample (or SRS) of n individuals. See section **c** above to review the definition of SRS. Then the confidence interval formula is

$$\overline{x} \pm z^* \frac{\sigma}{\sqrt{n}},$$

where $\bar{x}$ is the mean of the individuals in your sample, and z^* is determined by what level of confidence you want. If you want a 95% confidence level, then you pick z^* so that 95% of the area under the standard normal distribution is between $-z^*$ and z^*. (For 95%, the value of z^* is about 1.96.)

So, if you took an SRS of 10 adult men in your town, and you measured the average height of your sample to be 173.2cm, and you knew the standard deviation to be 7cm, you would calculate a 95% confidence interval as

$$173.2 \pm (1.96)\frac{7}{\sqrt{10}} \approx 173.2 \pm 4.34 \text{ cm}.$$

To interpret this, there is only a 5% chance that our sample mean was so extreme that our confidence interval did not capture the true average height of adult men.

3. How do you calculate a confidence interval for a population proportion?

Suppose you are trying to determine the value of p, the proportion of the population that is in some group (like is female, or voted for a certain candidate, or has blue eyes, etc.). Under some mild assumptions (like that we are not sampling too large a percentage of the population, that the individuals sampled are independent and randomly selected, and that the numbers you expect to meet the condition are neither too small nor too large[3]), we can calculate a 95% confidence interval for the population proportion:

$$\widehat{p} \pm z^* \sqrt{\frac{\widehat{p}(1 - \widehat{p})}{n}},$$

where $\widehat{p}$ is the sample proportion, n is the sample size, and z^* is the same as above.

So if you randomly sample 500 adults and asked them if they attend church weekly, and 203 of them say yes, then you can calculate $\widehat{p} = \frac{203}{500} = 0.406$. Then the 95% confidence interval is

$$0.406 \pm (1.96)\sqrt{\frac{(0.406)(0.594)}{500}} \approx 0.406 \pm 0.043.$$

To interpret this, you could say that you have a 95% confidence level that the true proportion of weekly church-goers in the population is between 36.3% and 44.9%.

4. Sample Problems

(a) Suppose that a study is conducted asking families of four how much they spend on groceries every week. The results of the survey indicate that the 95% confidence interval for the average amount of money that a family of four spends on groceries each week is $205.60 \pm $14.93. How would you interpret this result?

(b) Suppose that several fields are planted with corn. You select an SRS of 12 fields. The yield from each field varies, but the average yield from these fields is 125.8 bushels per acre. Assume that the standard deviation, σ, is 10 bushels per acre. Find the 95% confidence interval for the mean yield for corn. Interpret your result.

---

[3]Consult a good statistics text for more specifics on the limitations of confidence intervals.

(c) Suppose that you take a random sample of 121 faculty members at a large institution and you find that 73 of them have children. Find the 95% confidence interval for the proportion of faculty at your institution that have children. Interpret your result.

(d) Is a 99% confidence interval larger or smaller than a 95% confidence interval? Explain.

5. Answers to Sample Problems

(a) Suppose that a study is conducted asking families of four how much they spend on groceries every week. The results of the survey indicate that the 95% confidence interval for the average amount of money that a family of four spends on groceries each week is $205.60 \pm$ $14.93. How would you interpret this result?

This means that the average spending of the families that were sampled is $205.60. There is a 95% chance that this interval (from $190.67 to $220.53) will contain the true average weekly spending on groceries for a family of four.

(b) Suppose that several fields are planted with corn. You select an SRS of 12 fields. The yield from each field varies, but the average yield from these fields is 125.8 bushels per acre. Assume that the standard deviation, σ, is 10 bushels per acre. Find the 95% confidence interval for the mean yield for corn. Interpret your result. The 95% confidence interval is

$$125.8 \pm (1.96)\frac{10}{\sqrt{12}} \approx 125.8 \pm 5.66 \text{ bushels per acre.}$$

This means that there is a 95% chance that this confidence interval, obtained from our sample, will actually capture the true value of the mean yield for corn. In other words, we are 95% confident that the mean yield for corn is between 120.14 and 131.46 bushels per acre.

(c) Suppose that you take a random sample of 121 faculty members at a large institution and you find that 73 of them have children. Find the 95% confidence interval for the proportion of faculty at your institution that have children. Interpret your result. The 95% confidence interval is

$$\frac{73}{121} \pm (1.96)\sqrt{\frac{\left(\frac{73}{121}\right)\left(\frac{48}{121}\right)}{121}} \approx 0.6033 \pm 0.0872.$$

This means that there is a 95% chance that the actual proportion of faculty that have children is between 51.61% and 69.05%.

(d) Is a 99% confidence interval larger or smaller than a 95% confidence interval? Explain.

A 99% confidence interval would have to be larger than a 95% confidence interval. If you wanted more confidence that your interval contained the true mean, then you would need to have your interval cover more values. Another way to think about it is to think that z^* for capturing 99% of the area under the normal distribution curve would have to be bigger than z^* for capturing 95% of the area.